# Managing the One-Person Library

# Managing the One-Person Library

Guy St Clair

Joan Williamson

**Butterworths**

London   Boston   Durban   Singapore   Sydney   Toronto   Wellington

First published 1986

© Butterworth & Co (Publishers) Ltd, 1986

---

**British Library Cataloguing in Publication Data**

St. Clair, Guy
  Managing the one-person library.
  1. Libraries, Special.  2. Library
  administration.
  I. Title.  II. Williamson, Joan
  025.1'96  Z675.A2

  ISBN 0-408-01511-X

---

**Library of Congress Cataloging in Publication Data**

St. Clair, Guy.
  Managing the one-person library.

  Bibliography: p.
  Includes index.
  1. Library science.  2. Small libraries.
I. Williamson, Joan.  II. Title.
Z665.S774 1986  025.1  85-30965
ISBN 0-408-01511-X

---

Phototypesetting by En to En, Tunbridge Wells
Printed in Great Britain at the University Press, Cambridge

# Forewords

Dr David R. Bender
*Executive Director, Special Libraries Association*

Many librarians consider the one-person library as a stepping stone to loftier professional goals. Others consider it a necessary evil. Neither view is correct, for in one-person libraries the librarians are satisfied with the work environment and describe their professional activities as an exciting challenge, free from bureaucracies and burdensome organizational structures.

In 1976 Guy St Clair published in *Special Libraries*, the quarterly journal of the Special Libraries Association (SLA), one of the first articles on one-person libraries to appear in library literature. In 'The one-person library: an essay on essentials', he defined a one-person library as '. . . one in which all of the work is done by the librarian'. The article added: '. . . In a one-person library there is no distinction between clerical and professional duties; Management is not involved in policy making in the library; and the librarian, in terms of actual operations of the library, is answerable only to himself.'

This essay was, and continues to be, widely circulated. Little did anyone realize, in 1976, that it was an early step on the long road to the formulation of the book that is now before you. In its most basic terms, the advice presented was that the 'keys to success in a one-person library are effective self-management and good communication between the librarian, his clientele and management'. Since 1976 those basic principles have changed little.

What has not remained static is the number of one-person libraries. In 1972 one study indicated that 32 per cent of all libraries were staffed by one person. It has been said that by 1982 this figure had risen to an astonishing 50 per cent, although the actual figure, in all likelihood, is nearly impossible to ascertain The point remains that there are thousands of individuals relying upon their expertise as librarians to manage effectively all aspects of their operation – issues that typically are not covered in library/information schools.

What tools are available to professionals? Until this publication, very few. Occasional articles have appeared in the library press and some professional development opportunities have been sponsored. A quick literature search shows that there has been a dearth of useful books for individuals staffing one-person libraries/information centres.

One of the earliest discussions on one-person libraries took place in 1972 at SLA's Annual Conference. Guy St Clair led a roundtable discussion on 'one-man libraries'. Although the title was changed quickly, the enthusiasm generated remained. In fact, organizers quickly recruited additional speakers and seating to accommodate the overflow crowd for a subject which, until then, was greeted with the response, 'Who cares?'

In 1984 Guy St Clair, in collaboration with two of his colleagues, undertook the publishing of *The One-Person Library: A Newsletter for Librarians and Management*. This newsletter is an invaluable tool and on the 'must read' list of one-person librarians. Additionally, he has developed and taught a number of professional development courses geared specifically to meet the needs of the one-person librarian.

These events set the stage. In 1982 Guy St Clair was first approached to co-author a book on the topic. Ironically, it was the first time that he was not employed as a one-person librarian. Work began.

*Managing the One-Person Library* is comprehensive – it covers everything from the basics to automation and the nuts and bolts of management, collection development and time management. For those professionals involved in a one-person library, it provides a method for acquiring needed knowledge and skills.

This indispensable publication – backed by a decade of practical, first-hand experience, teaching and interaction with professional librarians – expands the tenets first published in 1976 to provide a flexible guide for those choosing to work in this specialized area of librarianship.

I congratulate Guy St Clair and Joan Williamson on providing this book. It has long been needed and will long be the source of assistance to those working in one-person libraries.

**Dr Dennis A. Lewis**
*Director, Aslib – The Association for Information Management*

The basic definition of a 'one-man band' or OMB (that is, the one-person librarian as described in the UK) is that it is a very small unit, managed by one person, albeit with clerical or secretarial help. The greatest problem which besets the OMB is not necessarily, or only, the shortage of resources or constraints on policy matters. Generally, it is isolation.

OMBs suffer from both professional isolation and organizational isolation. The former arises from the OMB's inability to participate in anything other than the most marginal way in library/informational professional affairs because of shortage of time and also because the professional bodies are not geared to the OMB's particular needs – or were not, until the Aslib OMB Group was formed.

The organizational isolation within the OMB's employing body arises generally from the management's lack of awareness of the significance of information as a manageable resource and also because the OMB him/herself is usually well down the pecking order and therefore is not seen as having a role other than the passive provision of information. Clearly, there are exceptions to both of these, but usually they are few and far between.

The main objective of the OMB Group must be therefore to overcome the sense of isolation. To this end, the Group has created opportunities for people to maintain their awareness of what's going on; to share problems, ideas, resources, to extend the network of colleagues; to gain mutual encouragement and support; and finally, of course, to draw upon the considerable resources available from the parent body.

My guess is that the number of OMBs is increasing, first because of reductions in the number of staff of existing units, and second because of the establishment of OMB 'libraries' in emerging service-based companies in the expanding 'information industry'. Also, it appears that an increasing number of OMBs who are managed by unqualified (in library/information terms) staff are getting to hear about the Aslib OMB group and are joining.

The growth of one-man bands is, I believe, a phenomenon of the 1980s and I further believe that such growth, matched by reductions in the larger libraries and information units, will characterize the 1990s and will go on well into the third millennium. The reasons are clear to see and include:

- Increasing pressure on resources in both public and private sectors.
- Greater demand for higher cost-effectiveness.
- Increased managerial awareness of the value of information as a resource.
- Increased availability and assessibility of information and data via electronic systems.
- Increased user-friendly desk-top computing power available.
- Increased complexity/diversity of systems, leading to a need for professional guidance.

All this may be summed up in the phrase 'effective information management'. The availability of relatively low-cost Information Technological solutions to both information and management problems provides hugely challenging opportunities for all the library and information-resources professionals. The opportinities for the OMBs are no less. In fact, the really opportunistic OMB should find him/herself in a position where the controlling influence is exerted through his/her knowledge of the organization and its requirements, on the one hand, and the sources and availability of information resources on the other – maybe OMB should be amended to mean 'our managerial broker'!

I am delighted to have been asked to write this foreword. It gives me the opportunity to acknowledge the entrepreneurial spirit of many of my colleagues in the UK, and I commend them on the success of their group.

# Contents

# Introduction

A one-person library is one in which all of the work is done by the librarian. In some libraries this work is limited to professional duties, with support staff to handle clerical routines and other tasks around the library. In others the librarian literally does *all* the work, from readers' services to emptying the waste-paper baskets, Between these two extremes are many people, some trained, some not, who have the title 'librarian' and who perform duties related to the library in the parent organization in which they are employed (or serve as volunteers, for many one-person librarians, working in such institutions as small museums, churches, historical societies, charitable organizations, etc. do not receive remuneration for the work they do).

This book has been prepared for them. It is an attempt to provide guidance for the librarian who works alone, and the authors' goal has been not so much to provide a handbook or 'how-to' manual (although dealing with the basics of librarianship is certainly an important part of this book) but to give the reader a sense of order and direction in the performance of those duties which fall outside the give and take of librarians working in larger groups. The success of a one-person library and its services is often a direct reflection of the attitude and personality of the librarian who is in charge. We have made an attempt to describe for English and American librarians some of the situations in which they will find themselves and to provide some suggestions on how they might deal with these situations.

The book is written for librarians on both sides of the Atlantic, and considerable attention has been paid to those administrative and professional situations which are different in the two countries. For, as alike as we are, there are definite differences in librarianship in the United Kingdom and in the United States. We have tried to make the British concepts understandable to Americans, and vice versa, but we must recognize that sometimes our familiarity with a situation on one side may cause some confusion on the other. We hope we have avoided the worst pitfalls. Similarly, there is some concern about terms. In the United States a 'graduate' librarian means someone who has a master's degree in library science from a school or university accredited by the American Library Association. In the United Kingdom that librarian is called a 'chartered' librarian because the Library Association has granted the person a charter to serve as a professional librarian. In the United States a person who runs a single-staff library is generally called a 'one-person' librarian. In the United Kingdom that person is usually referred to by the acronym OMB, which stands for 'one-man band'. There is, in the United Kingdom, a professional group known as the OMBs, part of Aslib, and the acronym has caught on as a descriptive term. In the United States OMB is an acronym for an important government agency, often in the news and frequently in news of special interest to librarians, so using OMB as a library term would have been confusing for Americans. For that reason, and with apologies to our readers in the United Kingdom, we have chosen to refer to our subject as the one-person library and to its practitioners as one-person librarians.

The subject of the sex of a person plays an important part in any professional publication today, and works on libraries are particularly vulnerable to misunderstanding, for the library profession is made up primarily of women. Yet most of us were taught in our earliest composition classes to refer to the sex of the person we were writing about in the masculine, unless we knew it to be feminine. Obviously that cannot be done today, so in the interest of fairness we have varied the personal pronouns throughout this book. For consistency, however, we have used accepted British spellings of words which are spelled differently in America, as alternation of forms was distracting and unnecessary.

As for the intended audience for the book, we have taken care *not* to write it for librarians in any particular library setting but have tried to make reference to the many different kinds of institutions in which librarians are performing their duties. While most one-person librarians obviously work in special libraries, and since most special libraries are perceived to be connected with business or technical organizations, it might be expected that this book would be intended for those in commercial or for-profit firms. However, we became aware that many one-person librarians work in small non-profit or not-for-profit organizations; in fact, many of them are untrained or unchartered and, as mentioned above, many are volunteers. It is hoped that this work will be of particular use to them, as well as to the professional, chartered librarian who has not been specially trained to work in a small, one-person unit, the untrained non-professional who has been promoted to a position of librarianship, the student who is interested in one-person librarianship but who has not had any courses in the subject, and the entry-level librarian, While we have written for a professional readership we have remembered that some readers may not be trained in librarianship but are professional nevertheless, and we have accordingly tried to avoid being too simplistic in our approach.

We are indebted to a great many people who have cooperated in this project. Large numbers have responded to authors' queries in the professional media, and we are grateful to them all. Also, many people, both in the United Kingdom and in the United States, completed questionnaires and sent additional comments and suggestions, all of which were read carefully and considered. Those attending our lectures and seminars have frequently offered helpful suggestions and comments, and we thank them for their interest.

Several friends and colleagues should be thanked for reading the manuscript and making helpful suggestions, and even though they eschew public acknowledgement we are appreciative. We are deeply grateful to Erla Zwingle for editing the first draft, and to Andrew Berner, who read the manuscript for professional content. Finally, staff and management personnel and committee members at the University Club and the Agricultural Training Board have been most supportive and enthusuastic. Needless to say, however, the opinions expressed here are our own.

## A brief history of one-person librarianship

One-person librarianship as a management concept is fairly recent, and apparently came about when the record-keeping functions of businesses and organizations merged with the historical and archival activities of those same organizations. This has not always been the case, however; the tradition of a library run by one person is an old one, and is traceable with certainty as far back as medieval days. Even earlier, of course, the ancients had libraries, and because the quantity of materials housed in the library was small, we may hazard an educated guess that the organization and care of the collection was the responsibility of one person. The libraries of Greece and Alexandria are known to have been taken seriously as collections of books (though not books as we know them). Sulla's acquisition, in 86 BC, of Aristotle's library was so significant that he put it in the charge of two librarians ('Andronicus of Rhodes, who undertook to establish a correct text of the Aristotelian corpus, and Tyrannion, formerly Cicero's literary advisor, who became custodian of the collection').[1] If a collection as important as Sulla's had only two librarians we can safely infer that it was not unusual for other collections to have only one. Another clue to this acceptance is the fact that the librarians who are named in history are named alone, with no mention of assistants, clerks and such helpers. These men, whose names have come down to us as organizers and administrators, may well have been working in one-person libraries.

Even among the early Christians, who were not especially interested in books and record-keeping (primarily because they expected the Second Coming to take place in their lifetimes), there are references 'not only to single books but to groups of books which may be regarded as rudimentary libraries'.[2] Might Timothy have been one of the early Christian one-person librarians? St Paul asks him to 'bring ... the books, especially the parchments' which he had left behind.[2]

Skipping ahead a few centuries, the growth of the monastic communities, each with its own library, meant that the size of the monastic libraries serving those communities also grew. However, staffing for the libraries did not grow. Even though many monks might be employed in copying and other work in the scriptorium, which was attached to the library and frequently under the authority and responsibility of the monk in charge of the library, the responsibility for the collection and, indeed, for the assignment of reading materials, continued to be the duty of one person:

> Benedictine monks were expected to spend some time in reading and study. [Archbishop of Canterbury] Lanfranc's *Constitutions* set out that one day a year 'the librarian shall have a carpet laid down, and all books got together

upon it, except those which a year previously had been assigned for reading. These the brethren are to bring with them when they come to the chapter house, each his book in his hand . . . he whose conscience accuses him of not having read the book . . . is to fall on his face, confess his fault and entreat forgiveness . . .' after which the librarian made a fresh distribution of books.[3]

The collections of these libraries seldom numbered more than a few hundred volumes, and one monk or librarian was responsible for the books, which were usually stored in great wooden book chests, examples of which can still be seen today in Durham Cathedral and other medieval places of worship. Most of the libraries of this period were ecclesiastical, in monasteries, cathedrals and universities (as at the Oxford and Cambridge colleges), and all would have been looked after by that single person. In some larger libraries, such as those in the cathedrals of Hereford and Wells, the books were chained to a lectern or desk for their protection, and users – the monks or the cathedral or diocesan clergy – were required to go to the shelves to study the books they needed. Not all libraries were chained, of course, and as time passed, not all users were necessarily members of a religious community or organization. Dr Johnson is known to have borrowed from Lichfield Cathedral library while compiling his dictionary of the English language.

The first public library in Britain was bequeathed to the City of London by its most famous mayor, Richard (Dick) Whittington, who died childless and left his huge fortune to charity. His executors joined forces with a wealthy London mercer named William Bury to establish and present a library to the City of London. This collection was situated in a building adjoining the Guildhall and, as was common at the time, the library was chained; it was looked after by one person, the chaplain of Guildhall College. Similar libraries were later established at Worcester and Bristol, and regulations drawn up proclaimed that 'the books should be chained and catalogued, and that the librarian should be a Bachelor of Divinity, or at least a graduate . . .' Thus we find another prototypical one-person librarian, and an early example of the requirement equivalent to that of our own time: a proper education for the librarian.

One-person libraries have continued throughout history, especially as the growth of commerce and the invention of printing created the incentive for those who could afford it to build their own private libraries. These libraries were not large enough to require staffs of library administrators, but for noblemen, ecclesiastics and ambitious and educated merchants who wanted someone to look after their books, one person would suffice. Thus did Casanova serve as librarian to Count Waldstein, only one of many examples of this kind of one-person library service in Western history.

As the level of literacy continued to rise in Britain, grammar schools multiplied in number until there were about three or four hundred by the end of the sixteenth century. Each of these schools, of course, had its own small library, usually in the charge of one of the masters, but in the grammar school libraries, as is sometimes the case today, the master in charge of the library had other duties as well.

Subscription libraries began to appear in the eighteenth century, and while these forerunners of the public library systems were controlled by a board of directors or overseers, who chose to involve themselves in hands-on activity and thus participated in financial affairs, book selection, etc., the day-to-day operations required the services of a single staff member, almost always hired by the library's lenders. Even Benjamin Franklin's Library Company of Philadelphia, founded in 1731, had as an early order of business the hiring of a librarian (*after*, it might be noted, the raising of funds, the purchase of the books and the beginning of work on the catalogue): Louis Timothée, a protégé of Franklin, 'a young French refugee recently arrived from Holland',[5] was chosen.

The subscription libraries developed because of the demand from lay people, particularly the middle classes, for access to literature of all kinds, both religous and secular. Books were very expensive, and so the idea of clubbing together to subscribe to a collection of books seemed a practical one. Probably the first library of this kind in Britain was at Norwich, a cathedral town in East Anglia, where in 1716 subscribers were allowed to borrow books from the old town library, which was originally for the use of students only. However, the typical 'gentleman's subscription library' of the eighteenth and nineteenth centuries was completely separate from the public library and the earliest examples of these gentlemen's libraries were in Scotland. The stock tended towards *belles lettres*, history, biography, travel, science and some fiction, if it were of literary merit, e.g. Defoe, Richardson or Fielding. The library would have been small in size, containing not more than a few thousand volumes, often set up on premises hired for the purpose, and frequently over a bookshop, with the bookseller acting as librarian.

These libraries were followed by the mechanics' institutes (the forerunners of the modern adult education organizations) and working-men's subscription libraries; these, too, were organized and run, as a general rule, by one person. The list of examples goes on, especially in America and the United Kingdom, where any roomful of books, particularly in the nineteenth century, had one person whose role was not only to watch over and care for them but even to bring together user and book.

By the time of the great library revolution in America in 1876 the one-person library, though still an important part of librarianship, especially in private collections and small academic institutions, was beginning to give way to the library in which several librarians, with specialized tasks performed in conjunction with general library service, were the more accepted form of librarianship. From 1876 onwards the idea of library work as a service profession began to take hold, and teams of librarians were required to provide library services to those many people who were without them. There were, of course, those small rural libraries where the librarians so sweetly and charmingly portrayed in musical comedies and films held forth alone and did their work as a strong force for moral order in the community, but even the fictional librarian began to be part of a team rather than a loner, as demonstrated by Katharine Hepburn and her associates in the film *Desk Set*.

However, not all librarians worked in teams. In fact, the *Desk Set* librarians would seem to have been an exception, particularly in special libraries. Librarians in public and academic libraries were usually part of a larger organization, but in special libraries and school libraries the single librarian remained the standard. Today the library operated as a one-person managerial unit is still usually found in a non-public situation. In the United Kingdom and in the United States, one-person libraries exist in such varied organizations as legal, accounting and computing firms, learned societies, agricultural institutes, engineering and chemical companies, research institutions, hospitals and schools, food and drink companies, cathedrals, marketing organizations and as small offshoots of larger governmental libraries. Frequently a technical or specialized library is created when the organization suddenly discovers the need to set up a small library and information unit at a modest cost. A pile of books, journals and legal papers suddenly must be put into some sort of order, and the parent institution employs a person to do the job. (While usually referred to as a 'library' from the time the suggestion is made to establish such a unit, the library is seldom appreciated immediately as a professionally organized and administered operation. In fact, it might be some years before its value becomes apparent to the management.) As a start, an attempt to supply materials for the proposed facility is made, often by gathering non-essential items which are in the way in offices and laboratories, which gives the space for the proposed library the air of a storeroom or warehouse even before the first applicant has been interviewed for the job of caring for the collection.

One-person libraries are not always organized after the fact, however, and it would be misleading to imply that such is always the case. Many institutions and corporate bodies are aware from their inception that a library is a necessary adjunct of their operation, and as plans are made for founding such an institution a library and a professionally trained librarian are included in the initial planning. Thus historical societies, advertising firms, small museums, clubs and professional associations, trade unions, publishing firms and performing-arts companies are all examples of the kind of parent institution which have some sort of library and librarian included in their start-up plans.

Then, unfortunately, there are those one-person libraries which are created negatively, because of budget cuts or redundancies. It is a sad fact that in times of economic stringency it is often the library or information unit which must suffer first. The unit already exists as part of the managerial structure, but suddenly there is only one person left to do the work formerly assigned to two and sometimes more employees. This situation is the most difficult one-person library assignment of all, for what has gone before has created a standard which will be practically impossible to maintain and, no matter how well-intentioned the surviving employee may be, there is little he can do to prevent a deterioration in the care of the collection or the quality of service.

In all three situations – where the library has always been part of the parent organization's structure, where one was created where it did not exist before, and where one has been created negatively – management has the responsibility for the quality of service, and it is the level of seriousness with which management regards this obligation that determines the role of the library in the parent organization,

## References

1  Thompson, James Westfall, *The Medieval Library*, University of Chicago Press, Chicago, 1939, p. 5.
2  Ibid., p. 14.
3  Rousham, Sally, *Canterbury: The Story of a Cathedral*, The Dean and Chapter of Christ Church, Canterbury, 1975, p. 26

4  Kelly, T. and E., *Books for the People: an Illustrated History of the British Public Library*, André Deutsch, London, 1977, pp. 16-19.
5  Gray, Austin K., *Benjamin Franklin's Library: A Short Account of the Library Company of Philadelphia: 1731-1931*, The Macmillan Company, New York, 1937, p. 11.

# The one-person librarian: a profile

Little has been written about the one-person library and the work done there, so it is with some lack of precise statistics that we attempt to profile the one-person librarian. However, working in a one-person library is closely akin to working in any other small business with a specific subject focus, and some generalized characteristics may be derived from that analogy. As for specific features, there have been a few studies and reports based on questionnaires, including that of the authors, and certain quantifiable characteristics may be described.

The British Library Research and Development Report by R. Serjean entitled 'Librarianship and Information Work: Job Characteristics'[1] draws on the 1972 census carried out by the Department of Education and Science which states that 32 per cent of library and information units employ one person either full- or part-time. The 1981 census shows that the figure has grown to about 50 per cent.[2] Considering the advances in modern technology and the reluctance of contemporary management personnel to add staff to library and information units, it is unlikely that the proportion of one-person librarians in the profession will fall to less than the one-third figure. In fact, it is probably safe to assume that the number of one-person library operations will continue to grow, as management comes to realize that one excellent, efficient and enthusiastic librarian or information specialist is preferable to two or more who do not provide the same level of service for users.

As we discuss numbers, however, we should consider that the Library Association in the United Kingdom had just under 25 000 paid-up members in 1984, and other organizations such as Aslib with a membership of 2082 (some from overseas) and the Institute of Information Scientists (IIS) with a membership of 1950 in 1983 account for the majority of persons working in library and information services. In the United States, the American Library Association lists a membership roster of some 40 000 librarians and information specialists, and the Special Libraries Association, which is roughly comparable with Aslib in the United Kingdom in that its members are generally (but not always) employed in non-traditional library situations, claims some 11 500 librarians and information specialists as members. There are, however, people in charge of one-person libraries who do not belong to any of these professional bodies. When we also remember that there are organizations such as the British Association of Law Libraries, the School Library Association, the Society of Archivists, the Private Libraries Association and, in the United States, specialized professional groups such as the Art Libraries Society/North America, the International Association of Law Libraries, the International Association of Music Libraries, the International Society of Jewish Librarians, the Music Library Association, the National Librarians Association, the Society of American Archivists, the Theatre Library Association, the Western Association of Map Libraries, the Church and Synagogue Library Association and any number of organizations with other special subject interests (representing picture, rare book, historical, legal, science and technology, education and various other types of collections), the number of one-person libraries is seen to be enormous, even taking into consideration the fact that some librarians may hold dual memberships of some of these professional bodies. There is, in the United Kingdom, one professional group devoted to the needs and interests of one-person librarianship (the 'one-man band' group of Aslib), but no such group exists, as yet, in the United States.

Many of these small libraries have grown up in the last decade or so to meet the information needs of various concerns. A high proportion of work in these small units calls for generalists and all-rounders; the need for functional specialists, the bibliographers and cataloguers, is basically limited to the larger library units, although many one-person librarians do have some sort of subject degree or qualification, depending on the kind of work performed in the parent organization.

In the one-person library the work will include everything, from the most senior tasks to the most menial, and any attempt to divide duties into professional and non-professional, as in larger libraries, would not make much sense. In the variety of tasks to be completed in a day, the well-trained one-person librarian can also be an educator – to management as well as to staff – and a consultant, teaching non-library staff how to use the library and to make better use of its services. As they learn to do things for themselves, the librarian is then able to pursue more challenging tasks.

There are, of course, unpleasant aspects of library work, just as with any job, and the one-person librarian must also perform these tasks. Serjean states that the most unpopular activities in a one-person unit are those associated with clerical and administrative routine. More serious problems may include lack of status; limited time for planning; reading of professional journals; and further training or personal contact with other professional librarians and information specialists: in sum, frustrated professional development. Hence the establishment of the OMB group as a part of Aslib, a group which effectively cuts across the boundaries of various professional organizations and even includes those who do not qualify or cannot justify membership of Aslib. This variety is inevitable, as, according to Serjean, only 38 per cent of staff in one-person operations have subject degrees and only 31 per cent have professional qualifications.

Conclusions similar to Serjean's were reached from a study conducted by Janet Shuter and Judith Collins for the British Library Reference Division (BLRD).[3] The first phase of the study surveyed two populations: recipients of the Department of Employment (GB) Work Research Unit information systems publications, trades union libraries and community research units, and members of the Aslib OMB Group. It resulted in a response rate of 15 per cent of those contacted, including 52 employees in one-person libraries. A second survey had a response rate of 59 per cent, with a usable response rate of 47 per cent, or 76 employees in one-person libraries. The content of the study ranged over various aspects of work, working conditions, qualifications and career history, revealing a picture of the information worker in isolation. As the results were compiled, groupings were made of those who were 'extremely satisfied' and 'very dissatisfied', with an 'average' group in between. When we look at the job factors which the three groups felt most came up to expectations we see that, among all one-person librarians – the 'average' group in the middle – organizing one's own time was at the top of the list, followed by the autonomy of the position, the interest level of the work, the fact that tasks requiring specialized and professional or paraprofessional skills do not have to be delegated, and the variety of the work done in the library. For those one-person librarians who are satisfied with their work the interest level of the work was at the top of the list of job factors which came up to expectations, followed by the pleasant situation of being in a position to try out new ideas, being appreciated for the work they do, the variety of the work they do, and the satisfaction they take in their work. On the other hand, when they listed job factors which most came up to expectations, dissatisfied one-person librarians thought that not delegating skilled tasks was the primary attribute of their work that came up to their expectations, telling us, it would seem, that when they accepted their positions in one-person libraries they expected not to delegate skilled tasks. For this group, the other factors which they expected included organizing one's own time, the people with whom they worked (presumably users and other staff in the parent institution, not other staff in the library), the autonomy of the position, being kept busy, and the security of the job.

It is interesting that the satisfied group singles out three factors closely related to the job itself, plus two other motivation factors. Two positive aspects cited by the whole group – interest and variety – relate to the content of the job, while the top six cited by the dissatisfied group relate mainly to working conditions. This distinction is interesting. Are the most satisfied one-person librarians more motivated because they have better status etc. as a result of performing more interesting tasks, regardless of the working conditions? Or do they attain better status because they are *more* motivated and market the services of the library better? Which comes first?

On the other hand, the factors which all three groups regarded as the 'worst' aspects of the job are also of interest. For all of the one-person librarians responding to the survey, lack of training was considered the main problem. This same characteristic was at the top of the list of 'worst' aspects for the satisfied one-person librarians, but after that the lists varied. For the total group, the remaining problems with the job had to do with reliability (or lack of it) of management support, not knowing what is going on in the parent organization, the physical working conditions, the lack of interest (presumably by management) in contributing to personal development, and low pay.

Interestingly, for the satisfied one-person librarians the second 'worst' aspect of the job was the amount of pay (presumably insufficient) for the work done, followed by concern about fair company policy and administration, lack of agreement with organizational objectives, job security, physical working conditions and, again, not knowing what is going on in the parent organization.

For the dissatisfied one-person librarians the order is very different, and there is one new aspect not mentioned in the primary list of the total respondents or in the responses of the satisfied one-person librarians. It comes at the top of the list: the organization as employer. Does this mean that for dissatisfied one-person librarians their main concern is that they do not approve of the work the parent organization is doing, that they actually disapprove of the primary mission of the parent organization? The other 'worst' aspects of the dissatisfied one-person librarians were also mentioned by the other groups but in different order of importance. For the dissatisfied librarians, after the organization as employer, the aspects listed were not knowing what is going on in the organization, the amount of (or lack of) pay for work done, being appreciated, lack of interest in or contribution to personal development, and lack of training.

Three characteristics are cited by all three groups: pay, training, and knowing (or not knowing) what is going on in the organization. It is interesting to note that no group seems happy with senior management! Is it a coincidence also that 59 per cent of satisfied one-person librarians and only 30 per cent of non-satisfied one-person librarians belong to a trade union? It is thus indicated – though not proven – that there may be a correlation between trade-union membership and job satisfaction. Another possibility is that highly motivated one-person librarians are using trade-union membership as a means of overcoming isolation, improving communication within the workplace, and obtaining union-provided training. Thus they seem to be able to obtain equal status with qualified staff in other areas, rather than being on a lower rung, as often happens.

It might not be unfair to suggest that perhaps library schools are somewhat at fault for producing the wrong type of graduate to enter the small technical or commercial library field. There seems to be something anomalous in library education – many library schools are still educating students to be library managers in charge of several staff and thus teach no clerical skills at all. The market indicates that schools should really be training at least some of the students to become *all-rounders* – bright, adaptable, trainable, able to innovate and cooperate, and with good *social* skills. Many one-person libraries need entrepreneurs, not bookish and introverted subject specialists. They need to be dedicated, professionally motivated, adaptable and keen, and must not mind a little drudgery at times. Personal development and growth can be as important as academic training, and we should expect the graduate library schools to develop these traits in their students. When this area becomes part of the graduate programme those students who accept employment in the one-person library world will find more career opportunities and be less threatened by economic fluctuations.

Generally speaking, if one wishes to advance in the parent organization the one-person library is not the place from which to begin one's climb. Career advancement from the smaller library and information unit is virtually impossible unless one is prepared to move away from purely library and information work into administrative or general management. It might be possible to 'empire-build' and thus create a two- or three-person operation for the library and information needs of the parent organization, but in times when the economy is tight such expansion is difficult and not a little dangerous. Management may perceive that the library is taking up too much of the organization's budget and close it altogether, although such a reaction would be extreme. There is a very delicate balance to be considered here. Does one offer a very full service and push for the necessary extra staff, or provide the bare minimum with only one person? It is a difficult choice and one which may be made only by considering seriously the circumstances of the parent organization and its information needs. Frankly speaking, promotion in the one-person library situation requires a willingness to switch employers: never easy, especially when times are bad, but not impossible either. Thus in the last few years we have seen the rise of a virtually new industry that has grown up offering career options for dissatisfied librarians. Further reading on this subject, especially for the one-person library employee, may be found in *What Else Can You Do With a Library Degree?* by Betty-Carol Selben.[4]

An informal survey conducted by the authors (questionnaire and conversation) revealed some further features of the profile. For example, more than 80 per cent of one-person librarians have the title 'Librarian', although other titles, such as 'Manager', 'Supervisor', 'Director', 'Media Specialist' and 'Information Officer' are also used. By type of library, the range is wide: more than 25 per cent work in the corporate world, and in the United States (but not in the United Kingdom) almost as many work in public libraries, especially in rural communities. About an equal number (approximately 11 per cent) work in academic and school libraries, a few work in medical or health sciences libraries (approximately 9 per cent) and law libraries (approximately 6 per cent), and somewhere between a quarter and a fifth of these librarians work in libraries which resist classification by type, such as societies, charities and volunteer organizations (quite a large number in the United Kingdom), museums, private organizations of one sort or another, churches and synagogues, etc.

There is no question that the one-person librarian works hard, and we discovered several telling facts: 70 per cent of them have between 1000 and 15 000 volumes in their collections, pretty equally divided between those with 1000–2500 volumes, those with 5000–10 000 volumes and those with 10 000–15 000 volumes, adding up to about 70 per cent of those with whom we spoke or corresponded. Occasionally we would run into someone who ran a very small library (under 1000 volumes) or one with over 25 000 volumes, but these were decidedly the exceptions. Depending on the kind of work done in the library, it seems unlikely that one person can handle the work involved in running a library containing more than 25 000 volumes.

When we asked one-person librarians how many books they added annually we found that about a quarter of them add betwen 1 and 99 titles to the collection. Fewer librarians add 101-200, 201-300 and 401-500 volumes, respectively. Some 11 per cent each add 501-750 or 751-1000 volumes annually, and a small number of one-person librarians add 301-400 or over 1000 volumes annually.

Describing one-person libraries by the number of periodicals to which they subscribe leads to the fact that more than a quarter of them receive between 51 and 75 titles; 16 per cent of these libraries receive between 26 and 50 titles and 13 per cent receive between 76 and 100 titles, so we can conclude that most one-person librarians do not have to deal with voluminous subscription mail. (We are not referring here to the other kinds of mail that come into the one-person library.) A very small percentage receive fewer than 25 titles or more than 100 titles, although there is the occasional library which reports that it receives as many as 250 subscription titles. None, in our survey, receives more than 250 titles, a fact for which we are sure those one-person librarians are most grateful!

When we asked about the status of the libraries in which they were employed we found that the great majority of them (66 per cent) work in a unit supported by an institution. Some few one-person librarians reported that they were employed in libraries that are part of a larger library system, and 27 per cent reported that they work in independent libraries. When we asked if they were literally a one-person library almost 60 per cent of them reported that they do, indeed, supervise someone, from 'Student', 'Secretary', 'Volunteer' or 'Prisoner', to 'Library Assistant', 'Clerk', 'Assistant Librarian' or 'Research Librarian'. In these situations we must assume that the one-person librarian is, in fact, what we would call a 'one-professional' librarian, since the distinction seems to be made here that the librarian is the only staff person with a graduate degree or chartered status and is thus the only 'librarian' in the library. Whether this person is in fact responsible for running a 'one-person' library is more a matter of semantics than managerial categorization. The fact that a librarian with assistance thinks of himself or herself as working in a one-person library means something, and it may be helpful to that librarian to identify with those who work in true one-person situations. However, it is interesting to note that, of those who reported that they supervise someone in their 'one-person' libraries, fully 56 per cent of them were *not* responsible for hiring or choosing that person. Perhaps this tells us more about the relationship between the librarian and his or her management than it does about the benefits of assistance to one-person librarians.

Another way of viewing the one-person librarian is to see if there is a library committee or board involved in the library's work. It is not so common in the United Kingdom for libraries, especially small units, to have committees, and only about 23 per cent of the libraries surveyed in the United Kingdom did, in fact, have committees, practically all of which were simply advisory. The practice is somewhat more prevalent in the United States. Of the American librarians who told us about their work, we estimate that about two-thirds do not work with a library committee or board; where they do, the majority of the committees (approximately 71 per cent) are simply advisory. About 6 per cent of the committees have a supervisory role in the library, with approximately 23 per cent characterized as partially supervisory.

For those librarians whose libraries are part of a larger institution, about half of the Americans and more than half of the British told us that they are included in non-library decision-making, the rest not. Not unexpectedly, when asked if they are regularly included in institutional staff meetings, about half said that they were and about half said that they were not. Some 53 per cent said that their jobs included tasks other than library work, but there is no apparent dissatisfaction with this arrangement. However, when asked if they had to perform non-library-related tasks which seemed to just 'fall their way' (being in charge of the coffee fund or supplies, organizing the annual Christmas party, collecting money for staff retirement parties, etc.), approximately two-thirds of the responding librarians said that they do not do such jobs, including several who responded most emphatically that they would not consider doing such tasks. Thus we find an interesting picture here: there seems to be a perception that many one-person librarians view the performance of these duties to be a problem, but in fact most one-person librarians are not asked to or do not accept such tasks. Perhaps those few who are put in this position are simply people who complain loudly and frequently and therefore create an invalid perception. They are not, it would seem, representative of the majority of one-person librarians.

When we asked the one-person library employees about their working conditions we found fairly predictable responses. About half of them think they have enough space and about half of them think they do not. Fully 98 per cent of the respondents told us that they have a telephone in the library, an obvious aid to combating the proverbial isolation if the librarian will see it as such.

A role in formal policy-making in the one-person library is pretty evenly divided between those who have it and those who do not. Of the librarians asked, 45 per cent have a written acquisitions policy and 55 per cent do not. However, 34 per cent of these same librarians have their selections reviewed by a committee or other administrator before the materials are ordered. Of those one-person libraries which circulate materials, 61 per cent have a written circulation policy and 39 per cent do not. Borrowers are allowed to check the circulation files in approximately one-third of the libraries surveyed, but usually only under extraordinary circumstances.

It is possible, within the limitations of this informal poll, to characterize the type of reference service that takes place in the library. When asked if they accepted telephone reference enquiries 83 per cent of the one-person librarians said that they do, and several implied that they do so most enthusiastically. Most of these librarians conduct manual bibliographic searches for their users, about one-third of them conduct computerized bibliographic searches, and approximately 70 per cent of them belong to or participate in formal or informal networks, consortia, etc. Fully 90 per cent of the one-person librarians contacted said that two-thirds of the librarians provide formal bibliographic instruction to library users.

In the final analysis probably the only way to characterize the one-person librarian is to go to each one and ask him or her to express an opinion about working alone. We found that 60 per cent see themselves as working primarily in public services, while only 40 per cent considered themselves as primarily technical services employees. This, perhaps, is as good an informal portrait of one-person librarianship as any. Most see themselves as employed to serve their users, or at least as employed to facilitate getting the appropriate information or material to their users. They are, indeed, service oriented and expect to be part of the team which supports the organization's corporate goals.

# References

1 Serjean, R., 'Librarianship and information work: job characteristics and staffing needs', *British Library R&D Report 5321 HC*, London, 1977.

2 East, Harry 'Changes in the staffing of UK special libraries and information services in the decade 1972-1981: a review of the DES census data', *Journal of Documentation*, **39**, 4, 247-265, 1983.

3 Shuter, J. and Collins, J., 'The isolated professional', *Information and Library Manager*, **3**, 4, 106, 1984.

4 Selben, Betty-Carol (ed.), *What Else Can You Do With a Library Degree?* Gaylord Professional Publications in Association with Neal-Schuman Publishers, New York, 1980.

Chapter Three

# Professional isolation and independence

There are advantages to working in a small library, and a one-person situation offers even more attractive advantages. Certainly the independence (for those who prefer working independently) can be a very special inducement for providing first-class work, an opportunity many in the workforce do not have. When one-person librarians are asked what is the best thing about their work – the one thing they would not change – the answer invariably has to do with their independence. Yet these same people, when asked to comment about the worst part of one-person librarianship, give the same answer, or a variation of it: 'professional isolation'. It would appear, then, that these two characteristics of one-person library work are two sides of the same coin. What can be done to alleviate the problem of isolation while enhancing the benefits of independence?

The answer depends very much on the personality of the librarian, and his willingness to seek out others who may be in a position to advise, consult, discuss and/or simply listen to the problems and pleasures of one-person librarianship. Occasionally, of course, there is someone on the staff of the parent organization who is in a position to listen, a co-worker, perhaps, or a supervising management person, or a user who enjoys the library and spends much time there. Possibly even a member of a committee or board which plays a role, advisory or supervisory, in the library's management can be one who comes to the library as much to listen as to work. If there is such a person, the wise librarian will go to him or her occasionally to seek advice, to inform and certainly to share some of the more theoretical and problematic questions that come up from time to time in the running of the library. It goes without saying that this kind of involvement on the part of interested people is certainly good public relations, probably second only to the quality of service provided by the library in encouraging people to think positively about the library and its services.

There are dangers, however, and the layman, no matter how interested he might be in the workings of the library (and many laymen seem to think running a library is a pretty simple task, akin to keeping orderly files in an office), can only advise from the point of view of a non-professional. The layman, despite the best intentions, is not qualified to understand many of the librarian's concerns, and it is in the librarian's best interest – and that of the parent organization – for him or her to seek such advice elsewhere.

So we should look to other professionals for advice and comfort, but in the one-person library how do we do this? Communication plays a vital role here, for the librarian who works alone has no-one to turn to – for professional concerns – except other librarians, often others who work alone, but just as often librarians who work in larger institutions who are willing to give of their time and energy, usually on a very personal, one-to-one basis, to discuss and describe how they handle some of the problems that are common to all librarians. It is through setting up lines of communication with other librarians that we find a solution to the problems of professional isolation.

There are several ways in which the one-person librarian can seek out other librarians with whom to associate. Before those means are described, however, some consideration should be given to the subject of the independence of the one-person library employee, since that independence often lays the groundwork for the pattern of communication set up later on with other librarians. The librarian who works alone is, of course, on the job for most of his or her work shift, and one of the problems of this situation, as we shall see, is the difficulty of getting away to meet with others, to attend professional meetings and seminars. On the other hand, one of the advantages of working alone is the opportunity one has of setting up the work patterns, managing time and arranging one's routines in such a way that one benefits from the schedule. Although there are certain duties that must be performed at prescribed times, there are others that are more flexible, and it is these duties that the librarian who works alone arranges and rearranges to suit his or her own schedule. Even the librarian who is unable to get away from the office for outside meetings with other librarians can arrange some of the duties to make time to get on the telephone to talk to others.

As we discuss the independence of the one-person librarian we must consider how that independence can be used to professional advantage. How can the independence of the one-person librarian be used to open up the lines of communication with other librarians? There are three factors: an understanding of the role of professional associations for the librarian, the importance of personal contacts, and the utilization and implementation of connections and/ or networking, formal and informal, which are exploited for the benefit of the librarian and the parent institution.

Why do we join professional associations? Indeed, what are professional associations and what do they mean for the librarian working alone? Ferguson and Mobley tell us that 'associations exist in almost every conceivable field of human knowledge and activity',[1] and so they do. For librarians, and most especially for one-person librarians, associations not only have practical value but are often the means by which professionalism is affirmed. Ferguson and Mobley assert that 'one important mark of a profession is that it has an organization addressed to its concerns', and they characterize membership in a professional organization as 'vital' in developing a professional career.[1] In the preceding chapter, in which we drew an informal profile of the one-person librarian, we listed some of the many professional associations available to one-person librarians in the United Kingdom and the United States. Each of these exists to play a particular role in the professional lives of working librarians, and if it is doing its job right, according to Dennis Lewis, an association should be providing the following back-up services: education, training, conferences, seminars and meetings, groups, branches, a professional register of members, research and development, a library for its members, and publications.[2] The wise librarian will take advantage of the opportunity to belong to such groups.

What are the benefits of belonging to several professional organizations? Obviously, membership brings professional literature, the reading of which is necessary for the librarian who is interested in knowing what is going on in the profession and who appreciates that there will be new developments, new technologies and different approaches to library management, even for the small, single-person unit. To join one's national association will enable the librarian to know what is happening on the national level. Further, membership is an advantage in a local association or in a local chapter of a national organization, because their meetings, particularly those held after business hours, are more convenient, and can lead the one-person librarian to people who may prove helpful.

There are other reasons for joining a professional association. Many such groups are subject oriented, so the one-person librarian employed in a law library can benefit from knowing what is going on in the professional law librarians' group; and similarly with theatre librarians, picture librarians, etc. Other groups may be organized by areas of professional interest, such as library-management groups, rare-books groups or private-libraries groups. Finally, some one-person librarians find it advantageous to belong to the societies which support the specific subjects dealt with in their libraries. Thus librarians in historical societies belong to historical and genealogical groups, chemical librarians belong to chemical groups, and so on. All of these will provide material and contacts to aid the one-person librarian.

While these library associations will bring a wealth of materials across the desk of the one-person librarian – often more material than one can possibly absorb or even find the time to read – there are other advantages in belonging to professional groups. In addition to professional affirmation the library associations provide members with the opportunity to interact with one another, probably the most important asset a professional association may offer for those librarians who will take advantage of them. Certainly the one-person librarian who can justify the time and can do the work should get on committees, be part of workshop planning groups, give papers, etc. Frankly, if one is serving, management is more likely to accede to your request for participation. This does not, however, imply that one must be a 'doer' as well as a 'joiner'. Serving on committees and task forces and boards is not the primary objective of most people who join professional groups. If one does become involved, so much the better for the organization, but as long as the dues are paid up, one does not have to feel guilty if one merely attends meetings and reads the journals. It is not written anywhere that active participation is the only way to benefit from belonging to a professional organization. It seems that those who do participate are usually 'doers' anyway.

However, there is a more practical side that should be considered. If a one-person library employee recognizes the advantages of belonging to a professional organization, going out to meet people, attending conferences and seminars, visiting other libraries to see how they work, etc., how does one go about it? First of all, make a serious attempt to convince management that one's participation will benefit the parent organization. The object is to persuade management to support, with a commitment of funds and time, the librarian's participation in professional associations. For, as in any business or profession, the better informed the employee is, the better an employee he or she will be. It is the librarian's duty to discuss frankly and openly the advantages of membership for the organization itself and to assess the benefits that such activities – through the librarian – bring to the organization as a whole.

If management is receptive to the idea of some professional participation for the one-person librarian, it is better to treat each meeting separately rather than seek a blanket absence, such as suggesting that one must be away at a certain time each year for a particular conference. Since supervising personnel can be better informed about the specific advantages of each meeting if permission is requested separately, the librarian is not perceived as putting attendance at the meeting before the subject matter.

In addition to management support and approval, there are other practical considerations in the one-person librarian's participation in association activities. One, of course, is the scheduling of meetings and events. It is difficult for the one-person librarian to get away during business hours, but most professional groups seem to try to plan at least some of their meetings and programmes in the evenings and/or at weekends, and in the US there is now a trend to schedule breakfast meetings. Such scheduling should be encouraged by the one-person librarians who are members of these groups.

For the one-person librarian who has difficulty in getting away from the office to attend meetings or seminars, perhaps thought should be given to treating these absences in the same way as any other absences from the office. After all, one has to determine, with management, how to cover the library when one is out sick, when one goes to the dentist and when one is on holiday, and perhaps the same solution can be applied to the library when one must be away occasionally for a professional absence. It is a subject which should be discussed with management, and both the librarian and the librarian's supervising personnel should have a clear understanding of what the organization's policy is about professional absences.

Finally, consideration could be given (perhaps as a last resort for the librarian who is not totally committed to thinking about her work even in her free time) to the possibility of using holiday or vacation time for attending professional meetings and conferences. Unless one is in an academic library and the meetings take place during break periods, it might not be such a bad idea to use one's vacation for such activities. This is an idea not commonly accepted in the American labour force, but for professionals it is not to be dismissed out of hand. Professional meetings, certainly the larger ones, are generally held in places which are attractive to tourists, so one can combine work and pleasure, if one is inclined to do so.

In any case, it is communication with supervising personnel which determines the extent of one's participation, and even if that participation must be limited it is to that librarian's advantage, at the very least, to hold membership of the appropriate professional associations.

The discussion of the role of professional associations for the one-person librarian leads directly to a consideration of the importance of personal contacts, for it is in the professional associations that we first become acquainted, and perhaps even friendly, with the people we want to know when we need to call upon them. It is not at all uncommon for librarians, gathering for a meeting, to have a few minutes to socialize before the programme begins, and it is in those few minutes that we can make the personal contacts which can be so useful. Librarians do not necessarily have to go to one another's libraries to interact profitably; their friendship, developed from casual meetings at professional gatherings, can lead to confidence about ringing up when they have a question to ask or another's opinion to seek.

The idea of connections is not a new one, but it was given new impetus and a sort of formalization a few years ago when Carol Nemeyer, Associate Librarian of Congress for National Programs, used it as the theme during her term of office as President of the American Library Association.[3] Nemeyer, of course, was discussing how more formal connections (with the business community, for example, or the heads of state library agencies) can be useful to the profession as a whole, but her theme inspires us to look at what connections we can use. When one seeks connections one simply observes which people or organizations may be useful in one's work, and when the need arises they are approached. If a user needs to see a particular type of material not collected at one's library, for example, but the librarian has recently been introduced to another librarian whose library does collect the needed material, it is far simpler for the user, and for the parent organization employing the librarian, to be put in touch with the librarian who has the material. It is not a complicated idea, and it is certainly one which most of us exploit informally from time to time, but it is something which should be considered as a regular resource for the innovative librarian. Connections can make our lives much easier, and certainly improve the results for our users. The goal of the one-person library is a simple one: to get the information to the user. If one has to use connections to do so, it should be done. There is nothing wrong with this, and there is no reason to be reluctant, as long as each librarian is courteous and is prepared to be as generous with his or her specific subject specialities and professional time as he or she expects others to be. One does not have to apologize as long as one is willing to share one's own strengths in the same way.

The more formal networks require a different kind of consideration because they are joined, usually at some cost to the parent organization of which the one-person library is a part, and their utilization must be justified in terms of value for money. 'That no library and information service can be self-sufficient, but needs to become involved in the exploitation of shared resources, has been an established fact since the early 1930s.[4] So writes J. Burkett in Aslib's *Handbook of Special Librarianship and Information Work*, and the picture in the United States is not much different: 'Librarians in general, and certainly special librarians, take pride in cooperating well with one another ... No special librarians think of their resources as limited to their own institutions.'[5]

What, in fact, is a network? In the United States it is defined by the National Commission on Libraries and Information Science (NCLIS):

> Two or more libraries and/or other organizations engaged in a common pattern of information exchange, through communications, for some functional purpose. A network usually consists of a formal arrangement whereby materials, information and services provided by a variety of libraries and/or other organizations are made available to potential users.[6]

It is commonly accepted within the profession that networking is still evolving, but for the one-person librarian there are many useful networks. These are often affiliated, in the United States, with a regional library system or a group of libraries within an industry or corporation, and formal participation in such networks provide such benefits to the one-person librarian as the free exchange of photocopies, hand-delivered interlibrary loans, etc. Some networks are more useful than others, often depending upon the quality of materials available, so it is up to each one-person librarian to decide if participation in such networks is advantageous or not. The evaluation of networking activities and the significance of such programmes to the one-person library is often an extremely subjective decision and one which is not arrived at without a great deal of thought and care. Here again, the experiences of colleagues and friends in similar libraries can be beneficial.

Finally, as we think of the one-person librarian's concern with professional isolation we must admit that the situation itself is one of simply being alone. It is up to each individual librarian to take that liability – the isolation – and turn it into an asset. The above suggestions will help some, but in the final analysis, it is the librarians themselves who have the ability to change how they think about their work. It is they who must assume the correct attitude, to see their working alone as another side of their independence. For the librarian working alone, her sense of professional self-worth is often neglected. She is a professional, specially trained to do the work she performs. Yet because of the circumstances of the job, there is no immediate interaction with other professionals and, as we have seen, the library's clients and the other employees of the organization do not think in terms of such distinctions. Thus if the librarian is to carry out her duties successfully the professional affirmation each of us needs must come first from inside. It will, if we follow a simple rule: always think of yourself as a professional, even when performing non-professional tasks. This is a subject we have entered into before:

> In speaking of professional and non-professional roles, it is easy to lapse into semantics. The terms have been defined and redefined, so it is not necessary to go into those details here. Yet there is one distinction which might be appropriate: the non-professional works a set number of hours, but a professional, generally speaking, works on a particular job, and works until

the job is done. This is not to say that a professional does not work set hours. Of course he does, but his concern is more with the project or piece of work itself than the hours on the job.

In the one-person library, it is essential that the librarian be aware of the distinction and think of himself as a professional. He needs it for his own professional affirmation and also to keep the level of service where it should be. Even when doing clerical tasks, he must think of himself as a professional doing clerical work, not as a clerk working in a library.[7]

## References

1 Ferguson, Elizabeth and Mobley, Emily R., *Special Libraries at Work*, Library Professional Publications, an imprint of The Shoe String Press, Inc., Hamden, Connecticut, 1984, p. 161.

2 Lewis, D. A., 'The role of the professional organisation', *Aslib Proceedings*, **35**, 2, 108-121, 1983.

3 'President Nemeyer: seeking good connections [1982 ALA Annual Conference Inaugural Address]', *American Libraries*, **13**, 9, 531, 1982.

4 Burkett, J., 'Library and information networks', *Handbook of Special Librarianship and Information Work*, Aslib, London, 1982, p. 377.

5 Benson, Joseph, 'Networking: the new wave for special librarians', *Special Librarianship: A New Reader*, The Scarecrow Press, Inc., Metuchen, New Jersey, 1980, p. 380.

6 Rouse, William B. and Rouse, Sondra H., *Management of Library Networks: Policy Analysis, Implementation, and Control*, Wiley, New York, 1981, pp. 4-5, cited in Ferguson and Mobley, op. cit., p. 147.

7 St Clair, Guy, 'The one-person library: an essay on essentials', *Special Libraries*, **67**, 5/6, 234-235, 1976.

# Managing the library

It is a commonly held notion that managing a one-person library is like running any other small office, but librarians know that this is not the case. In fact, it is this kind of thinking on the part of management and others not familiar with the requirements of good library management which seems to cause many of the problems found in one-person librarianship. Too often, the general administrative staff seems unaware of the value of a library. While the library must maintain the same business-like administrative procedures to be found in any office, librarians recognize that a library, as an organizational unit, is different from an office. Yet we must also appreciate that the library is part of the parent organization and, in the case of many (if not most) libraries run by only one staff member, the library is thought of administratively as just another office. Therefore, a recognition of the role of the library in the parent organization's administrative structure is the basis for a successful and productive relationship between the librarian and management.

## The role of the library

What is the role of the library in the parent organization? Perhaps the best way to find an answer is to seek a definition of what a 'special' library is, for most one-person librarians are employed in what would be called special libraries. Indeed, even in academic and public situations, when the provision of library service is the responsibility of only one staff member, the library is usually what is called a 'special' library. Wilfred Ashworth, in *Special Librarianship*, defines a special library as 'one which is established to obtain and exploit specialized information for the private advantage of the organization which provides its financial support ... '[1] Sylvia Webb, in her book on setting up an information service, suggests that such libraries result from 'the realization that the organization needs information regularly, and is aware that having a central point of reference for information enquiries is likely to be more efficient and effective than the 'shot in the dark' approach'.[2] In the United States, Elizabeth Ferguson and Emily R. Mobley, in *Special Libraries at Work*, establish a standard definition of the library and the librarian:

> A special library is characteristically a unit or department of an organization primarily devoted to other than library or educational purposes. A special

librarian is first an employee, a staff member of the parent organization, and second, a librarian. 'Special' really means library service specialized or geared to the interests of the organization and to the information needs of its personnel.[3]

Grieg Aspnes, in a classic essay on the philosophy of special librarianship, makes reference to another difference between special library work and that in the traditional library setting: 'The special librarian's methods may be less formal, more experimental, with a greater tendency to use short cuts or adopt novel techniques', and he adds one more important element to the special librarian's role: responsibility for providing a total information service.[4]

Thus we can see that the role of the library in the parent organization is directly related to the work of this organization, and the library is there to provide the information needed to support that work directly. When we look at the vast array of types of service provided in such libraries we are impressed, first, with the variety of organizations which use libraries and information centres to support their work and, second, with the incredibly wide range of research materials which these librarians handle. For example, the library for a costume company supplying costumes for films must maintain large collections of pictures and drawings, as well as basic books and periodicals. A library supporting the technical curriculum in a two-year college must provide reports and government documents as well as books, but for this library the greater emphasis might be on current periodical holdings, as they are the most up-to-date medium for the work the students and faculty must perform. The same is true for the information centre supporting the work of a scientific or technical research organization. The variety is endless, but the role of the library remains the same: to support the work of the parent organization. The library, by its very nature, means nothing by itself. Its value is its use to the organization which it serves.

In addition to understanding the role of the library or information service in the parent organization it is also to the librarian's advantage – for the successful management of the library – to know the organization itself. Elizabeth Orna, in 1978, identified this knowledge as the basis for the strategy of an information service in an organization:

Although the aim is a productive interaction between the service and its users, it would be a deception to think the way to it lay through concentration on human relations, 'interactive skills', 'sensitivity', and the like. Good personal and professional relationships between information workers and their colleagues elsewhere in the organization are a necessary, but not a sufficient condition for ensuring effective information use. They cannot be purposeful unless they are backed by a strategy which derives from thorough knowledge of the organization. Knowing the organization provides a frame of reference against which the various options open to the service, the allocation of resources, the priorities of individual demands, and ways into contacts with users can be evaluated and decisions taken.[5]

Orna then lists three things which the librarian must know about the parent organization: its structure and how power is distributed in it, the way information flows in it, and its purposes and aims. Why does a 'thorough knowledge of the organization' matter? Orna replies: 'It can help us to judge both the constraints and the opportunities which the information service has – and among the opportunities, whatever the form of the organization – is that of becoming skilled in making the organization work for us, and learning to play it as a responsive instrument.'[5]

## The business of librarianship

An important key to successful management of a one-person library is in the librarian's attitude. The library must be run in a businesslike manner. This point, which seems obvious, is often lost on librarians and their management. For many reasons, libraries are often run as if they were somebody's hobby, and such practices are not only unfair to the users but especially unjust to whatever source is supplying the funds for operating the library. It behoves us, regardless of the kind of library in which we are employed, to consider carefully the harm which can result when a library is not run in a businesslike way.

There are those who object, saying that the library does not exist to show a profit, nor do its users pay (in most cases) for the information they obtain. Nevertheless, the library is a business organization, and while its product is a service and not something which can be measured by standard profit-and-loss ratios, it is nevertheless an operation in which money is being invested, and it is the obligation of the librarian and the library board or committee and management to see that the monies are used in the most efficient and productive way. True, there is not a profit posted at the end of the fiscal year, but the service of librarianship, the information disseminated and the books borrowed all add up to a product which ought to be provided with the same efficiency as in any business. The difference is that in the business world a lack of efficiency can destroy the market and thus bring about the failure of the business. In the library world, unfortunately, bad business practices are sometimes tolerated because, even though the services may deteriorate, the library will generally be allowed to continue to exist. This is a problem in librarianship and one against which library administrators, even the employee of a one-person library, must constantly be on guard.

## The lines of authority

We can safely assume that every one-person library is part of a parent organization. The supervising authority may not always be on the same premises as the library (for example, the very small public library run by one person, or the departmental library located across the campus from the main college library), but there are few, if any, situations where the librarian has absolute authority. The public librarian is responsible to whatever governmental unit – town council, mayor's office, etc. – has the authority for overseeing the operation of the library. The small departmental library, of course, is supervised by some section of the college's library system. What the library can or cannot do for its users depends on the librarian's relationship with that managing authority.

The first consideration, then, for the employee in a one-person library is to seek out and to understand clearly to whom he or she reports. This may seem obvious, but, as is frequently the case in the world of one-person librarianship, there are so many variations and so many different types of parent organizations that what may seem obvious is not necessarily so. For example, in an information unit in a research and development department of a large commercial firm one might expect that the managers of the research unit would supervise the librarian. Yet the library might be part of an administrative services unit, along with the secretarial pool, the mail room and/or the personnel unit. On the other hand, the director of the executive library in a major corporation might report to the head of public relations. These are the types of unusual alliance which may be found in organizations which have one-person libraries.

If the structure is unclear, how does one find out what it is? In many cases asking to see a flow chart of the organization's departments and their relationships is enough, but a little delicacy and tact might be needed, depending on who can provide the information you are seeking. If the parent organization is large enough to have several departments it is likely that, at some point in its history, flow charts have been devised, and this information can be useful to the librarian. If a chart is not available, the librarian must get the information from her immediate supervisor, since one cannot really contribute successfully to an organization without knowing what the lines of authority are.

## The role of management

The term 'management' is usually used to refer to those senior administrators whose duties include supervising the several departments which make up the organization. By this definition the one-person librarian is not management, although his or her duties are clearly to 'manage' the library (in the sense that 'manage' might mean to organize, to control or to oversee the materials and the operations in the library). This would seem to be the sense that Helen J. Waldron gives to the term 'management' in her essay on running a special library. As she describes the role of the special library in the organizational structure, she says:

> For one thing, special libraries tend to be small – there are literally hundreds of them that operate as one-man libraries; that is, one professional, and

perhaps some clerical help and perhaps not – and many hundreds of others that can be classed as two- or three-man libraries. Anyone finding himself in such a library situation is forced into being a manager whether he likes it or not. This can be a frightening experience, but it can also be a very exhilarating one – depending on how much the librarian knows.[6]

There are exceptions, and our research tells us that many OMB/one-person librarians do, indeed, have another person in the library to work with them: a clerical assistant, a part-time typist, a shelver or a student assistant. Thus they could qualify as 'management', in the sense that we define it here. Strictly speaking, however, the librarian in a one-person situation is not management (in organizational terms) and, if she has some assistance, her role is more supervisory than managerial. Decisions of policy will be made, more than likely, at another level in the organizational hierarchy (with, it is to be hoped, the advice and agreement of the librarian). Sometimes, because of the education required, the salary paid or some other consideration, the employee of a one-person library is carried on the employee roster as a department head or middle manager, but these considerations are basically cosmetic. In fact, it is the employee of the one-person library who is being supervised, and the relationship established between that employee and her supervisor is essential to the successful operation of the library.

The librarian's effectiveness in the organization is often directly related to her place in the organizational hierarchy, and for this reason it is to the organization's advantage to give the librarian real, rather than *de facto*, managerial status. Ashworth makes a strong case for such status:

> The ideal situation is for the head of the library service to have managerial status through which he will derive the necessary knowledge (directly as part of the management team) of the continually-changing aims of the organization, of the potential for future growth and of the constraints under which the organization has to operate. This will enable him to assess which information can be profitably used; and also that which is unlikely, from the lack of proper resources, to be exploitable.[7]

Although it is *desirable* for the librarian to be part of the management team, it must be recognized that in most organizations in which the library is small enough to be run properly by only one employee it is unlikely that managerial status will be accorded the librarian. The librarian simply is not perceived by senior personnel as important enough in the organization's overall structure for such status.

Such status can be achieved, however, depending upon two factors: the rank and position of the person to whom the librarian reports, and the effectiveness and energy of the librarian herself. It is not uncommon for a new librarian to come into an organization in which her predecessor was a long-term employee, possibly a redundant older employee, who had been asked to 'set up a library'.

This person ran the library sufficiently, but not efficiently, under non-professional circumstances until his or her retirement. When the new librarian comes in and is able to enlist managerial commitment and support to match the enthusiasm and professional expertise which she brings to the challenge, we find that senior management is often impressed and soon the librarian is in that position of understanding, reacting to and anticipating Ashworth's 'continually changing aims of the organization'. When this happens the librarian is indeed *de facto* management and, combining the proper communication skills with a positive relationship with the immediate supervising management personnel, is often able to translate such status into legitimate and formalized status. It does not always happen, but it happens often enough to enable librarians to know that they can be considered part of the management team if the quality of their work warrants it.

It should also be kept in mind that the position of one's supervisor in the organizational structure is an important factor in the recognition of the librarian as management. If, for example, the library is part of the administrative services unit or the public relations staff, and if, as is often the case, that section is headed by a staff worker who has worked his way up to that role and is not a professional manager, it is highly unlikely that the library or its role in the organization will be recognized as the professional managerial unit it could be. On the other hand, having the librarian responsible to the head of research or the manager of a specific department can lead to unbalanced service and expectations from that particular department which cannot be met if one is to give service to the whole of the organization. Other sections of the organization could be neglected, a situation which Ashworth suggests will not occur if the library is part of the managerial responsibility of a neutral supervisor, such as a director of the company or a senior vice-president.[7]

It is frequently said that one of the appeals of one-person librarianship is the independence one has. Frankly, it is lack of supervision on the part of management which brings about this state of affairs. There are many reasons why management prefers to leave the library employee alone: often a lack of knowledge about librarianship inhibits the manager, or other demands keep the interest elsewhere. It is not inconceivable that a plain lack of interest in the library makes management keep its distance; conversely, the manager may not feel a need to follow closely the workings of the library due to confidence in the librarian. Whatever the reasons, management is frequently faulted for being uninterested in the library unit.

From management's point of view, such distance is not unreasonable. Management's role is generally limited to administrative supervision, and aside from some basic scheduling and personnel or custodial procedures, the focus of the library operation is on library activities, which, of course, are the responsibility of the employee in the library.

Nevertheless, management does have the administrative responsibility for the library unit, and some working relationship is required. If necessary, the library employee must seek to encourage management interest in the library, even if in limited form. For the librarian who needs an advocate, an educated and committed manager can be of use. Finally, as management must supervise expenditures (regardless of the source of the funds), it is wise to maintain a dialogue in order to offset any potential adversarial situation. Negotiations for a library operation are never easy – even when the parent organization realizes a profit from the information provided by the library – and enthusiastic management is certain to be a good support for the library.

## Using management

Having established what the lines of authority are, what do we do with this information? We use it for communication, necessary for educating management and developing the kind of dialogue which leads to support for the library's activities. For many, the activity between librarian and management is one-sided, as we receive management memoranda, personnel notices and procedural directives but are seldom expected to provide self-initiated material in return. Stories abound concerning the lack of recognition some librarians receive from their own organizations. In a survey conducted several years ago the directors and the librarians of several small museums were asked questions about the management of the libraries in the museums in which they were employed. While the librarians presented responses, three of the directors replied that their institutions had no librarians. Fortunately, few librarians have suffered these humiliations.

Frequently, employees of one-person libraries do not know their organizations' lines of authority because they do not receive anything from 'above' except through the next authority up, which, as we have seen, might or might not be the appropriate managerial unit for supervising a library. Once she knows what the lines of authority are, the aggressive one-person librarian will try to use that line by submitting booklists, notices of special purchases, requests for suggested acquisitions and internal 'press' releases of events and other news items, such as the librarian's participation in a conference or meeting. Monthly, quarterly or, of course, annual reports can be useful by describing not only the library's collecting activities but its administrative activities as well. These specific communications procedures are the kinds of thing which can be used to keep management advised of what is going on in the library.

All of this is well and good, but what about the manager who returns documents unread, or tosses them out, or, worse still, complains that the librarian is sending too much material? This is a problem which does exist in many organizations, particularly where management is unconcerned with library activities and (especially in profit-making organizations) sees the library as a non-productive drain on the parent organization's funds. In these cases it is time for an advocate, for some person or group who feels positively about the library and can carry that message to management. There can be two resources for such support: the users (who can be guided by the librarian to play both informal and formal advocacy roles) and the library board or committee. Both groups exist for other reasons, and few librarians, users or board or committee members see themselves as operating in any kind of advocacy relationship, except peripherally. However, the fact is that when library service is exceptional, users are pleased, the board or committee is pleased, and management, whether it want to be interested in the library or not, is forced to recognize the worth of the library to the parent organization.

## References

1 Ashworth, Wilfred, *Special Librarianship*, Clive Bingley, London, 1979, p. 6.

2 Webb, Sylvia P., *Creating an Information Service*, Aslib, London, 1983, p. 1.

3 Ferguson, Elizabeth and Mobley, Emily R., *Special Libraries at Work*, Library Professional Publications, an imprint of The Shoe String Press, Inc., Hamden, Connecticut, 1984, p. 4.

4 Aspnes, Grieg, 'A philosophy of special librarianship', in Jackson, E. (ed.), *Special Librarianship: A New Reader*, op. cit., p. 1.

5 Orna, Elizabeth, 'Should we educate our users?' *Aslib Proceedings*, **30**, 4, 132, 1978.

6 Waldron, Helen J., 'The business of managing a special library', in Jackson, E. (ed.), op. cit., p. 146.

7 Ashworth, op. cit., p. 12.

# The library board or committee

To begin a discussion of the library board or committee we should point out that this subject exemplifies one of the primary differences between libraries in the United States and in the the United Kingdom, especially those with limited or one-person staff. Small libraries in the United States, even in the corporate, scientific and technical worlds, frequently have a formal or informal group of users who serve as a library committee, but this is not often the case in the United Kingdom, and much of what is said here might not be seen to be applicable to British libraries. This difference, however, gives us the opportunity to consider the value of such a committee or board.

It is imperative that the employee in the one-person library understands clearly the duties, responsibilities and authority of the library board or committee in relation to the librarian and to management. If possible, at the time of employment the librarian should be given in writing a statement describing the board or committee's role. If it is not offered it should be requested; a written policy is not only useful for the protection of the person managing the library but clarifies for each member of the board or committee what he or she is expected to do. This is not to suggest that an employment relationship should begin in an atmosphere of distrust, but simply to recognize that while management personnel and the library staff have accepted their positions and responsibilities as permanent, most of those who sit on boards and committees are appointed for a finite, and frequently clearly defined, period. Thus the committee's level of commitment can be expected to change as its membership changes, but the librarian and the managerial staff will continue on a longer-term basis. To have a clearly stated and simple document outlining the obligations and responsibilities of the committee or board will, in the long run, make the librarian's organizational tasks considerably easier.

What is the role of the library board or committee? 'The principal purpose of the committee is to advise, support, and guide the library director and to serve as a linkage among the users, the library, and the management', says Jane H. Katayama.[1] In other words, the committee, in most cases, serves in an advisory capacity, or to set policy, or to supervise the expenditure of library funds, or to select materials – indeed, to work in every way with the librarian in guiding the direction of the library and the services it offers. Katayama continues: 'It is essential to distinguish between advisory functions, which are in the domain of the library committee, and administrative functions, which belong to the library manager.[1] The committee or board does not (and should not) involve itself in the day-to-day operation of the library, and its public role, in all cases, should be one of support for the librarian and the work he is doing. Such a role might seem unobjectionable, but the temptation of power, however limited, can be irresistible to the layman who has been appointed to a library committee or board, and there will be times when the librarian must educate the board or committee in its understanding of its obligations and limitations.

As examples we might look at the boards or committees connected with some types of one-person libraries. If the informational unit in a research and development department of a large firm has a library committee it probably exists to advise on acquisitions. Most commercial enterprises would not encourage much more involvement than this, simply because the library is there to serve a for-profit organization and the people on the library committee will have many other duties. As users it is the responsibility of these people to know the literature, so their role as acquisitions advisors is of prime importance to the librarian, who cannot always have the time to know the literature (much as he or she would like to).

Similarly, the museum library board or committee is generally going to be concerned with acquisitions. The museum library is probably heavily used by the curatorial staff, and the library committee will be largely made up of curatorial people, with perhaps a museum trustee or management employee included for 'balance' (and often more cosmetic than not). There are times when the museum library committee can get involved in such projects as fund-raising, special maintenance, etc., but primarily it will exist to advise the librarian about acquisitions.

In a departmental library of a college or university, where there is only one person to manage the library, the library committee can be expected to take a more active role. Like the professional researcher in a commercial firm, the faculty of the department is required to know the literature of the subject and will be expected to advise on acquisitions; in fact, the committee will usually bring the acquisitions list to the librarian, rather than the other way round.

This situation is not as negative as it might seem, for it should be recognized that in many small organizations the librarian is not a professional or chartered librarian, is not trained in library management, and would generally be reluctant to accept such assignments as recommending titles for the professional users of the collection. A small law firm, for example, has a library and an employee who serves in a custodial or clerical position, filing reports and performing other routine and important, but certainly non-professional, tasks. Often, indeed, the 'library' duties in a small law firm require only half of the 'librarian's' time, with the other half of his work day being used to perform the duties of receptionist, office assistant, etc. In this arrangement, obviously the firm's library committee or board, which might be loosely structured but must exist, will have absolute control of the library and will make all decisions affecting service, from scheduling hours of service to complicated procedural and/or policy matters which, in another firm, might be delegated to a professional or chartered librarian. In many small libraries it must be so, for the librarian is not qualified to make such decisions.

The same might be true in other small businesses or organizations, although it is possible that the librarian with some additional training in the firm's subject area, but not in library work, might become a more valuable employee to the library board or committee. The activities described in Don Lee's article[2] – arranging contacts between clients and specialists, compiling surveys, conducting in-depth studies, making field visits, recommending services and setting up discussions – are typical of the work which enhances the library employee's value to a library committee. While the actual decision-making responsibility regarding the library is the province of the committee, the data received from the library employee are vital.

In a more social organization, such as a church or local historical society library, the role of the librarian is not so limited. In such a setting, where the membership of the library committee is made up of interested laymen not necessarily knowledgeable in the subject specialities of the collection or in library management, the library employee takes on a dramatically different character in the functioning of the committee. It is he who is called upon to bring to the committee's attention specific goals, plans, ideas or problems, as well as to advise the committee of the various aspects of the day-to-day operations of the library. It is often in these situations that a particularly strong working relationship builds up between the librarian and the chairman of the committee. Whenever possible, the librarian should seek the opportunity to be useful to the chairman, as well as to other members of the committee. In fact, some of the chairman's work can be simplified when librarian and chairman offer mutual respect and support. One of the most effective ways for the librarian to gain this regard is to seek out the chairman and ask his or her opinion on subjects for discussion at committee or board meetings. The librarian should be in a position to make up the agenda for the meetings. Once the agenda is determined, it is wise for the librarian and the chairman to have a conversation (even if it is nothing more than a brief exchange of words on the telephone) to discuss it and to determine what areas might call for mutual support.

In an organization such as a church or local society the librarian is in the unique position of being able to determine most of what comes before the committee. It is good to bear in mind that members of the committee or board are usually not professional librarians. While they might take their positions very seriously (and, indeed, one sometimes encounters the amateur librarian, with all the good and bad that that concept implies), they are not qualified to make professional library-management decisions. Frequently, they have accepted the appointment as an honour or recognition and do not expect to take their work on the committee or board very seriously. In this case, two practical considerations are worth remembering: first, do not forget that the members of the committee 'come there to play'. They are not earning their living at the library (as the employee of the library is doing) and the funds which they are expending are not, in most cases, their own money. All they are obliged to give is time, which they do very generously, as we must remember that they are busy and successful people or they would not have been selected for the committee or board in the first place. Many of these people do take their work very seriously and contribute a great deal to the successful operation of the library. Nevertheless, in the final analysis on any question of procedure or policy, their jobs are not on the line (as the librarian's might be). The library committee and board members should be treated with this thought in mind.

A second consideration to keep in mind is that the board or committee will always want to look good, so it should be part of the librarian's political awareness to try to further that aim. When any member of the committee is called upon to explain some failure or lapse of service, the tendency, almost invariably, is to seek to place the blame elsewhere. For example, a particular user may not be satisfied with an answer to a reference question and will write a letter of complaint to the committee. To counteract such criticism it is wise to seek support in advance, which simply means that the librarian, whenever he has the opportunity, should do whatever can be done to make the board or committee look good. This does not necessarily mean that the librarian fawns over committee people or gives them special service or treatment which is denied to other users of the library, but only that the committee is made to know that its opinion is valued and respected. Thus, in the day-to-day operations of the library the librarian does what he can to see that the board or committee is given appropriate credit and appreciation. It may be as simple as using the phrase 'on behalf of the library committee' in acknowledging a gift to the library, or it might be just saying to someone who compliments the librarian on a good reference response that the compliment will be passed on to the library committee. The point is that the librarian and the committee support one another and are not shy about saying so in public.

The relationship between the librarian and the board of a small public library is very different from the private and quasi-private situations we have been describing, primarily because the legal structure of a public library involves a governing agency. This relationship has been clearly described by Dorothy Sinclair, who properly points out that the interest of the users and the board in the details of running a small library is one of the distinguishing characteristics of work in small libraries.[3] Similarly, other sources describe the relationship between library committees and boards for the one-person librarian who runs a school library, and since school libraries are more a part of the education profession rather than the library profession, the librarian who is responsible for managing a school library single-handedly is referred to those sources.

It is not difficult from the preceding to conclude that the librarian who supports his committee, who listens with respect when board members make suggestions and who goes to the committee for advice and reassurance will have established a relationship that will be very useful to the librarian. This is simply to recognize that these relationships are primarily human, and as such are subject to the same sort of reactions as other human relationships. If the librarian thinks of his work with the committee as mutually respectful and supportive, and not adversarial, much can be accomplished. When the librarian is on the spot, with management or with a disappointed (or even irate) user, it is a very consoling feeling to be able to say, 'Perhaps you should speak to the chairman of the library committee'. If the librarian and the committee or board can establish early on a relationship in which they see themselves working together as a team, the support from the committee or board will be there when it is needed, and the librarian will have the advocate for his or her support when it is needed. 'An active, interested committee can provide the library with meaningful support, sound advice and guidance, and act as liaison between the users and management.'[1]

The committee as advocate is especially useful in those situations when management or a user does not understand the limitations of the library and expects more in service than can be delivered. Most laymen think that they understand the running of a library but, as is made clear to most librarians on an average of about once a day, they do not. Frequently the layman will expect that a unit called a 'library' should be able to provide him with any information he may seek. It is not uncommon for a user, not understanding the limitations of a particular subject collection, to seek information that is outside the library's realm and to be highly disappointed when a suggestion is made that he or she will do better at another library. Just as frequently the user expects the librarian to obtain the information from the other source. Such limitations can be explained away by referring the user to the committee or board which, knowing the limitations of the library and the services offered there, will support the librarian. It is a common problem, and it is to the librarian's advantage to know that he or she can count on the committee or board for support. In summary, we once again quote Katayama: 'The relationship among library committee members, senior management personnel, and the library staff can best be described as a synergistic one, each bringing expertise and knowledge for a common goal – that of contributing to the fulfilment of the organization's mission.'[1]

# References

1 Katayama, Jane H., 'The library committee: how important is it?' *Special Libraries,* **24,** 1, 44, 1983.
2 Lee, Don, 'One-man operated – running an information unit for management in the public transport industry', *Aslib Proceedings,* **32,** 3, 114-117, 1980.
3 Sinclair, Dorothy, *The Administration of the Small Public Library,* American Library Association, Chicago, 1979, p. 24.

# Basics I: the one-person library

As we have seen, and as Dorothy Sinclair has so positively described in her classic guide for the small public library, there are certain advantages to working in a small institution. We are convinced that those advantages are added to when one is managing a one-person operation. The independence one has as a professional librarian in a one-person library can be a special inducement to excellence, an incentive many in the workforce do not have. Many one-person libraries, constrained by budgetary restrictions to hiring entry-level personnel for managing the one-person library, capitalize on the appeal of independence to new library-school graduates, which means that many professional librarians now managing one-person operations are in their first professional positions. What should this librarian expect on her first day on the job, or, if in the United Kingdom, in the second post after licentiate training has been completed?

The first advice that other one-person librarians would probably give is that the realities of the situation will have little to do with what you have been taught in graduate school or, if you are not a graduate or chartered librarian (as many employees in one-person librarianship are not), with your previous notions of what goes on in a library. When one works alone, the entire spectrum of objectives, duties and responsibilities is rearranged – not necessrily a bad thing, of course, but a situation which requires frequent adjustment from the first day of employment onwards. So the first thing for the new employee in a one-person library to remember is simply this: be encouraged. Things are not as overwhelming as they seem, and the theories, goals, ideals and aspirations you have been nourishing so carefully over the past few years are not to be thrown out. They are simply to be recognized for what they are, and while they are not to be forgotten (for one must think about them all the time), one must get on with the business at hand: getting the library up and running for the first day of work. Here we can cite Dorothy Sinclair, author of *The Administration of the Small Public Library,* an excellent guide for the beginning librarian. Even though she is speaking specifically about financial considerations and, of course, addressing the public library manager, the text is appropriate for what we are saying here to the one-person library employee:

> Every librarian with sound training and standards who comes to a library with a small budget is faced with the problems of reconciling theory with realities. The skill needed here is one not taught in all library schools – the ability to plan, to balance, and to compromise where it will hurt the least, while at the same time never forgetting that a compromise has been made.[1]

Once the position has been finally accepted there is a certain amount of thinking to be done about the job. Obviously some of these considerations will have been made upon applying for the position in the first place, and certainly some of the information will have been brought to the attention of the applicant during the interviewing process. So by the first day on the job the librarian will already know something about the objectives of the library, the role of the library or information unit within the parent organization, and who uses the library and why. Now the concept of ideal versus non-ideal situations should be given some thought.

What are the objectives of the library or information unit? How does one go about defining these objectives even before one has begun to work in the library? To begin with, the one-person library is almost always going to be one part of a larger administrative unit, the parent organization we have been referring to. As the objectives of these organizations vary, so will those of the library. We can safely state that all one-person libraries are 'technically' special libraries, and special libraries have historically been a part of librarianship known more for its diversity than for its sameness. One definition of a special library was given in 1966, and we still generally use it: 'A library maintained by a business firm, association, government agency, or other organized group whose collections are for the most part limited in scope to the subject area of interest to the sponsor.'[2] Thus we can quickly see that the objectives of the one-person library can be as diverse and as distinctive as the parent organizations which support the library. If the parent organization is a research arm of a government agency the one-person library is there to feed information to researchers. In this library, quickness of delivery may not be the prime objective of the librarian, but rather accuracy of information. On the other hand, the one-person library supporting the work of a financial institution (regardless of how small) must provide the information not only quickly but accurately as well, thus putting special pressures on the one-person librarian. In a museum library, where the emphasis is on research to support the work of the curatorial staff, demands are of a different sort. A small library in a church or synagogue has yet another objective, to provide spiritual reading material for the congregation or to support the reference needs of the clergy. The examples could go on if we wanted to attempt to define the various objectives of the many types of parent organizations which have small libraries as part of their administrative structure. For the librarian coming to a one-person situation it is imperative that he or she learn, as soon as possible, the objectives of the institution in which the work is to be done. Once the library objectives have been clearly defined it is time to turn her attention to the role of the library in the parent institution. While this is somewhat akin to defining the objectives, the emphasis here is primarily administrative, and for this we refer to the previous chapters. It is to her advantage to know to whom the librarian reports, the distinctions between the authority of the administrative management and the library committee or board. If there is no library committee or board, it is now that the librarian gives some thought to the political and administrative groundwork necessary to get such a committee or board created.

Finally, before the librarian comes to work in the library, he or she should spend some time quietly reflecting on the ideal versus the non-ideal. As a graduate or chartered librarian, or as someone with interest in and perhaps previous affiliation with a library, the new staff member has some notions, perhaps formal, perhaps not, of how a library should be managed and how it should fit into the administrative structure of the parent organization. Usually the new employee does not know exactly how things are, and she may well be in a good position to do things differently, perhaps a little better, and certainly with a new enthusiasm and interest that comes with being a new employee. This is not to say that the new librarian will come in and change everything around, for such activity is neither appropriate nor desirable, but at this point, before the librarian has actually gone to work, it is time to study the situation, consider it in connection with previous experience and/or education and come up with some thoughts about how the library should be run. Now is the time to do it, for immediately upon reporting for duty there is going to be much to assimilate in such a short period of time that it will be some days, perhaps even weeks, before the new librarian can go back to thinking about the ideal goals and directions he or she might be interested in bringing to the library.

A word of caution is in order here, simply because the very nature of seeking ideals is risky and can lead to disappointment. In thinking about what the library should be the new librarian is not necessarily determining to achieve these ideals. We and the new librarian are aware that the very nature of ideals, especially in management situations, is fraught with danger, simply because we are perhaps setting ourselves up to be disappointed. However, we must recognize these ideals, and we must point our work in their direction, even if we know they are unlikely to be realized, simply because a professional librarian is obliged to do the best he or she can under the circumstances. In this context a consideration of the ideal in library planning is an important part of Dorothy Sinclair's exposition of the planning process. Although planning as an activity for the new librarian is to be discussed shortly, Sinclair's comments are worth quoting here:

> The librarian must plan at several levels. At the top, not forgotten though temporarily shelved, is the vision of the ideal service for the community. It is wise to start here, before returning to solid realities, for several reasons. The first is that the librarian should never lose his or her vision or high standards, never be content with compromises. Economy may be a necessity, but complacency is the enemy of all progress.
>
> A second reason for considering the ideal before grappling with the feasible is that the ideal may not be as unattainable as it at first appears. Perhaps there is a way to reach the quality of service the community should have. Unless this possibility is considered and all avenues explored, how can the librarian be sure? Even if the service contemplated in the vision is far off, it is closer than if no vision existed.
>
> In the third place, an ideal pattern is important for present planning. Without long-range goals, current decisions may be shortsighted. Definite,

attainable stages in the progress toward long-range goals can be set, and pride can be taken in the realization of these intermediate objectives. The trustees, staff and community share in the excitement of such accomplishments without the danger of settling back into complacency and self-satisfaction after partial success.[3]

The librarian going into a one-person library for the first time, especially if he or she has never worked in a one-person library before, will find a few interesting features in this line of work which are not often found elsewhere. For example, if the incumbent librarian is to be on duty for a few final days to give the new librarian some guidance, not only is the new person going to be caught up in the unusual working conditions of an employee's leaving but he or she will be left alone for some of the time because the other librarian simply does not have the time to stop and actually work with the new person. On the other hand, if the incumbent librarian has left the position and the new librarian comes into an empty office, again he or she will have some time to become oriented to the new situation. It is in this 'learning' time that the new librarian must look around, take stock of the situation and proceed to learn what he or she can about the library and the work which is done there. Quite frankly, no new job has ever appeared, on the first day, as good as it seemed in the interviews. There are always little surprises, some of them rather nasty, and the new librarian in a one-person library needs to be prepared for them and not to be discouraged.

When the surprises come, the first thing one must do is to consider what the job will be like after some time has passed in terms of improvements in service, a different atmosphere in the library (and perhaps a totally new attitude towards the users), etc. The new librarian can see the job as one of challenge and opportunity and not one of drudgery. A few basic rules will have to be set, as pleasantly as possible, for some of the users and other staff of the parent organization. For example, one of the oldest gambits is to ask the new librarian to do a typing job, say, or another task which is not only not in the purview of the librarian but which would not be an appropriate request in any case. Such a request, even from management, will sometimes be accompanied by an insinuation that the previous librarian did this work, or that any reasonable person could not possibly object. Firmness is called for, with politeness, in refusing: at the very least, the new librarian may simply reply that, as a new staff member with so many duties not even yet defined, it would be impossible to take on an outside task at this time. It has to be said, or the librarian will end up doing work he or she was not hired for and the work of the library will be hindered.

There are three areas of interest which the new librarian needs to consider, in the early days on the job, and it is important that they not be forgotten in the myriad other tasks which are being learned at the same time. In any new library position, but perhaps more so in a one-person library, the daily duties for the first few weeks seem to be staggering in number and complexity, and it is easy for the new librarian to forget that there are broader areas which must be given some thought. The three immediate things to keep in mind are: what has gone before, the library's immediate needs, and planning for the future. In other words, if the new librarian in the one-person library would try to think of himself as a sort of in-house consultant hired to study the library and determine what can be done to make its work more efficient and productive, and at the same time learn how to carry out the regular duties of managing the regular and routine work which must be done in the library, in a very short period of time the librarian will have a solid grasp of the work of the library and will be in a position to guide its future development.

To determine what has gone on before will be the easiest of these three broad tasks, for the librarian's predecessors will have left trails of clues for the new person to follow. In addition, users will be quick to help the one-person librarian learn some of the procedures. Also, of course, one's supervisor, if interested in the library, plus the library committee and board, will all be helpful in describing what the library was like prior to the new person's arrival. A considerable amount of tact and discretion is necessary here, for the previous librarian, despite possible obvious inefficiencies which might have become apparent on the first day of the successor's work, was perhaps also a favourite employee or special friend of some of the users. The predecessor may have been an excellent librarian, about whom no-one had any complaints, but with a very different style from that of the new librarian. What we are talking about here is simple courtesy on the job, and while it will probably be necessary to make some decisions to do things differently, one must move slowly and with a certain amount of consideration for those who were used to the library before the new person arrived.

Having spent some time analysing the previous procedures the new librarian is in a unique position to study what needs to be done, both in the short- and long-term future. The immediate needs will become apparent almost from the first day, when the new person discovers such things as the copying machine being located on another floor, despite the fact that journal articles are copied on a regular basis and the amount of time consumed in going back and forth to do the copying is a large drain on efficiency. Such obvious anomalies were probably not dealt with because the former librarian had no choice but to go to another location to make copies for the library (after all, he or she was probably running the library when there was *no* copying machine) and if the amount of time spent in this work had become onerous by the time the previous librarian had made a decision to leave, it was a problem the new librarian could be left with. Many such situations will arise in the daily routine, some of which can be corrected immediately and some filed away for discussion with management and/or the library committee or board at the proper time. Also, incidentally, the first few weeks on the job are not the best time to make drastic recommendations for change, or even recommendations which might be perceived as drastic. It is better to go slowly, to observe carefully and to correct what can be corrected without causing too much disruption (or what would be perceived as disruption) and to save the big battles for later, after the new librarian has built up a reputation for cooperation, efficiency and a pleasant attitude. By setting the stage carefully, the new librarian will find management and the library committee or board receptive to change when the time comes to seek it.

There is one area where management and the library committee or board can be approached, after a short period of study and adjustment, and that is in the area of planning. Before you can hope to give good service to your users you must give some thought to planning. When working alone, planning is very important but, sadly, it is the one activity which is most neglected, to the eventual detriment of the quality of service. Whether you are accustomed to it or not, you must set aside a certain amount of time each day or week to plan ahead. This can only be time well spent, and it will result in increased productivity and efficiency, thus increasing motivation and job satisfaction. One complaint among one-person librarians is that there is never time to draw breath, much less plan for future activities. Indeed, some one-person librarians complain regularly that there is not time to think about purposes and goals. This attitude is in itself self-defeating, for the librarian who does not engage in some forward planning and systems analysis is doomed to provide a service that is inefficient and counter-productive. The service will not be cost-effective and will not change with the needs of the organization, and the library itself will be top-heavy with out-of-date material which has not been discarded or even organized in the first place. The administration of any small library, and most especially a one-person library, requires that time be available not only for the required day-to-day professional effort but for planning as well. In short, a one-person librarian, like any other administrator, needs time to think. So says Tom Whitehall in his article on the systems approach to problems in the one-person library,[4] and it is advice well taken.

As the first few months of the job roll along, the new librarian managing a one-person operation will soon begin to discern what the real goals are (as opposed to the stated or perceived goals, which might be different) for the users, the management and the committee or board. It is possible that these goals may vary considerably, and the new librarian might find himself in the position, as with an in-house consultant, of preparing a project proposal of what the library might be doing for its users five, ten or twenty years in the future. Such a proposal will require some time for interviews with users, perhaps some special meetings with management and the library committee or board members (although these latter meetings might not be necessary if the facts of the situation are clear enough to the new librarian to make a case for the proposal), and certainly some quiet time for thinking about the ideal library situation and the situation as it exists in the present circumstances. Thought must be given to such areas as sympathetic management, resources to do the work demanded of the librarian, and financial support to provide at least minimal services (including proper equipment, lighting, space, furniture, etc.). The librarian working alone will be forced to spend a certain amount of his personal time thinking about these subjects. After they have been studied and discussed with users, a document, appropriately presented to both management and to the library committee or board, will not only give the one-person librarian direction for his or her efforts over the next few years but will enhance the reputation and value of the librarian as seen by users, management and the library committee or board. In other words, by providing a document showing a serious approach to what the library can be for its users the librarian has established himself as a serious professional administrator who works in a manner that is not only seldom found in library work but is not expected there. The library can only benefit from such conscientious effort.

Now, without undermining the importance of planning (for it must be done, as is so clearly demonstrated by the long quotation from Sinclair earlier in this chapter), we must return again to Sinclair's important work on the small public library and borrow another of her principles for the management of the one-person library: 'Perhaps the most important matter for consideration of the board and administrator of the small library is this matter of limitation. What shall this particular library try to do and be?'[5] Limitations are something none of us is particularly interested in addressing, primarily because, as practitioners in a service profession which many entered in order to help people, to guide users to the information they need and, even when called upon, to help them interpret the material, we do not like to think of ourselves as denying any request. However, today no library can be all things to all men, and indeed none tries. Even the New York Public Library has subject areas in which it does not collect. This is not so serious a problem in business or other corporate libraries, probably because they are created and designed for specific purposes, but it is not uncommon in the museum library, the library in a historical society and libraries in cultural organizations for the library to try to have broad coverage of many subject areas that are not unique to their collections. The limitations of a library, especially one small enough to be managed by one person, are not cause for apology. Indeed, by limiting what they do, one-person libraries are often in the position of doing those things better than some of the larger organizations which try to cover too many subjects.

At this point, before the specific duties of the librarian are described, it is appropriate to look at what the librarian is supposed to be doing in the one-person library. Since a one-person library is a special library it is necessary for it to be judged by the standards of special librarianship, and there are two sources for defining the responsibilities of a special librarian. The first is an essay, in *Special Librarianship: A New Reader,* edited by Eugene Jackson and published in 1980. That the essay, 'A philosophy of special librarianship', written by Grieg Aspnes, is the first in a book of essays attests to its importance in describing some of the functions of the special librarian. The things he says about special librarians are true of employees working in one-person libraries, whether they are graduate chartered librarians or not, and Aspnes begins by pointing out that special librarians share 'with all other librarians the unique quality of their profession: the ability to organize graphic records of human thought and experience for the benefit of human use'.[6] Having so given us an overall view of the work, he gives a list of the librarian's primary responsibilities: classification, cataloguing and indexing are the basic responsibilities of all librarianship, and the special librarian must guide the growth of the collection, be able to distinguish the outdated or less valuable from the more useful, and know at all times where the materials under his control can be found. The combination of these responsibilities, Aspnes correctly asserts, is the main reason for the 'special librarian's being – the responsibility for providing a total information service'.[7]

Such a list of responsibilities is fine as far as it goes, but for the special librarian who is managing a one-person library there is one additional aspect of special librarianship that must be included. Helen J. Waldron discerned it in her essay in 1971 (also included as a chapter in Jackson's compilation). In describing what elements differentiate special librarianship from other forms, she states:

> First – and without a doubt the most important – is a very specialized and personalized service, which is both a philosophy and a practice. I certainly do not imply that other kinds of libraries are not concerned with service, but providing *special* services is a primary function of all special libraries, regardless of the kind of organization with which they may be associated.[8]

These thoughts are particularly appropriate when applied to the employee in the one-person library, for his or her role is very much as a provider of information. The librarian is not there primarily to do the many things that he or she must do simply to keep the library going. The administrative functions can (and will) be turned over to someone else when they interfere with service, and in the one-person library that service is noticeably personal and special. It is not fawning, and it is not provided from a subservient point of view (or, if it is, there is something wrong in that library or the parent organization). It is a service provided by a professional library manager who has skills and abilities which make him an asset to the parent organization, so much so that, without that personalized and specialized service, the work of the parent organization could not be done. The responsibilities of the employee in the one-person library are indeed built around his organization of the collection, but that organization is complemented and, indeed, enhanced by the librarian's special skill in providing personalized library service.

For the special librarian employed in a one-person library it is the diversity of duties which appeal most about the work. One never hears such an employee complaining of being bored with his job, because the demands on one's time are so many and so varied that one does not have the opportunity to be bored. The duties of the one-person librarian can be categorized in a number of different ways, but the method most chosen is to describe those tasks which are user services and those connected with support services. While the time devoted to the latter is considerably out of proportion spent on the former, it is the user services which define the librarian's job, at least as far as management, the committee or board and the users are concerned.

Various services for users in the one-person library can be: circulation (the lending of books, periodicals and other library materials), request services, scanning and routing periodicals and SDI (Selective Dissemination of Information, in which the librarian reviews the literature, 'filters from it items of significance and sends these directly to various individuals according to their personal interests'[9]), photocopying, interlibrary loan activity, abstracting, indexing, performing searches (by whatever means), information and reference work, and project work and report writing. All of these are services offered for users and must be provided efficiently, accurately and quickly. Support services are those activities in the library which the one-person librarian must perform when he or she is not working with a user, and are those services which provide the organization and the efficiency required for the successful management of the library. These include book ordering and the necessary research in determining that a book is available and can be ordered, classifying and cataloguing the collection, internal accounting procedures, administrative tasks involved in working with the board or committee, and, of course, keeping loan records, reservation requests, shelving, labelling, filing and the many other 'little' tasks which, when left undone, can seriously hamper the efficient operation of the library.

These support services are not the only tasks done for this purpose, but in the one-person library there are other duties which, if possible, should always be contracted out to jobbers who do these types of work for libraries. These include journal subscription order and fulfilment, book and journal binding, conservation and restoration work, secretarial tasks (typing, correspondence, etc.) when there is a secretary in another department whose services can be used by the library, and any printing which has to be done for the library (accession lists, guides, annual reports, etc.).

Thus we can see that whereas the *Oxford English Dictionary* defines the librarian as the 'custodian' of the books, the actual professional definitions are not so simple. A librarian/information specialist in a one-person library must be a generalist. When we look at the tasks listed for user services and support services it is not difficult to see that the librarian in a one-person library must be able to do a little of everything (hence the expression used in the United Kingdom to describe a librarian working alone: 'a one-man band'). This librarian may have to abstract, index, catalogue and classify books and journals, perform literature searches manually, online or by teletext, scan and route literature, compile bibliographies and reading lists, write reports and assess information found in searches performed. In addition to these tasks, usually called 'professional' because they require special education and skills, the librarian in a one-person library must handle the myriad clerical tasks that keep the library running smoothly. Reference queries (another professional task for which special education is required) also must be answered, and the modern qualified librarian may regard the library much more as an information centre, containing as much non-book material as actual shelved books. In some professions (e.g. teaching) libraries are also known as 'resource centres', because they contain not only texts and other reading materials for both staff and students but also audio-visual materials, sheet music, posters, photographs, flip-charts, reading lists, gramophone records and cassettes, etc.

In the world of libraries and librarianship there is much discussion about the distinctions between clerical and professional work. It is commonly agreed that professional work requires special education, skills and abilities, and the library employee who has attained the status of graduate librarian (in the United States) or chartered librarian (in the United Kingdom) is generally accorded the distinction of being a 'professional'. His or her duties in the one-person library are going to be the user services and management of the library which require the special ability achieved with graduate study. On the other hand, many of the tasks described above certainly do not require special education and ability. The skills for completing these tasks are generally called 'clerical'. The question thus arises: should a professional librarian be doing clerical work? Conversely, should a clerical employee be doing professional work? The answer cannot be a simple yes or no, for there is no place for such a distinction in the one-person library. When there is only one person to do all the work the distinction between clerical and professional is really no longer relevant. We admit, and we will be discussing, the fact that non-professional tasks are great time-wasters for professional, chartered librarians. At the same time, we are obliged to recognize that many employees who run one-person libraries are not graduate or chartered librarians, for the economies of many of the businesses and organizations which often most need the services of a staff member do not allow for hiring a trained professional. Thus we have to conclude that the major difference between professional and clerical work in a one-person library is determined by one's attitude. How the librarian feels about the work he or she is doing becomes much more important than whether this task is clerical or that one professional. In the one-person library the employee is required to provide his or her own professional affirmation. Thus, even when doing clerical tasks the librarian in a one-person library must think of himself or herself as a professional doing clerical work, not as a clerk working in a library. The standard of service in the library requires it, and the librarian, as an employee making a contribution to the parent organization and its goals, should accept nothing less.

# References

1 Sinclair, Dorothy, *The Administration of the Small Public Library,* American Library Association, Chicago, 1979, p. 9.
2 American Library Association, Statistics Coordinating Project, Joel Williams, Director, *Library Statistics: A Handbook of Concepts, Definitions, and Terminology,* American Library Association, Chicago, 1966, p.143.
3 Sinclair, op. cit., pp. 2-3.
4 Whitehall, Tom, 'Time to think: use of the systems approach to the problems of the "one-man" information unit', *Aslib Proceedings,* **19,** 12, 406-414, 1967.
5 Sinclair, op. cit.
6 Aspnes, Grieg, 'A philosophy of special librarianship', in Jackson, E. (ed.). *Special Librarianship: A New Reader,* 1980, p. 3.
7 Ibid., p. 4.
8 Waldron, Helen J., 'The business of managing a special library', in Jackson, E. (ed.), op. cit., p. 142.
9 Aspnes, op. cit., p. 10.

# Basics II: self-management

The list of duties in a one-person library is enormous. Not only is the librarian responsible for the full range of professional duties, such as readers' advisory, answering reference questions, selecting and ordering materials, cataloguing and classification, collection review and similar tasks, but he or she must also fit clerical duties in the schedule, including typing, filing, circulation counts, shelving, etc. Even occasional custodial duties such as cleaning shelves or shifting books are often done by the librarian, who quickly learns that the fastest way to get something done is to do it herself. To do *all* these jobs and to do them well requires a level of self-management that none of us is taught in graduate school and few of us learn even later. It is easy to say we can manage our time, especially if we are part of a staff and duties are defined; but it is difficult when everything must be done by one person. There are no rules imposed by management, there are no time-sheets, there are no supervisors looking over one's shoulder.

The key to self-management is to establish priorities. There are certain jobs in every library which must be dutifully performed; otherwise a backlog accumulates, and what has been a daily routine can quickly become a monumental project. So the first rule of self-management in a one-person library is obvious: get the housekeeping done first, do it early each day and get it out of the way. The librarian who skips the circulation count on Monday will find herself with twice as much to count on Tuesday, and Monday's efficiency will be reduced by worrying about not having done it.

A second rule continues the establishment of priorities: concentrate the effort on those activities which call for immediate action. Of course, the choice is obvious if one is deciding between answering a reference enquiry or working on the index to the organization's archives. The librarian must answer the enquiry first. However, he will be aware that producing the index, even though it is the kind of task which does not satisfy an immediate need, is a valid and professional activity, and the conscientious one-person librarian will try to find some time each day for precisely this type of work. This choice is easy. It is more difficult when the librarian must choose between two equally essential tasks. This is where one's professionalism is called upon. The librarian's experience and background will enable him to establish proper professional priorities.

In all libraries there are professional duties which call for an immediate response, such as readers' advisory and reference. However, many tasks in a library are not so pressing, but these projects, upon completion, will enable the librarian to respond to requests for immediate information more successfully. These are valid professional activities and the librarian should be aware of them, of their demands on his time and their eventual contribution to the library operation. She does not need to apologize for such activities, and even if they are so esoteric that only the librarian will know about them (and use them if they are, indeed, these index-producing types of activity), they are nevertheless part of her job and she should feel free to plan time for such activities. The service to the users of the one-person library will be better for it.

Once determined, specific work in every library must be considered in such a way as to be performed effectively and efficiently. Unfortunately, many people often approach their tasks in an entirely wrong way, with the common approach being to achieve, complete and remove the task, whereas the first thing which should be done is to plan the task and to think about how it should be completed. While planning, in the broadest sense, was discussed in the previous chapter, it is suggested here as one of several approaches to effective self-management and time management. Probably the best way to do this is by using the systems approach, particularly suitable for a small library because the librarian is often entrusted with two jobs – the collection and storage of materials and the exploitation of the contents of the materials on behalf of those who use the library. To begin with, these are two questions to ask when setting up or running a small library service. First, what are the basic requirements of the organization? Second, how can these requirements best be satisfied with the existing resources (or building on the existing resources if the library service is new)? It is a commonly accepted notion in the profession that many library systems come about because a member of management 'thought it was a good idea at the time'. We cannot stress how wrong this thinking is, because an arbitrarily chosen system can have more influence on the library operation than the real requirements. Thus systems planning requires that you discover the real needs of the organization before you set up the library. Often, because of lack of time to think through the potential need and uses for a library service, the service provided is unrelated to the actual requirements of the users. For instance, management might have an uninformed understanding – or misunderstanding – of the services a library can provide for an organization, perceiving a library as simply a book-ordering service, perhaps, and not being aware that the requirements of the organization can be better served by the use of online databases for speed of retrieval, or utilizing Viewdata, or taking advantages of the capacity of a microcomputer for cataloguing. Management might never have heard of an SDI service, or considered how it could benefit the staff, or thought of allowing the staff to use a departmental word processor for producing booklists and bulletins. In short, you must put a great deal of thought into the planning of a small library service, and you must be able to convince management that the old traditional systems are not necessarily the best as far as cost-effectiveness and time saving are concerned. It is thinking and planning for these eventualities which makes them happen, and while the one-person librarian is carrying out her daily tasks it is also imperative that she be engaged in a continuous thinking and planning process.

Effective self-management is basically good time management, and there are two approaches to time management which can be considered here. One is KISS, an amusing but nevertheless worthwhile operational technique which has been espoused by managers since at least World War II. The second is an analysis of time management for industry as described by Ian Barclay at a gathering of librarians.

KISS – an acronym for 'Keep It Simple, Stupid' – is a theory of business management that has been described occasionally in the media. While its light-hearted tone might be offensive to those who prefer their management theory couched in more pompous terms, it is precisely the kind of management theory needed by one-person librarians, and its acceptance, or at least its consideration, can be beneficial to the library and management alike. While the ideas it incorporates are hardly new or overwhelming as management goals, it is a system which, when applied felicitously by one-person librarians, can be an enormous time-saver. The best way to save the librarian's time is the most obvious and the most difficult to achieve: simplicity. We are, by nature, the most complicated profession. If ever a history of mankind is written that breaks us down by profession, librarians will probably be characterized as the most careful, the most particular, the most specific of all. In many respects that is what draws us to the profession: we want to organize, to categorize, to analyse, and then to reorganize whatever we come across, but in so doing we sometimes tend to lose sight of what should be the goal of any librarian, but most particularly of the one-person librarian, which is to get the information to the user.

One of the articles which describes the KISS theory of management[1] points out that a key feature of well-managed  companies (and, by implication, for the employee in a well-managed one-person library) is that they keep things simple in spite of almost overwhelming pressures to complicate things. In a one-person library the librarian frankly does not have the luxury of complication. There is not the time, when you are doing what you must do, which is everything. The one-person librarian simply does not have the time to get bogged down in references and cross-references and the 'where-might-the-user-look?' kind of thinking. The material in the library has to be accessible, and for the librarian working alone KISS is an acceptable approach to doing it.

There are four basic components to KISS, according to Peters and Waterman, as described in the *Wall Street Journal*. First, paperwork is kept to a minimum. Second, the small size of the operation is recognized as an asset, not a liability. Third, the recognition of limited objectives is seen as an incentive to more satisfactory work. Finally, the recognition of a simple, dominating businesslike and efficient value for the library is seen as a necessary goal for the librarian and for management.

Whenever possible, paperwork is eliminated or minimized. All memoranda, with no exceptions, are limited to one page. For the one-person librarian who is called upon to write grant proposals, reports to management, research assignments, etc., such a rule would seem to have been created to be broken. However, it is a valuable discipline. The one-person librarian really does not have the time to sit down and be creative whenever she is called upon to prepare project proposals, user studies, etc. So as far as the minimum paperwork part of the KISS concept is concerned, the one-person librarian is (or should be) already incorporating it into her own regimen. If it is not part of one's normal procedure, it should be.

Keep a very simple ledger to keep track of office and library expenditures. If you have a microcomputer, adapt one of the electronic spreadsheet programs for the library, just as you would for your chequebook at home. It does not have to be complicated in the one-person library, and if it is, perhaps you should look at some of the work you are doing in this connection. Is it worth the extra time and effort? Use form letters whenever necessary. It is not rude to send a form letter to acknowledge a gift or to remind a committee about a meeting. You do not have time to write a separate letter each time a recurring event comes up. Most important, avoid purchasing agents if you have any say in the matter at all. One of the unvarying rules in the corporate world is that the use of purchasing agents increases the price of anything that is bought and at the same time adds to the amount of time necessary to obtain that item.

The second part of the KISS rule has to do with size and the advantage, no matter how large the corporation, of keeping departments of manageable size: 'Well-run organizations keep crucial parts of their enterprises small, even if the entire organizations are large and far flung. As a result, they encourage a personal touch, highly motivated cultures, and unusual entrepreneurial spirit.'[1] A well-run one-person library also must have the personal touch, and the personal enthusiasm of the librarian, so that the patrons are encouraged to use it. It is because one-person libraries are so small that they can be so good. In fact it is now becoming recognized that this entrepreneurial spirit can bring success to those large companies that are willing to break up into smaller units:

An American corporate orthodoxy that was suited to mature, stable markets turned out to be ill-suited to a dynamic marketplace characterized by a tremendous pace of innovation and change. And big companies began to wonder whether their very structures inhibited their ability to adapt in a dynamic marketplace ... American business has discovered that small is beautiful.[2]

We have earlier described some of the advantages of a small library, but here we can give some attention to the personality of the librarian. For many managers the concept of a small library and a one-person library staff automatically includes the stereotypical librarian, and managers are delighted and pleased when they discover that the person running the library is *not* an on-the-job reader (the most typical stereotype) and is, in fact, as highly motivated and self-motivated as many of the finest members of other departments of the parent organization. When the librarian is discovered to be an efficient administrator, research guide, teacher and office manager all in one, the library's role in the work of the parent organization will be greatly enhanced.

High motivation grows directly from the circumstance of self-motivation. For the librarian in a one-person library there is no choice but to be highly motivated, because he or she has no-one else to turn to (or to blame, when things go wrong!). Every decision must be made in terms of 'how can I accomplish this task?' or 'how does this fit into *my* schedule of activities?' There may be several choices for how to perform a particular task, but the one-person librarian limits those choices to those which get the job done most quickly and efficiently.

It is this self-motivation which leads to the unconventional entrepreneurial spirit in the small organization. The one-person librarian has to know to whom to turn when his resources fail, to know how to seek (and to justify) managerial support for outside expenditures, for new technology, for labour-saving devices. Often the librarian has to know how and when to seek support elsewhere, when to go around management and find another way to get what is needed. The use of volunteers is one such example of this kind of entrepreneurial spirit in the one-person library. Obviously not appropriate in the for-profit sector, volunteers have, nevertheless, been a boon in other types of one-person libraries. Librarians frequently comment on how volunteers enable them to perform tasks and to offer services which literally would not be available if management had to pay for them. While the role of volunteers raises serious questions about the value of services rendered, equal pay, etc., there is no question that the use of volunteers is one way to get a particular job done. This is the kind of thing the one-person librarian must think about: how to manage successfully with whatever resources are available. Often the stimulus for finding and using resources must come from within the librarian herself. The one-person librarian, more than any other library administrator, must be an entrepreneur.

Another part of running the library by the KISS method of management is the determination of the objectives of the managerial organization. Here, 'keep it simple' means exactly that. We also ask ourselves a primary question: what are the objectives of the one-person library? Some management-by-objectives programmes will include lists of twenty or more objectives for a single manager. It is easy to imagine what it would be like in a one-person organization if there were twenty or more objectives for that person's work! There would be no real sense of accomplishing anything, and probably very little would be accomplished, except that the librarian would feel pushed around by an over-defined job description and frustrated because some nebulous 'they' expected these tasks to be performed. A sincere and honest analysis of the necessary tasks and a direct discussion between librarian and supervisor will usually reveal that much of the one-person librarian's frustrations are self-manufactured.

Our advice for a one-person librarian is to have one objective – something like 'get the information to the user'. Then the librarian and the person to whom he reports can discuss broadening the activities of the department. However, the librarian will be wary. There are many people (including, unfortunately, management personnel from time to time) who do not understand library tasks and who think librarians do not do anything but sit around and read. The librarian in a one-person library cannot allow herself to be talked into something that cannot be handled. In this respect we should keep in mind the company that reminds its managers: 'More than two objectives is no objective.' These executives have discovered that it is not effective to try to keep one's attention on more than one or two priority matters at any given time.

Here again we come upon the nettlesome subject of professional versus clerical duties, and when clerical duties are not appropriate for the one-person library. There is no question that clerical duties are time-consuming and, for the chartered, graduate librarian, are taken on with somewhat less enthusiasm than the range of professional activities for which special skills, education and intellectual abilities are required. Yet it must be recognized that many librarians who work alone are not specially trained. In fact, many one-person librarians are people who have been asked to take over the library or information service because they demonstrated special expertise in some other aspect of the parent organization's structure. For organizational reasons their positions were realigned and they were directed to manage (or in many cases to create) the library. For these 'librarians', the conflict between professional and non-professional tasks is not a real concern, for they are doing what they were hired to do, i.e. manage a library or information unit. Whether they do it as well as a chartered, professional librarian would do it is not a question for discussion here. We can only address the situation as it exists, not as we would have it exist, for no matter how strongly we may feel that only professional librarians should be employed as librarians, some organizations simply do not have the work or the need for a professional, chartered librarian on staff. Thus we are in the position of advising the one-person librarian, regardless of her professional qualifications, that clerical work, if it is part of the job description, must be accepted. If it is not formally part of the job it must be re-assigned so that the professional, chartered librarian can use her time more professionally. The professional role of the librarian will be determined by the objectives of the organization, and it will be those objectives which will determine the objectives of the library and the one-person librarian who is employed.

Having brought up this subject of limited objectives for the one-person library how do we apply this concept to the management of the one-person library? First, of course, the librarian must have a sense of priorities, as we described earlier, and once the tasks are defined in order of importance it is necessary to remember that the librarian can do only one task at a time. We will see, as we describe the specific tasks in the technical processing work in the library, for example, that it is not always possible to work uninterruptedly at one task while ignoring everything else. In the one-person library, which is a service organization just like any other library, the librarian will almost always be interrupted just when a particular task is about to be completed. This is one of the characteristics of one-person librarianship – it comes with the territory. However, accepting this fact does not mean that the librarian works in an unstructured fashion. Just like any other serious business person, the librarian in a one-person library begins her day with a list of tasks to be performed, accepts each interruption with as much grace and politeness as she can muster, and then goes back to the task at hand. There will always be days when even the interruptions are interrupted. On these occasions the librarian simply has to acknowledge it, accept it and put away the materials for the original task, to be taken out again tomorrow, when, one hopes, there will be an opportunity to finish the work. The point is to organize the tasks, to know, and to accept, which ones have to be dealt with sooner than others, and to attempt to complete these tasks (incorporating the interruptions) in the proper order.

Finally, in discussing the applications of the KISS theory of management to the one-person library the librarian must recognize the business value of the organization. Work in the library must be kept simple. Yet for many libraries, especially one-person libraries which are part of larger organizations, the business end of running a library is often dismissed. if the parent organization has a separate business manager, accounting department or purchasing agent the librarian is often in the position (or is put in the position) of not knowing how the money is spent or whether thc library is getting value for the money spent in purchases for the library. In technical processing procedures the librarian therefore tries to job out as much of the work as possible, relying on commercial agencies to supply materials, preferably already physically processed for the library, so that time and money is not consumed in the library itself. The library must be organized and managed just like any other business, as we shall discuss in greater detail in a chapter devoted to this subject. For now, we can simply recognize that although the librarian is not selling a product in the literal sense, nevertheless information is obtained and delivered, and it must be produced in a businesslike and professional manner. When non-library personnel in management criticize librarians, the one attack that is delivered most frequently is that librarians do not manage their departments in a businessslike way. Such a charge may often be true, but for the serious librarian, especially in a one-person library, the lack of businesslike practices is dangerously inefficient. The article on the subject written in 1974 by Shirley Echelman[3] is recommended for the valuable insights it can provide the one-person librarian who may not understand that her operation is to be managed in such a way.

One of the most obvious goals for the one-person librarian who is trying to manage her time carefully is to consciously seek short cuts. A good place to begin is with an analysis of the tasks which are routinely performed in the library. Wherever possible, those tasks which are done more than once at different times in the work flow should be combined. To determine what these are, it might be necessary to refer to your procedures manual for the library. For example, if you find that you are entering bibliographic data about certain materials or titles into your system more than once (whether it be on correspondence for ordering the materials, cards for the catalogue, booklists for users, etc.), analyse why this information must be entered more than once and make some attempt to combine some of the paperwork. Can the order cards be duplicated and used as temporary 'in-process' records for the catalogue? Can that same information be used as a booklist for users? However arranged, it is always worthwhile in the one-person library to combine record-keeping whenever possible.

The physical organization of the library can have much to do with how library time is used – or abused. If the library is organized well, both the users and the librarian will be able to find things with the least expenditure of time and effort. Give clear guidance to shelves, catalogues, etc., so that if you are busy the readers can help themselves. Similarly, have regularly used items readily available, though the librarian's desk should be free of unnecessary clutter.

Another commonly accepted time-saver for one-person librarians is a record of useful telephone numbers kept always at hand. If the librarian does not have time to look for a specific answer to an enquiry, or if the particular reference which contains the answer is not handy, a call to another librarian who can supply the answer is in order. In most cases, the user does not care where or how the librarian obtains the answer, he just wants the answer. Perhaps a digression will illustrate this. In New York, practically every one-person librarian has a couple of telephone lines and it is not uncommon for the librarian to take the call on one line, put the user on Hold, use the other line to call a public or other telephone reference service, get the answer and go back to the other line; the alternative is to take the number when the user first asks the question and then call him back with the answer. In nine times out of ten, the user does not care where the answer comes from and the librarian does not need to tell him. Just let him praise the good service in the library. If the librarian feels a little guilty about making other librarians do his work, perhaps a donation squeezed from the budget at the end of the year for a contribution to the most useful telephone reference service would be appropriate. It is worth it in time and energy saved.

Yet another good approach to finding short cuts is to join as many formal and informal consortia and/or networking groups as possible. For example, in New York, the New York Metropolitan Reference and Research Agency (METRO) exists for the purposes of enabling librarians and other information specialists to share resources. Similarly, in the United Kingdom librarians can get in touch with one another by telephone using the OMB network, the London business libraries network and other such informal groups. Especially in the OMB/one-person library, where the librarian has to be 'on duty' during business hours and usually cannot get away to go to use resources elsewhere, the availability of such an agency can pay for its annual cost many times over.

What is suggested here is something probably all librarians recognize, but some sort of built-in inertia seems to prevent us from doing: seek *connections*. As we have said, we use this term to speak about communications and professional interactions, and it is not an original concept by any means. There is nothing wrong with it, and there is no reason to be shy about it, as long as we are courteous and are prepared to be as generous with our subject specialities and our professional time as we expect others to be for us. In our profession we speak often about making professional friends and setting up connections; these colleagues, consortia and networks can all be useful connections to have, and in a one-person library one cannot be hesitant about using them. After all, our goal is simple and oft-repeated: *get the information to the user*. All the rest is background, support, organization and management, and as far as the user is concerned it really does not mean anything. The fact of the matter is that all of the background work is valid if it helps us, as librarians and information specialists, to meet that basic goal. One does not have to apologize to anyone, as long as one is willing to share expertise, resources and specific strengths in the same way.

Other connections can be found on the premises, and the utilization of these in-house resources can be a primary time-saver for the one-person librarian. We refer here to the users of the library, and who can be of benefit to you when you must make a decision. Decision-making can be a very time-consuming process. We know that two things are required for decision-making: knowledge and a framework on which to hang that knowledge. Decision-making becomes much more time-consuming when we suddenly realize that we have no facts at hand on which to base the decision, and it seems a matter of common sense to accumulate a steady stream of facts so that sudden panic decisions do not have to be made. In other words, when doing a job such as renewing certain journals on an annual basis, you should know automatically those which are still necessary to the work of the staff, those which can be cancelled and any new additions which need to be made. This will save much time, as the list can then easily be checked without recourse to running around and asking members of the staff to take a snap poll (which is likely to lead to wrong decisions anyway, as most people do not make very good choices under stress). Time spent talking to staff on a regular basis about their information needs is time well spent.

Similarly, the one-person librarian cannot buy a book just because a manager says he needs it. You have to weigh how many other staff might use the book, who will find it really useful, how much it costs, whether the library contains something of a similar nature which would do just as well and, most important of all, whether the work will supplement the existing collection. Similarly, decisions about whether to subscribe to certain journals can be handled by asking the same types of questions: is the item needed for current awareness, is it abstracted regularly, are the contents online or are much of the contents ephemeral but very useful? Any such decisions should not involve the one-person librarians in much soul-searching but can evolve naturally if you have kept a steady flow of information coming in from your users. Decision-making, though complicated, can be less stressful if you know your users, and if you know and understand the objectives of the library and the institution it supports.

There are a couple of other aids which can be mentioned. First of all, the librarian in a one-person library should job out as much of the time-consuming or clerical work as possible. If there is no-one else to paste labels in books or tape on plastic covers the librarian may elect to do it, but such tasks take her from the more important work and must, by their very nature, be thought of as distracting. For such tasks, the efficient librarian will find a book jobber who will provide the materials already labelled and jacketed. Similarly, if you have a pretty good rapport with management try to recruit temporary staff for special projects. If you have decided once and for all to organize those ten-year piles of corporate annual reports, or a mess of old periodicals, do not waste *your* time. Find a bright teenager between terms and let him do it. It may not be done *exactly* the way you would have done it, but it will be certainly more useful than it was as unorganized chaos.

The one-person librarian today is more fortunate than in years past in that technological advances make it possible to acquire things such as microcomputers, efficient copiers, etc. Actually, running a one-person library is a major organizational challenge. It was not so long ago that a request from a librarian for a microcomputer would have been an occasion for merriment among management, but today management has a vested interest in seeing that the library, like all other parts of the organization, functions in the most efficient and cost-effective ways possible, and this often includes acquiring and utilizing new technology. It also puts on the librarian the responsibility of keeping an open mind about the value of new technology and the advantages to which it can be used in the one-person library. This is not to say that the one-person library is the place for expensive experimentation, but we should be willing, as unfortunately many librarians are not, to consider how we can do our work better and more efficiently, even if it means that we must come to grips with some of our fears and reluctance about new products and services.

Another self-management rule which must be observed is to learn to say 'no'. For many persons, and for librarians especially, since we have been trained in a service profession, it is almost impossible to refuse to do a task, but there simply are not enough hours in the day to do all the things your clients and management would have you do. The librarian who has a supportive manager can confidently refuse requests that are not in his realm of service. There is no way, however, to convince everyone that the librarian has anything to do but sit and wait for questions. The librarian has to learn to do only those services for clients normally provided by the library, and work outside that limit is rejected with a firm but pleasant 'no' and, if possible, referral to an appropriate department where the work can be done. As for other employees (those who are not clients, usually secretarial or clerical workers), it may sound elitist, but the librarian should not even bother to waste his time trying to educate them. No amount of effort, however well-intentioned, will convince them that the librarian does not spend all his time sitting and reading. The best way to deal with this problem is simply a firm, but again polite, refusal when they come to the library to visit, gossip, kill time, or even to ask the librarian to do their son's or daughter's research assignments. Obviously a genuine query from a member of the secretarial or clerical staff will be honoured, and responded to like all other genuine requests for information, but inappropriate requests have to be discouraged. Such employees will soon get the message about what can and cannot be done in the library or by the librarian, and while these distinctions may not make the librarian the most popular person in the organization, she will, at least, not lose time dealing with inappropriate assignments. The ability to say no is an asset, tremendously difficult to achieve, but important if one is to provide a relevant library service.

In a one-person library it is particularly important not to be tempted to use library time for personal work. It is easy to forget, in a quiet time when the mail has been done and there is no-one waiting to be helped, that one is an employee and not on one's free time. Such activities as personal letter writing, bill-paying, telephone conversations, etc., can be tempting, but must be avoided.

Many one-person librarians solve the problem of personal tasks by working flexible hours, that is, being on duty the hours they are required to be in the library but also frequently coming in early or staying later or coming in on an occasional Saturday or Sunday to do those things which cannot be classed as 'job' but which are better done at the office than elsewhere. This is particularly true of work for professional organizations. Most of those who want to contribute to a professional organization cannot find time during their work days but are able to do something for the group by putting in time at the office after hours.

If you find you are going to be away from the library occasionally, whether it be for a trip to the dentist, a vacation, a professional meeting or conference, or even, if you can, for your daily lunch break, try to establish with management some sort of set procedure for relief from some other member in the parent organization who will come in regularly on schedule. This employee is not expected to know how to run the library, but only to sit at your desk and tell those who come in or call when you are expected to return. Do not glorify the employee as an 'assistant' and do not even expect him or her to be able to do simple library tasks. Just arrange to have someone available to cover for you.

Know your own skills. Be confident in what you are doing, and if the job calls for some skill that you have not mastered try to find out where and when you can learn it. Do not flounder around doing things you do not know how to do. It just wastes your time and costs the company money, and since the 'mysteries' of librarianship are not always known to those who supervise us, there are plenty of times when a one-person librarian can ride along on just looking busy. If you do not know how to do something that needs to be done in the library, seek some help. If you do not do this it will catch up with you sooner or later.

Finally, there is one last admonition we would make to anyone in one-person library work. You cannot be lazy. No matter how much you want to try to take it easy on the job, in the one-person library you just cannot. The work is there, it is always going to be there, and one-person librarianship is the last place in the world for an unmotivated, uninterested employee. It happens sometimes, and it is a mistake when management puts people like this in one-person libraries, because frustration all around is the end result. Get your energy together, be industrious, show your initiative, and you will like your job better.

## References

1  Peters, Thomas J. and Waterman, Robert H., 'Keep it simple', *Wall Street Journal*, 27 October 1980, p. 30.

2  Linden, Eugene, 'Let a thousand flowers floom', *Inc,* April 1984.

3  Echelman, Shirley, 'Libraries are businesses, too!' *Special Libraries,* **65,** October/November, 409-416, 1974.

# Basics III: time management

Time management, as it relates to one-person librarianship, essentially involves a consideration of one or more steps toward self-improvement, which in itself requires more than just a recognition of the need and a willingness to apply oneself to the task. It also requires an ordered system within which the most important aspects of work can be fitted and actions taken. When reduced to its most basic level, effective self-management is really just good time management, and there are three fundamental factors:

(1)  Recognition of the need.
(2)  Desire to do something about the need.
(3)  Well-managed time to allow (2) to occur.

Essentially, then, good time management means reorganizing your approach to work. We have already stressed the importance of planning and thinking, which must be included in one's daily activities. You do not have to look busy all the time. Take time to stop and think about what you are doing or what needs to be done. This alone will reap dividends.

Ian Barclay, lecturer in the Department of Industrial Studies at Liverpool University, suggests one approach to time management:[1]

● ATTITUDE to your job tasks.
● APPROACH to your job tasks.
● ANALYSIS of your activities.
● APPLICATION of techniques.
● APPRAISAL of effect.
● ENJOYMENT of achieving the main aim.

In discussing attitude we should keep in mind that personal characteristics have much to do with time management. By understanding your personality and how it influences how you use your time you can take steps to maximize the beneficial aspects and minimize the detrimental ones. Examples include the morning person versus the night owl, the extrovert versus the introvert, those who enjoy dealing with people versus those who prefer to work in the backroom, away from the public, struggling with knotty problems. If you are aware of these factors in your personality you can make them work for you.

As has been mentioned before, a recognition of the library's place in the organizational hierarchy can be helpful in determining what tasks should be done or avoided. You may get on well with certain people, but if they are not relevant to your work you should consider spending less time, rather than more, with them.

Task components also influence your use of time. You might be spending a disproportionate amount of time on tasks you enjoy to the detriment of other work. Clearly, the pleasant aspects of the job produce job satisfaction, but you must determine how much time you can justify doing what you like. One of the basic rules of the workplace is that no job, no matter how perfect it may seem to others, is going to be perfect in practice. Every job is going to have some part of it that is not one's favourite thing to do, but it has to be done.

Communication becomes important in the overall time-management picture. Ask yourself how you communicate with the various teams that you may have to deal with. What pressures do you experience in the library? Are they brought about by certain people with whom you work? What role does internal politics play in the organization and how does this affect your use of time?

Regardless of how much you like your work, avoid becoming a workaholic. You need your leisure, and you should make sure you get it. You will function better for it, and you will be able to make better decisions if you can clear your mind on a regular basis.

Working in a one-person library you have the advantage of arranging your time. There are any number of little rules which can be helpful here, but some of the most useful are:

- Do not waste time complaining about problems.
- Accept your limitations – perfection is not a useful standard in the workplace.
- Be friendly to your users.
- Keep calm and never panic – no-one can complete a task successfully in a panic situation.
- Think about your task more than once if you need to – but only do the task once.
- View problems as opportunities: do not just solve them – exploit them as well.

When we are dealing with the one-person librarian's approach to time management we first question the motivation. Why should a one-person librarian need to be concerned with time management? Because there is never enough time. This is the one common theme whenever one-person librarians get together, or when they respond to questionnaires about their work. Whether this is the actual case or not is not relevant here – most one-person librarians perceive that time management is their greatest problem, and if that is the case they are perfectly justified to study how better to use their time. A first question which might be asked is simply 'Does this task have to be done?' We have already pointed out that some tasks can be jobbed out to a vendor, or directed to another department, or the task may be a repetition of a step that was done earlier and could be completed at that time. In any case, if it is determined that the task must be done, the following questions can be addressed:

- What exactly is it that has to be done?
- Will completing this task solve a problem?
- How much has to be done?
- How long do I have to do it?

After quantifying the tasks it is possible to improve our methods of taking on a job. We begin by planning goals. In a one-person library there are two broad groups of task to be accomplished: the administrative tasks which are set by you or your management, and the problem-solving tasks, often set by others, either your users or management, if management is considered to be among the users of the library. The former are more flexible than the latter because you are not likely to keep a user waiting whilst you take care of administrative tasks.

Plan for specific results, first by trying to get a little more done each week than you did in the previous week, but also by planning ahead for the following week, month and year. You keep these goals in mind, even if they seem impossible at the time, and you chart them because giving yourself something to look at will enable you to see how your plans are taking shape.

From time to time you will run into problems, but these you should view as opportunities to be exploited. If you cannot cope with the number of manual searches you are having to complete, consider costing out the benefit of online searches and suggest to management that the workload justifies having an online facility in the library itself.

You should anticipate problems, accept that they will occur from time to time and attempt to deal with them before they arise. By maintaining contact with your regular users many problems can be avoided.

Another approach is to cost out your time use. Everything you do costs time and energy, which in organizational terms is money. If you work out how much it costs your organization to employ you in complete terms – not just salary – you will get some idea whether your employer is getting value for the money spent. This can be a very strong argument when suggesting innovations.

Finally, in discussing the approach of the one-person librarian to his or her job there are a few general tips which are worth remembering:

(1) If you have a problem, do something about it now – do not procrastinate.
(2) Do not pursue lost causes.
(3) Do not make excuses: do not say you will try to do something on time – just do it.
(4) Do not look for difficulties – they may never arise.
(5) Start something new each day.
(6) Finish something each day.
(7) Keep outside activities out of work.
(8) Ask others how they save time.
(9) Enjoy your work.

The one-person librarian is motivated to analyse his or her work because by doing so the following can be identified:

- Unused/wasted time.
- Time-wasting activities.
- Ways of changing procedures to improve efficiency.

From time to time, especially in a library where one has been the one-person librarian for a number of years, it is a good idea to conduct actual studies to analyse how one spends one's time. Just how much time is used for going through the mail, for ordering books, for answering reference questions? A time analysis is always little surprising because most of us do not realize how we use our time. The results of such an analysis can be an invaluable aid in helping the one-person librarian to reorganize her routine, for just being aware of how much time is spent on a particular task will frequently encourage us to do it in a faster and/or more efficient way, or to consider whether it is a task worth doing at all, and if it is not to abandon it.

It is not simple, but a time analysis can provide many answers to questions and frustrations. It means keeping a record of what you do and how long you take to do it, by writing down, for a set period such as a week or a fortnight, what you accomplish during every fifteen minutes of your working day. As you chart your progress you will find that certain activities keep recurring which, once they have been coded, you will be able to state in percentages of total time used. Typical findings are:

- Items that can be omitted altogether.
- Items that can be done by someone else.
- Unexpected events caused by bad planning (not necessarily planning in the library).
- Time-wasting people and events.

You will also analyse by activity and by omission. In the former you will analyse particular work episodes, questioning why you are doing a particular task, how long it took to do it, what methods are employed to complete it, etc. By concentrating on some of the more time-consuming work periods you may be able to eliminate them, consolidate them, or at least reduce them. Similarly, when you analyse by omission you will be asking yourself what you would like to have completed at a particular time and what tasks should have been considered had there been time. If you have been honest with yourself and cut out some of the things which you do not need to do, or can get someone else to do, you might be able to fit in some activities which you feel are necessary but have not yet been able to introduce. Choose the ones which will most benefit the service you provide for the organization.

The next step, as you apply these hints and tips, is to apply them. This, too, takes the form of list-making. There are any number of things which can be included on such a list, and our purpose here is simply to get you started. You will add more of your own.

(1) Be on time and stick to appointments.
(2) Do the hardest jobs first, when your energy is highest.

(3) Use selective delays – stop sometimes and think about the specific job you are doing at that moment.
(4) Use scientific techniques when appropriate.
(5) Ask other people how they save time.
(6) Recognize that you can do more than one thing at a time.
(7) Do it now.
(8) Do not reply to an assignment with 'holding the wolf at bay' memos.
(9) Do not miss deadlines.
(10) Be honest with yourself and with others – seek help if you do not know how to do something yourself.
(11) Budget well.
(12) Be composed.
(13) Bring any conflict out into the open.
(14) Improve your learning, concentrating and reading skills.
(15) Recognize stress and learn how to cope with it.
(16) Do not drink or use drugs during the work day.
(17) Stay fit.
(18) Develop a confidant or mentor – you need someone to talk to.
(19) Enjoy your job.
(20) Do not be lazy.
(21) Avoid negative and destructive thinking.

Finally, give some consideration to ways of dealing with management. The boss is there not just to supervise but to know what is going on, in your department as well as in the others for which he or she is responsible. Try to pick a good boss. Unfortunately, one-person librarians are often saddled with someone in the organization who knows little about libraries and information services, and who often has no commitment to the service provided by that department. In that case, there really is little that can be done, other than attempting to have yourself moved to another department or supervisor where there is management which is both interested and supportive. However, you might find it worthwhile to spend more time in upward rather than downward communication. For your management to know what is going on in your section it is up to you to initiate the communication.

# Reference

1 Barclay, Ian, 'Time management',
Paper delivered at the Library
Association Industrial Group Annual
Conference, York, March 1984.

Chapter Nine

# Collection development

In the one-person library collection development is that work which includes the formulation of and adherence to a library policy statement, the organization and development of criteria for the selection of materials for the collection, the understanding and utilization of the procedures employed in the acquisition process, and a continuous review of the collection. Each of these activities is a vital part of the librarian's administrative role in the library, and none can be ignored without influencing the effective service of the one-person library.

## Collection development policy

A logical starting point for a discussion of collection development, according to Andrew Berner in a presentation he made to a library Friends group, is to examine the question, 'What is a collection development policy and why do we need one?'[1] According to Berner, every library has a collection development policy, although in many libraries it may exist only as some informal ideas in the head of the librarian. Unfortunately, this approach has two significant failings: it is very shortsighted and does not look towards the ultimate goals of the library, and as staff changes (especially in the one-person library) the informal policy is going to change as well. Obviously, then, a written collection development policy is necessary as an aid to the librarian and the library's board or library committee. No library can be all things to all people, especially a library which is small enough to be managed by one person. That librarian is always going to be in the position of having to pick and choose the materials that are to go into the collection.

In the special library, what kinds of materials are collected and how does collection development begin? The American Library Association's *Guidelines for the Formulation of Collection Development* categorizes five codes or levels of collecting density (comprehensive, research, study, basic, minimal).[2] According to Susan Gensel and Audrey Powers, most special libraries, which we have to recognize include most one-person libraries, collect at the research level, with timeliness the important characteristic of the collection. 'Current periodicals and online services comprise a major portion of the budget, and weeding becomes one of the most important activities in this research atmosphere.'[3] Yet there is a place for a seriously thought-out collection development policy even in those one-person libraries which are not in research institutions and which serve a more general group of users, such as small public libraries or libraries in cultural institutions, religious organizations, etc. While Gensel and Powers were addressing special libraries when they outlined their list of steps to be taken in order to begin collection development, it seems to us that all types of one-person libraries can benefit from following these points:

- Understand the goal of the parent organization.
- Examine the budgetary process.
- Examine existing materials.
- Identify other research needs.
- Determine any peripheral needs.
- Establish mechanisms for selection.
- Establish mechanisms for acquisitions.
- Develop inventory and replacement procedures.
- Prepare criteria for weeding.

Berner has also made a list which, because he is addressing a lay group whose members are not professional librarians, is somewhat broader in approach, and his seven topics for consideration[1] are more applicable for the traditional one-person librarian who might not be faced with the demand for immediacy required in the special library:

- *Acquisitions.* This involves determining the types of items which will be purchased for the collection.
- *Maintenance.* Once items are in the collection how will they be cared for on a day-to-day basis? This includes such seemingly mundane but important items as having the shelves regularly straightened and dusted.
- *Housing and storage.* This is an adjunct of maintenance, although it deals with more long-term considerations such as temperature and humidity controls, ultraviolet filters for lights and windows, etc.
- *Preservation and conservation.* This addresses the question of preserving items which are already in the collection, and includes repairing those volumes needing work, phase boxes for those beyond repair, acid-free sheets to retard deterioration, etc.
- *Replacement.* Those volumes which have been lost over the years may be replaced (in print or microform), but decisions must be made as to which books will be replaced.
- *De-accessioning.* The removal of volumes which are no longer of value to the collection. This helps to solve another problem which virtually all libraries face – the lack of shelf space.
- *Gifts.* Gifts can provide a major supplement to acquisitions. However, decisions must be made as to what types of gifts will be accepted, whether or not any conditions will be allowed with gifts, how they will be processed (i.e. with large gifts, is additional staff time available for processing?), how they will be acknowledged, etc.

Thus we can see that simply creating a collection development policy is a step of some importance for the one-person library, and will require serious concentration and support from management, the library committee or board, if there is one, and ideally a representative goup of users.

Berner concludes his suggested directions for formulating a collection development policy with three considerations: the inclusion of the library's statement of purpose, the wording of the policy itself, and the listing of those subjects which make up the strengths of the collection. The statement of purpose, whether a memorandum from senior management creating the corporate or departmental library or a printed document published by a town's board of managers, will list the concrete goals for the library and spell out exactly what that library is supposed to be for. The wording of the policy should be specific enough to offer guidance, but not so specific that it removes all options or initiative from the staff and the governing body of the library. Finally, the policy should give indications of the specific subject areas which are of the greatest significance to the library and its users, based on factors such as use and demand, the rate at which materials become dated, ease of referral to other libraries, and an analysis of the present collection. When all these are considered, the librarian and his governing board or management are in a position to create a written policy statement for the library, a statement that will be useful not only to the present librarian and management but to those who come after them. Gensel and Powers bring their paper to a conclusion with an admonition to librarians to use their policies, and we can only offer the same advice to one-person librarians who have worked to create a policy:

> Once your policy is recorded don't leave it up on a shelf. Make it an active extension of your operating procedure. It should be fluid enough to reflect changes as the organization grows. Whether you actually write it down or not – the exercise of preparing such a procedure will become an intuitive part of your thinking. Be practical![4]

How does the one-person librarian organize and develop criteria for the inclusion of materials in the collection? The first step, obviously, is to look at what is already there. Unless you are starting a new information service there is already something in the library. What types of materials are there? As you look over the collection you will find that materials fall into broad categories which can include, in an established library or information service, the full range of someone's collecting instincts: books, certainly, and magazines, and critical file materials (pamphlets, clippings, reports, correspondence files, etc.), plus, if research is done in the parent institution, research reports, company files and similar materials (including, often, such things as archives, photographic or other two-dimensional graphic material). Then, too, there will be the peripheral material, often ephemeral, but items which someone at some time used in connection with his work for the parent institution and, when the work was finished, did not know what to do with and gave to the library. These include such things as consultants' reports, files relating to activities of one employee or another in professional or trade groups, supply catalogues and, oddly enough, such ordinary things as road maps, renovation diagrams, etc. Finally, because they require special attention, some materials come to the library because of their type: one institution may store all its audio-visual materials in the library, another may keep microfilmed copies of the minutes of board of directors meetings there, while a third might use the library as a storage facility for odd memorabilia: early medals, perhaps, or a couple of oil paintings, or copies of the speeches of some remote founder of the parent institution. The list can be endless, but if you prepare a simple inventory of the broad categories of materials in the library or information centre you will find you have at least a point of departure for your consideration.

Then, list in hand, you tick off each category by asking two questions: (1) how did (does) this material get chosen for the library and (2) who uses it? At this point, one rule comes quickly to mind: do not be sentimental. No matter how much we (or anyone else) may love certain types of materials, the one-person library is *not* the place to indulge that affection if that category of materials does not meet the first requirement of collecting: does the material support the goals of the parent institution? Therefore, as you look over the list, you must cold-heartedly question the value of each category of materials, and the first step in the process becomes easy: if the material does not support the goals of the parent organization and/or if the material is not used, do not consider that category for future inclusion.

This step really solves two problems for the one-person librarian, for it enables him to determine how certain categories of materials are chosen and who chooses them, and it tells him what materials are used and who uses them. With this information you can now begin to establish the criteria for inclusion.

When you are involved in choosing stock for setting up a library, refer to Sylvia Webb and the excellent guidelines in *Creating an Information Service.*[5] Webb suggests interviewing all the prospective users of the service and ascertaining their needs. By doing this, not only will you appear to likely users as a positive, helpful person, but they will be impressed by your knowledge and perhaps surprised by what a library service can do. Also they will be flattered by having their opinions sought and will be a great help when you are selecting future stock and need help with subject coverage. Additionally, by seeking help from potential users you may prevent some of the negative attitudes towards libraries and information services developing and avoid the *non-user* syndrome. When you have seen all the staff who are likely to use the service, and have drawn up the budget, then this is the time to compile a core list of the items which are likely to be needed, e.g. reference works, standard textbooks (if they are to be included), statistics, journals, etc.

As you conduct the interviews and think about the materials for the collection be guided by three steps suggested by Gordon Ambach in a presentation at an American Library Association Annual Conference:

(1) Sharpen objectives.
(2) Adjust directions to needs.
(3) Share resources.[6]

Although you, your management and your users have general ideas about the goals of the parent institution, as you discuss the library and information centre, tighten up on those and think about how the library can *specifically* support those goals. Be prepared to accept that the needs of the organization will not always be the same, and when they change, management and the librarian must be prepared to change the library's collecting activities with them. The luxury of retroactive storage is not in the purview of a collection small enough to be supervised by one person. Finally, you must look about you in the library community to see if you need to collect exactly what others are collecting. Unless you are in a highly competitive industry where secrecy and privileged information are required, it is to your advantage and that of your parent institution to know what is available in other libraries and to make whatever arrangements are necessary to share materials.

As you interview management and users about the library collection two rather personal considerations are raised at this point. First, and again, avoid sentimentality. No matter how much you like the person you are interviewing, keep reminding him that the library or information service is there for a specific purpose; it is not there to provide personal reading materials or information unrelated to the work of the institution. Certainly, library funds cannot be used to support purely personal interests, and in a more general type of one-person library the librarian will be in a position to make this point clearly understood. The special-library world is difficult, and we must agree with Alan Spooner's point when he spoke to a group of special librarians about communicating with senior management:

> Forget everything you ever learned about fundamental fairness. All your customers are not created equal, and it simply makes no sense to tell the company president that he can't have a book until the mail clerk has finished reading it. . . . Time allocation also is not predicated on fairness. The Chairman's request for information on a particular economic policy issue should take priority and, if necessary, utilize more time and manpower than a sales representative's request for the complete roster of the 1955 Brooklyn Dodgers.[7]

However, once you have learned these tastes and reading interests, *as long as they are in agreement with the goals of the parent organization*, there is no reason why these interests of senior management cannot be incorporated into your library's collecting scheme.

The second personal consideration has to do with your own abilities and expertise. When you are interviewing users and management do not lose sight of the fact that your training, especially if you have special education in your institution's subject specialty or specialties, is a valuable resource to the library, and your collecting opinions are as valid as those of your users and management. In the one-person library you may be put in the position of educating some of your users to the situation, but your persuasive skills can serve you well if you choose to use them. Your knowledge and input in the development of criteria for the inclusion of materials in the library is important to your parent organization and you must put yourself in the position where your expertise is recognized and utilized. It is when you bring together your knowledge of the library's subject, the thoughts and ideas of your users and management, and your findings about the kinds of materials already in the library, that you can develop the criteria needed for collection development.

## Acquisition procedures

The acquisition procedures are fairly straightforward for the one-person library. Once you have a good understanding of the types of materials you will be acquiring you can set up routines for their selection. These routines will, of course, vary with the kind of library but, generally speaking, materials will be chosen by you based upon input you receive from your users. There may be a selection committee, made up of representative members of the users, but even here you will probably be expected to provide lists of materials, with some supporting documentation, such as reviews, requests from specific users for specific projects, etc. More than likely, however, you will be expected to select the materials based upon your research, your knowledge of the needs of your users and your understanding of the ways in which the library supports the goals of the parent organization. This means that you must be aware of current trends in publishing in your library's subject specialties. You must know what is being published and by whom, you must read reviews and other promotional materials about the subjects and you must, as much as possible, read some of the materials your users will be reading. This does not mean, of course, that you will sit at your desk reading the library's collection of books (no one-person librarian can afford that luxury!), but it does mean that you will know your stock by title and try to find time to scan items, know the tables of contents of books and journals coming into the library, glance over research reports and generally do whatever you can to be knowledgeable about what is in the library. In the more traditional library you will, of course, rely on your catalogues, whether they are card catalogues or computerized, to provide you with a handy guide to what is in the collecton; after working in the library for a few months you will be surprised at how much of the collection you know by title, certainly as many as several thousand titles. In the technical library, where you are concerned with sending selected materials out to your users, you will organize a system of scanning materials to know what is needed and what is not. For the one-person librarian, using some of one's own time for professional reading is required simply because there is not always time to do the amount of reading and study needed for the job while at the office.

As you become knowledgeable about the kinds of materials to go in the library you will pick up other techniques which will aid you in your selection activities. One of the most useful is to consult other librarians whose stock is similar to yours. These librarians can give valuable help and save you some very expensive mistakes, and you will be establishing an informal network which will be mutually beneficial. Obviously, being a trained librarian, you will rely heavily on the many subject guides and bibliographies for building up the collection, when you have access to them. One of the problems of a small library, especially one run by just one person, is that many of the subject bibliographic tools simply are too expensive for the library's limited acquisitions funds. Thus you will not be able to achieve anything like perfect coverage, nor should you attempt it, but there are many ways of filling in the gaps. For instance, if it is not feasible to have every reference book in the library totally up to date and if you can manage with slightly out-of-date copies, do not be embarrassed to ask users to donate such materials when they are discarded from offices and research collections located elsewhere. If your use of, say, *The Hotel and Motel Redbook* is only for addresses of hotels and if the latest room charges are not required for your users, perhaps the corporate travel agency or department will donate the superseded volume from that office each year. Similarly, if the only current use for *Statistical Abstracts* is for the cost-of-living increases published monthly in the Department of Labor's *Survey of Current Business* and the abstracts are referred to only for historical data, why buy a new *Statistical Abstracts* each year if the marketing department will give you last year's for no charge? As a final example, if you find that you do not need a standing order for *Ulrich's International Periodicals Directory* or *The Encyclopedia of Associations* and you can get by with purchasing it individually on an occasional basis, you will save a considerable amount of money in your annual serials budget. Hang on to copies already in the library for a little longer; as long as your users are made aware of the fact that the reference tool is not the latest edition, you can spend the money on something that you are required to update annually.

When it comes to selecting materials most non-librarians think of book selection as merely the acquisition of *new* books and journals. This is not so, and it is up to the librarian in the one-person library to educate them. First, there is the acquisition of stock for a new library which is being set up from nothing. Here lists of essential materials can be drawn up and added to gradually. Second, there is the continuing selection of stock for the existing library, expanding and contracting various sections according to need, and building on existing stock as necessary. Third, the process of stock-weeding needs to be taking place constantly.

In a one-person library, shortage of space means that items are rarely removed to secondary stock but are disposed of to another library or otherwise removed from the site, even sold as waste paper when necessary. Lastly, any journals which are no longer relevant to the needs of the organization are discontinued. Many libraries are having to discard back runs of journals because of lack of space, cost of binding, etc., and rely on back-up or loan services. It is, however, a good idea to keep back copies as long as possible because of citations thrown up by online searches and bibliographies.

Selection of book and journal stock is now controlled by four factors:

(1) Library budgets
(2) Space.

(3) Changing needs of the organization.
(4) Interloan systems.

Thus book selection can be seen to be a skilled task if it is carried out in a thoroughly professional manner. You need to be aware of the present needs of the organization by liaison with staff, by attendance at meetings, etc. You also have to know your organization's subject interests well enough to be able to anticipate future needs of staff. No mean task this, but if you attempt to do it and sometimes succeed, you will gain status within your organization.

You will also need to get to know a great deal about the book stock and have a positive approach to stock weeding. If a book is worn out or damaged, consider replacing it with a new edition if there is one or, if not, binding it if the book is in frequent use. You could find that another work has taken over the field, and this should be a consideration. Remove out-of-date and unused books regardless of condition. If the book has been on the shelves unused for months there is probably a reason for this, and you may not need it in your collection. Set yourself a standard for use and beware of sentimentality, especially in a special library. You may worry that you could throw an item away and that the next day a client may arrive asking for just that very thing, but this occurrence is quite rare. Remember that the majority of books – except for classics and valuable antiquarian books and incunabula – were not meant to be enduring and should be replaced as necessary by newer and more up-to-date stock. However, you should know which old editions and items to keep – certainly not everything that is old is out of date and worthless. Old editions can give certain misleading facts and figures which can give rise to faulty conclusions, but they are often useful for comparisons of data, etc.

Materials that should be retained in a technical library are those which give a history of the organization, details of the set-up, etc. These often are mistakenly thrown away, but they should be kept because of historic value. When a centenary comes around someone will be detailed to write a history of the organization and the library is the natural place to look for suitable material.

A good librarian knows the stock by title and, as we indicated earlier, tries to find time to read or scan as many items as he can. It is tempting to cut corners and send out items to staff without scanning them first, or without digesting the table of contents of a new book. Do not be concerned if you have management which shortsightedly criticizes the fact that you appear to be reading books and journals in the course of your work. When you have the opportunity, try to explain, in as natural a way as possible, that your particular work requires that you know what is being written and that you must know what is contained in your library if you are to do your work properly.

A good way of assessing items you think you need is to visit a specialist bookseller covering your subject areas if you are located in an area where these booksellers can be found. Otherwise you may wish to set up an examination procedure with return privileges with your bookseller. There is no better way of judging a book than by actually looking at it. You can use your bookseller's approval service, but do not misuse it. A busy bookseller will not thank you for continually returning items, especially if they are specialized and difficult to dispose of. Only use the service when you really need it, or else you will get a reputation for poor judgement. Of course, accidents will happen when you are busy but do not let them be too frequent.

In reviewing books check the quality of the print – is the type large enough to read without eyestrain and is it pleasant to look at? Are the margins wide enough and is the quality of the paper good? What are the illustrations like? Remember that the standards laid down for paperbacks are not necessarily as high as those for hardbacks, as these books are not meant to have as long a life. What is the quality of the binding of a cloth book? Is it durable? Check the date of publication and make sure that an item is not out of date. Look at the qualifications of the author and the authority of the publisher in that particular field. Beware of letting your own views predominate when selecting stock. Remember that the library exists for the users, whether they be technical staff, members of a subscription library, faculty of a college or university department, or the general public. The presence of the wrong books can do almost as much harm as the lack of the right stock.

Get to know your bookseller, talk to him and try to visit personally as much as possible. Do not forget to look at second-hand books when gaps need to be filled and money is tight, and if possible establish a relationship with a second-hand dealer who will search for titles when you need to replace an out-of-print title. Shop around for a bookseller who gives you the best service; even the smallest library can hardly use one bookseller for all the items needed. Have two or three in use, including a local one if possible, to impress the users with instant service should they require something urgently. Unfortunately, this latter service is usually only possible in larger cities and towns, but if there is a local bookseller who can serve as your library's quick-response source, by all means establish a relationship and give him business when you can. If for no other reason, it will pay off in the long run in good public relations with a satisfied user. Unfortunately nowadays much book ordering has to be done by post, telephone and telex, and this invariably means delays, but if you have to use these methods, organize your part of the operation in the most efficient and least time-consuming way possible. Keep online book ordering in mind. It is now feasible, and worth considering, although it may be beyond the budgets of many one-person libraries at present. Finally, some items can be ordered through such systems as Prestel, so you should keep an eye out for this service.

Do not forget standing orders for certain reference books and standard works, those items which you acquire unquestioningly evey time a new edition is published. Books such as *Who's Who*, the various almanacs and the many special-subject reference annuals are best acquired through a standing-order procedure, not only for the time saved by the librarian but also to ensure that the materials are available for the library's users as soon as the work is published. In other words, standing-orders, if carefully arranged, take one more tedious chore from the librarian. Unfortunately, standing-order programmes may not be worthwhile for many one-person librarians because of smaller budget allocations. However, this is not always the case, and you would be wise to investigate the possibility of using standing orders whenever you can, except for those reference items you are required to review for purchase every year. In any case, a standing-order programme is worth considering if there are certain titles that you find you must acquire annually. You can also take advantage of publishers' offers to order before a certain date, thereby gaining a discount. Unfortunately, the Net Book Agreement is limited to libraries which are open to the public, and it is not always available to smaller libraries because they do not purchase in large enough quantities.

Lastly, convince your management that book and journal ordering is best done directly through the library and not by the central purchasing agent. Not only will ordering through the central purchasing department be time-consuming, but that department's forms will not be suitable for book ordering and the staff will not have your expert knowledge of booksellers and suppliers. You may choose, of course, to use a jobber or a subscription agency, but that would be your decision and would involve dealing with someone who is accustomed to working with books and periodicals. That is not the same as having your purchasing done through a departmental or corporate purchasing agent.

When it comes to purchasing journals and serials, you will need to make a selection of newspapers which provide up-to-date facts as well as news and figures which quickly become out of date but which are essential on a temporary basis. They also provide some good in-depth articles which can be extracted and indexed. Weekly journals keep the reader up to date in their appropriate specialist fields but it should be remembered that some of the items are news items and soon become out of date. There are, nevertheless, substantive articles which are important and worth preserving for an appropriate period of time, provided they are indexed or an index is available online for the materials in these weeklies. Monthly, bi-monthly, quarterly and annual serials which aim to be less newsworthy and more technical in nature are often abstracted by major services and frequently cited by online services and databases. There seems to be a core of these journals which are cited most frequently in each of the various subject fields, and by keeping an eye on these and consulting your various subject specialists you should be able to provide a good cross-section aimed at filling in the gaps left by abstracting services and bibliographies.

Once you have decided on a selection you can order either direct or through a subscription agent. You may, of course, obtain some of your journals through membership of a society or body, and there are a large number of controlled-circulation journals. In the case of ordering direct this can entail much work if you have a lot of titles, but it does mean that you can liaise directly with the publisher in cases of missing issues, incorrect invoicing, etc. You may be able to get some of the more popular titles through your local newsagent, together with the newspapers. Subscription agencies will accept a single annual order of all titles required and invoice you accordingly. They will send you an annual alphabetical list of all the journals you require at a certain time each year (usually July or October) and you are then free to amend accordingly.

Remember that this list must be reviewed carefully each year to make sure that all journals are still relevant to the needs of the organization. New items may need to be ordered and others cancelled. The objectives of the organization for which you work may have changed, and this should be reflected in the contents of items received on a regular basis. You can keep the top copy of this list (which is usually supplied in duplicate) for your own reference, having recorded on it details of when invoices were received and paid and a note of the new price of the journals. Over a period of time these lists will give you an idea of price fluctuations and are a useful budget-reviewing tool. The second copy is marked up with any cancellations and amendments and returned to the agent.

A small library cannot be exhaustive in its coverage because of space, time and finance. Therefore, in addition to borrowing, obtaining items by gift and exchange is another good way of economizing. See if you can swap an item which you do not need with another colleague who does. That librarian in turn may be able to provide you with a missing copy in a run of journals or something similar. The British Library Gift and Exchange Scheme is an excellent way of obtaining back copies of expensive reference books or runs of journals which you otherwise might not be able to afford. In return you can unload anything which may be useful to them.

You may be able to exchange new publications produced by your own organization for those of another with similar interests. This is especially useful for obtaining items from abroad, and saves the hassle over foreign exchange. You will also be able to obtain useful publications through memberships of various organizations and groups. Encourage staff to donate items which they may obtain through personal memberships, attendance at conferences, symposia, courses, etc. No doubt a lot of ephemeral material will come your way but there is always the waste basket. Encourage users to make the exchange of information a two-way thing. If they come across something which is new, encourage them to tell other users and yourself (except for strictly confidential information of course). A two-way flow of information does away with the mistrust and mismangement which seems to persist in some organizations. Remember: *what you do not know can hurt!*

## Information sources

Make use of free literature – advisory pamphlets, leaflets, bibliographies, government literature, trade journals, college prospectuses, etc. These items of 'grey literature' are often difficult to trace, but the term is something of a misnomer, because, though often of an ephemeral nature, this material is usually well presented and extremely useful in the short run. A good source of this type of publication is Prestel, from whom you can also obtain publishers' catalogues.

Other sources of publications are bibliographies, publishers' catalogues and trade literature, book reviews in journals and newspapers, government lists, indexes of conference proceedings and periodicals lists, including controlled-circulation journals. The best known of the British bibliographies is, of course, the *British National Bibliography* (*BNB*), which is available from the British Library on subscription. There are weekly, monthly, quarterly and annual cumulations with five-year cumulations also. *BNB* is also available on fiche. Almost as well known is the *Cumulative Book List* (*CBL*), published by Whitakers of London. This is an alphabetical author/title/subject listing of books. It starts as the weekly *Bookseller* and continues as *Books of the Month* and *Books to Come*, which gives information about books published in the month of issue and those projected for publication in the next two months. The *CBL* is published quarterly and there is also a five-year cumulation. The American equivalent of this is the *Cumulative Book Index* (*CBI*), published by H. W. Wilson in New York. This is monthly with annual cumulations. For retrospective searching, the bibliography *British Books in Print*, also published by Whitakers on an annual basis, is very useful, and there is an American counterpart, *Books in Print*, published by Bowker of New York. This also appears on an annual basis and is supplemented by *Forthcoming Books*, which lists books currently being published and to come for the next few months. There is an international publication available in microform called *Books in English*, which combines books published in the English language both in the United States and in the United Kingdom. There are also the MARC tapes, which are the machine-readable form of the *BNB*, and these also list stock added to the Library of Congress in the United States.

For directories and reference books, sources include *Walford's Guide to Reference Material, Current British Directories* and the *Top 2000 Directories and Annuals*, the last published by Alan Armstrong Associates in Reading. Some very good subject guides to start you off on the right track are the Library Association series of subject guides on various topics – these include books, reference works and periodicals on any chosen subject. There are also the *How To Find Out* guides, published by Pergamon Press in Oxford.

For publishers' catalogues you should ask to be put on the mailing lists of companies which publish books relevant to your needs. Certain booksellers compile specialist lists of what is available in certain subject areas. Examples of these are the Landsman's Bookshop in Bromyard, which publishes a complete catalogue of what is available in agriculture, horticulture and gardening, and the Business Bookshop (Alan Armstrong), which brings out lists of business books, reference books and books on the EEC. HMSO in London also produce excellent subject lists, though these are limited to those items published or sold by HMSO itself.

Book reviews come in all sorts of sources: the daily and Sunday newspapers, the *Times Literary Supplement* (*TLS*), the *Times Educational Supplement* (*TES*), the *Economist*, the *New Statesman, New Society, New Scientist, Nature*, etc. You should also read such publications as *The Bookseller, The Listener* and *British Book News*, and check such items as the ASLIB booklists. Subject journals also contain informative book reviews in your own fields, and thus are worth consulting. Library journals such as the *LA Record* and *ASLIB Information* also assess books in the library and information science fields and keep staff up to date in their outlook. Another useful tool is the annual compilation of book prices, published by The Library Association. This comes out for books and periodicals as well, and librarians in small libraries can benefit from consulting these.

For government publications obviously the best-known source is the HMSO *Daily List*, which can be posted to you on a daily or weekly basis, or is now available on Prestel. This lists all the House of Commons debates, Hansards, Command Papers, Government Acts, Statutory Instruments and Government Departmental Papers published by HMSO. It also lists some publications of international bodies such as the EEC, NATO, FAO, etc. What this publication does not do is list papers published internally by government departments. These are harder to trace, but there is now a good source of these in the Chadwyck-Healey *Catalogue of British Official Publications not published by HMSO*. This is also available on fiche. You can either order publications that you need through the catalogue or directly from the publishing body concerned. The catalogue does rely on individual bodies reporting their publications, and is not therefore exhaustive in its coverage. There is also a keyword index available which is designed to complement the catalogue. Some government departments publish sectional lists, e.g. Ministry of Agriculture, Central Statistical Office and the Department of the Environment. Eurofi publishes a useful monthly broadsheet entitled *Business and Government* which abstracts the most newsworthy government items and explains their implications, which for busy one-person librarians is very useful. There are also monthly catalogues of United States Government Publications, published by the Government Printing Office, and, again, separate departments of the American government bring out their own lists. Where United Kingdom statistics are concerned, do not forget *Guide to Official Statistics*. Some government items are listed in the British Library monthly *British Reports, Translations and Theses*. These often list many of the explanatory memoranda for the dreaded COM documents brought out with monotonous regularity by the EEC. The British Library compiles a list of its EEC holdings which also gives details of the EEC information centres in the United Kingdom and HMSO publishes EEC booklists.

Conference proceedings are reported in three sources:

(1) *Index of Conference Proceedings*, published monthly by the BLLD with an annual cumulation.
(2) *British Reports, Translations and Theses*, which is also published by the BLLD on a monthly basis and in fiche form.
(3) *BNB* and the Chadwyck-Healey *Catalogue*. Announcement of theses also appears in learned journals, and from the United States in *Dissertation Abstracts International*.

Periodicals are covered in a variety of publications, the best known of which are *Ulrich's International Periodicals Directory, Willings Press Guide, Benn's Press Directory, Blackwell's Periodicals List, Dawson's Little Red Book, Irregular Serials and Annuals* (an international publication appearing in New York and London on an annual basis), the union lists of large national libraries such as the British Library and the Library of Congress, and the subject lists compiled by the Science Reference Library in London. Any library with a subject bias similar to yours will also send you one of its periodicals lists so that you may make a comparison.

You may also have to venture into the sticky world of patents and standards. The Patents Office, which is part of the Science Reference Library (SRL) in Holborn (London), holds complete collections of United Kingdom and United States patents and produces the journal *Official Journal (Patents)*. This is a weekly publication giving details of patent applications filed, specifications publications and patents sealed. The Patent Office at St Mary Cray in Kent also issues a booklet for use in industry called *Patents: A Source of Technical Information*. Something like 23 million patents from all countries are available for reference in the SRL, and the provincial patent libraries (e.g. in Birmingham, Liverpool, Manchester, Leeds, Glasgow, Newcastle and Sheffield) hold patent specifications from the United Kingdom, Europe, the United States and Patent Cooperation Treaty (PCT), related patent journals and indexes. Should you need them, these libraries have photocopying facilities, and some offer access to online patent-searching services.

Standards are another area which you may need to know about. In the United Kingdom the British Standards Institution (BSI) is the body responsible for publishing standards. The essential reference source available from them is the *BSI Catalogue*, which lists all standards available and has a comprehensive subject index. It is updated regularly by the *Sales Bulletin*. Details of new and revised standards, as well as drafts and amendments, are available in the monthly *BSI News*, which is available to subscribers. If you are a subscriber standards can be bought at a reduced cost, but if you do not often need to consult these documents the BSI library is very helpful (reference only), and your nearest large city or borough library should also have a collection of standards which you can peruse for reference. BSI at Milton Keynes, Buckinghamshire, will also help you to trace foreign standards should you need these, and there is also the International Standards Organization (ISO) catalogue for international standards.

## Collection review

It is now commonly accepted that the selection and acquisition of materials is only part of the collection development activity for a library. Now considered to be equally important is collection review, that part of library work in which materials are selected for relegation, preservation or discard (to use the terminology of the American Library Association's *Guidelines*[8]). Most of us know this process by the less exalted but more descriptive term 'weeding', which has unfortunate negative connotations to management and users, and is, in fact, only one part of the review process. By whatever name, it is a subject which must be always at the forefront of any collection development policy in a one-person library. The ALA *Guidelines* state:

Most libraries are or will soon be faced by problems of change of institutional goals or programs, space limitation, increasing collection size and cost, the impact of new programs or needs, the problem of accumulation of duplicates or obsolescent materials which may no longer be needed in the active collection, and by the aging and decay of library materials. There is no single, or simple, answer to any of these problems, but most of them can be alleviated or reduced by a systematic, judicious, ongoing program of collection review to identify items which may require conservation treatment, or which – for a variety of reasons – may no longer be required in the active collection. Materials review will provide better collection control, provide easier access to collections, and may achieve economies of space . . .[8]

To begin with, collection review should be established as part of the library's collection development policy and should be treated as a part of the library's administrative activity. Having established it, the librarian or his representative seeks review advice (and participation, if the library is structured to allow for it) from the library's primary users and management to determine what materials are to be considered for discard, preservation or relegated to an off-site storage facility. As we have indicated, it is generally not the practice in a one-person library to remove materials to a secondary collection because of shortage of space. The one-person library's collection will basically be made up of materials which are current and relevant to the work of the parent institution, and most one-person librarians will thus be dealing more with the questions of discard and preservation than with relegation. In the technical library, since most of the information dates quickly, only the most up-to-date material is kept, and the physical preservation of the collection is not a problem. It is really only the more traditional library collections for whom preservation is of interest.

Any library must formulate criteria for weeding the collection. According to Gensel and Powers, the monograph collection must be weeded constantly, with comparisons made between new editions of older works and the discard of even slightly out-of-date material: 'There is nothing more misleading to a researcher than to discover that the edition being used for a "new" technique is not the latest. This should be prevented by systematic weeding.'[9] Collection review for serial titles is a more subjective consideration, because so much of the literature used in the one-person library is in periodical or serial format. Here the librarian must think about how often a title is called for, whether it is available at a nearby library that retains a full run of the title, whether it is available under an arrangement for free exchange of photocopies between two libraries, etc. It is to the library's advantage for all arrangements to be examined before decisions are made about weeding the serials, but the primary focus must be on keeping the serials collection as current and up to date as possible within the limitations of space and use.

Again, consider the interlibrary loans and the borrowing of materials. If, however, you cannot locate the item after a few telephone calls you should resort to whatever union catalogue arrangement is available in your area. If you are lucky enough to be running a library which participates in one of the local consortia or networking arrangements, familiarize yourself with the procedures and try to use them often enough to justify your membership of the organization. There are a couple of ground rules to keep in mind. First, if the purchase price of the book is under a certain amount (usually agreed upon by practising librarians in the area), you should not try to borrow the book if it is in print. Also, keep in mind that the costs of the loan, including the paperwork and staff time, can be a deterrent: staff time spent on checking details, typing the form and envelope, etc., can be very expensive. If the book is not too expensive and is in print, it might be better to purchase it for the collection. Obviously, more expensive materials such as texts should be borrowed whenever possible, as they will not be necessary for the library collection, particularly if they are going to be used for only one specific project.

There is no question that the formulation of an appropriate collection development programme for a library is time-consuming and involved, but there can also be no question that it is necessary. It is only by creating and observing a carefully thought-out policy that the library can allocate its resources for its users in the most efficient and orderly way.

# References

1 Berner, Andrew, 'Collection Development', remarks delivered at The University Club Library Associates Meeting, March 1983.
2 Perkins, David L. (ed.), *Guidelines for Collection Development*, American Library Association, Collection Development Committee, Resources and Technical Services Division, Chicago, 1979, p. 3.
3 Gensel, Susan and Powers, Audrey, 'Collection development and the special library', *The New York State Library Bookmark*, 41, 1, Fall 1982, p. 11.
4 Ibid., p. 14.
5 Webb, Sylvia, *Creating an Information Service*, Aslib, London, 1983.
6 Ambach, Gordon M., 'Building on hard ground: strong foundations, broad support', paper delivered at the American Association of School Libraries, President's Program at the Annual Conference of the American Library Association, 10 July 1982.
7 Spooner, Alan, untitled remarks, part of a programme, 'Communicating with Senior Management', sponsored by the Business and Finance and Library Management Divisions, Special Libraries Association, 13 June 1984.
8 Perkins, op. cit., p. 20.
9 Gensel and Powers, op. cit., p. 13.

# Chapter Ten

# Technical services

In all library situations the relationship one has with one's users is of primary importance, and certainly this relationship is the best guide, both for users and management, to the quality of services available in the library. However, behind it is a variety of support activities which users, and often management, know little about and seldom have an opportunity to observe: the selection, acquisition and processing of materials, record-keeping for those materials, describing where they are located and who has them if they are permitted to be taken from the site, updating and processing serial materials which come out on a regular (or irregular) schedule, and more. The generally recognized term for these activities is 'technical services', that is, those services which exist to bring order to a collection of materials, often diverse in format, and which enable those who use the materials, both library staff and patrons, to have access to them in the most orderly and most efficient way possible.

The employee in a one-person library is in a unique and enviable professional position because she can establish priorities in the technical services area of the library's work and be answerable only to herself. Management and users usually have little interest in how the materials are organized as long as they are accessible. This opportunity to provide good service is one which many librarians embrace happily, and indeed it is high on the list of attractions that bring people into the field of one-person librarianship. Being able to set one's own standards of professional ability, and a lack of interference from others, are great rewards in a profession full of sad stories of individual put-downs. The high level of responsibility is equally attractive. To do the job properly requires a sense of responsibility and a level of self-confidence that is not required in many other types of librarianship, and nowhere are these traits more necessary than in technical services. In other library situations the way to make the library work is to hire a good technical services staff; in the one-person library the librarian herself must have high standards for technical services.

How do we deal with technical services in a one-person library? In this chapter we will discuss various methods of processing and organizing materials and making them available to the user. We will describe old and new methods, and allude to some procedures and methods which perhaps have not even been widely accepted yet. Our common theme will be to seek short-cuts: in the one-person library the quickest, most efficient method is not a luxury, it is a necessity. Thus in the technical services procedures one question must be asked at every step: is it necessary? The one-person librarian who answers this question honestly and unemotionally will manage a library in which there is time to do all the things that need to be done.

## Analysis of collection and users

The first task for the one person librarian, whether she has been given a new position as the employee in a one-person library or is reviewing the way things are done in the library in which she is already employed, is to analyse the collection and the people who come to the library to use it. Following the analysis of collection and users it is necessary to turn to the materials in the collection, for most libraries include a variety of objects to be used for research and study, and the way in which these materials are handled in the technical processing scheme will vary with the type of material. Is the bulk of the collection books, journals or reprints? Are there important collections in the vertical files, or does the strength of the collection lie in government documents, technical reports, annual reports of corporations or institutions similar to the one of which the library is a part? Are there audio-visual materials, records, tapes, floppy disks or diskettes, posters, art reproductions, slides? Are there special collections of rare books, manuscripts, archives and institutional memorabilia? Are there historical photographs, maps or other oddities which are unique to the type of institution of which the library is a part? Indeed, are there materials unique to this particular institution not found anywhere else? All these types of materials must be noted and analysed,. for each is handled differently in the technical services procedures and each will require, if not special expertise, at least some special handling and reference or guidance for the librarian.

Once an analysis of the collection, the uses to which it will be put and the users who will avail themselves of the collection has been made, it is possible to proceed to the actual processing of the materials in the collection. Here, two considerations can be made. In Chapter 7 there was a description of a management approach called KISS, an acronym for a light-hearted phrase, 'Keep It Simple, Stupid'. That description has particular relevance to technical services, for simplicity is essential. There is a corollary, too, in the questioning of procedures and techniques to determine if they are valid for the library.

For the employee in a one-person library who is daily confronted with the task of serving all her patron's library needs, taking care of all the technical processing for the collection and managing the entire operation in a businesslike and professional way, the questioning of procedures and activities is an essential part of her administrative routine. Chartered graduate librarians are trained to follow certain established procedures, and for many librarians it is difficult to question why a certain task is done a particular way. Yet for the well-organized and confident librarian working in a one-person library who is already seeking short-cuts, some of the accepted rules may not be applicable. Many methods continue simply as traditions. Working alone, the one-person librarian is frequently in a position where it is not inappropriate to ask himself why he does a task this way, or whether he might not do it another way. Once again, we can remember that the one-person librarian is in the unique and often enviable position of having no-one else to answer to about methodology. Such questioning is not necessarily a negative or contentious activity on the part of the librarian. It is a healthy and reasonable approach to one-person librarianship, for the librarian who can look at a procedure and wonder how it can be done more efficiently is not only doing his parent organization a favour but making his own job easier. By the same token, the librarian who refuses to think about such things, who is reluctant to question procedures and who blindly follows along, doing what has always been done in the past, is doing the library and the parent organization a disservice. There is a happy medium between change for its own sake and questioning if something can be made better.

## The use of modern technology

This leads us to a consideration of the uses of modern technology in the library. We have come to an age where we must accept and acknowledge that things are never again going to be the way they were, and for some such a situation might be seen as threatening. On the other hand, the new electronic age can be the beginning of a period of exceptionally good service to users and management by those who overcome their resistance to the new technology and see it merely as a new tool for expediting what we have always done. Nowhere will such an attitude of acceptance be more useful and more dramatically implemented than in the technical services work of one-person libraries.

Yet we must be cautious, for librarianship has not always been in the forefront of accepting new technologies, and especially in one-person libraries around the world there has been marked reluctance to deal with these questions. For a variety of reasons, the employee in a one-person library has not been able to seek and find new ways of doing things. Often this has to do with the attitude of management or the library committee or board. Occasionally, persons in these positions turn out to be uninformed amateurs unable or disinclined to accept the requirements of modern library management. Sometimes the problem is simply financial, since the small library in an institution with limited assets is usually far down the priority list for expansion. Also, bluntly, often the problem lies not so much with the institution or its board or its management as with the librarian in charge, for many, regardless of our business or profession, feel threatened when we feel pushed to learn new tools and procedures.

Whatever the reasons, it is clear that librarians have resisted, and the time has come to try to find out what new technology can do for us and our libraries. Obviously, not all of us are going to be in a position to accept all the new technologies, and as we are in a period of transition, many one-person librarians will not be utilizing new technologies for many years to come. Yet they must be acknowledged and prepared for, so as we describe procedures for organizing the technical services in a small library we must also arrange for those procedures to be adaptable to the new technologies.

We know that the computer is a labour- and time-saving device. From the point of view of even one of the simplest library tasks we have learned that a simple program, with a control number referring to author, title, class and basic subject entries, can eliminate the need for a card catalogue and provide users with a frequently updated book catalogue (or portion thereof, as required). In fact, such a simple inventory program can probably be designed for use with the library's parent organization's accounting or other record-keeping program, if the library itself cannot justify the cost of purchasing or leasing a microcomputer. However, with the decreasing costs and increasing sophistication of microcomputer technologies, especially as they relate to library operations, an individually designed program or system is seldom called for in the one-person library. Until just a few years ago the technology was too expensive and a one-person library could not consider acquiring it. As one manager remarked, it would have been like 'swatting flies with a baseball bat'. However, now there is no reason why the librarian in a one-person library has to spend her time typing and filing cards.

The same improvements have been made in the various database services. Many are now appropriate for the one-person library, and where there is an established need for such data there is no reason why files of back periodicals and reference books must be maintained. In these and in all technological developments, the rule, for the one-person librarian, must be: *if it saves time, get it.*

Thus the first question we must ask, in analysing the current operation of a one-person library, is whether or not any new technologies can be used. Planning is the key here, for any library, regardless of how small, or how poor, or how limited, will probably at some future date incorporate some aspect of these modernizations into its technical services operations. For those fortunate one-person librarians who are already using them or are on the verge of applying them to their operations, the present suggestions will, it is hoped, support the work they are doing.

Having established that there can be two ways of organizing and handling library materials, manually and with the aid of some computerized record-keeping technology, let us see how items are received into the collection, considering materials by type, as different items have to be handled somewhat differently.

# Accession numbers

The use of accession numbers is an accepted practice in most libraries. Simply defined, an accession number is a running number assigned to every processed item in the collection, beginning with the number '1' for the first item acquired (accessioned) in the library. In the one-person library most librarians assign that number when the item is ordered, thus giving the item a record number which can follow it through the entire processing procedure. There is a school of thought which recommends waiting to assign the accession number until after the item has been received, in the event that the order is not filled, but the advantages of having an assigned number from the beginning outweigh the single disadvantage of being obliged to re-assign the number if the material is not received.

When the item is ordered the accession number is assigned to it and the record of the order is entered. If the work is being done manually an accessions book register is generally used, simply listing the accession numbers, in sequence, and whatever order information is needed (author, title, publisher, price, vendor, date of order, etc.). Some librarians who keep manual records prefer to use cards for the order file. For the librarian using a computer (whether a mainframe, minicomputer or microcomputer) the same data can be entered into an accessions file. Here the accession number will be the 'access number', probably to be used as a masterfile by which data about that item will be accessed throughout its history in the collection.

When a new item is received into the library it is noted in the accession book, card file or computer accession file. Any invoices which accompanied the item are checked against the item for cost, edition, format, etc., and the invoice is approved and sent to the appropriate department for payment. A note can be kept in the accessions record of the date that the invoice is received and dealt with and the total amount paid. Some librarians in one-person situations simply photocopy invoices but this is not really necessary if the record of the invoice is at hand. Some librarians use the invoice photocopy as an additional accessions register, but this is unnecessary work and is not recommended. A simple notation in the order record is all that is needed.

The accessions register book can be a loose-leaf binder or ring file to which extra pages can be added. The following information must be included: accession number, classification number, cutter number (if used), author or authors, title, publisher, date of publication and date of entry. Some librarians establish an additional file here for source (e.g. vendor, gift, exchange, etc.), and it is not uncommon for the one-person librarian who is using a computer to include here subjects and cross-references so that this file can be accessed as the masterfile for the item as it is processed into the collection. In this latter case the file that started out as the order file becomes, in practice, the masterfile from which all other data files are read in the preparation of the material for accessing by various fields. From this file can be compiled a monthly list of accessions, either typed manually from the accessions register book or, if a computer is used, printed out from whatever file (author, title, subject, class, etc.) is desired.

## Catalogues

When these data have been entered, a classification number can be assigned and the item can be catalogued. For the one-person librarian it should be remembered that this is a small special library and it is not written anywhere that the librarian must adhere slavishly to the methods learned in library schools. In fact, this is the first of several occasions wherein the one-person librarian is encouraged to question whether the accepted practices learned in graduate school are necessary for this collection. Qualified librarians new to working in a system where time is of the essence may discover quite a few useful short-cuts here. Cataloguing and indexing enable both the librarian and the readers to find an item easily after it has been shelved or incorporated into a filing system. The librarian in the one-person library cannot forget the needs of the user when cataloguing and indexing. Each particular library must be organized not only to make systems very easy for the librarian but also for the users, should the librarian be absent or unable to assist them. Expecting a certain amount of 'self-service' might not be amiss in the very small library, and certainly users can be trusted and encouraged to help themselves to certain materials which they might need on a recurring basis, as long as they return them properly. Certainly one of the most frequently heard phrases from the patrons in any small library is 'I'm sorry to bother you, but…' or 'I know you are busy, but…' If the users can help themselves to certain regularly cited tools (dictionaries, indexes, directories, etc.) the librarian's time is saved and the users are not made to feel awkward.

It is a sad fact that many users are rather afraid of libraries, and indeed of asking questions, for they fear that they will be thought stupid or troublesome. Thus, in designing the catalogue, keep in mind that any person with reasonable intelligence and a little training should be able to use it without difficulty. This requires that the entries be consistent. In the smaller libraries in the United States it is an advantage that Library of Congress Cataloging in Publication (CIP) data is included in every book, for this provides a consistent and authoritative source for processing, as long as it fits into the library's own scheme of doing things. Conversely, there is no need to use CIP, or in the United Kingdom the BNB-CIP scheme, when classifying a book if it does not necessarily fit into the particular library's system. In the main, however, especially when the collection is a general one covering a variety of subjects, it is recommended that these systems of classification and cataloguing be used.

In the one-person library world most librarians find that they will always need to do some adapting of whatever classification scheme they use, whether it be an original system (highly unlikely in a new library but not at all unusual in libraries created in earlier periods, before library administration was considered a management science) or an adaptation of an accepted scheme. In any case, it must be a system which is easy to understand and to use, and, if necessary, devised for people who are not able – or inclined – to think through the logical reasoning implicit in an ordinary searching procedure. The basic question is always: *where can the librarian and/or the user find – quickly and easily – the item(s) needed?* After all, users are interested in the end and not the means of cataloguing, and the librarian should be, too. The catalogue is meant to give vital information about a particular item and to guide the librarian and the user to it. The catalogue is *not* meant to be a mine of useless information.

The catalogue is simply a list of books and other materials held in stock in the library. It can be on cards or in book form, in some sort of loose-leaf binder arrangement (a style found in many of the very old libraries of Europe), or it can have been generated by a computer, with the employee of the one-person library inputting once into the system (usually when the material is ordered) and then reading from various fields, depending on how the library has chosen to configure the different categories such as author, title, subject, etc. More sophisticated catalogues and techniques for their creation are discussed below.

It is not necessary in the one-person library to catalogue everything that comes into the library. Ideally, cataloguing should be kept to a minimum, and for the library using a card catalogue cards should be made only for books, possibly reprints, some specialized publications and some government reports. It should be necessary to *index only* material such as official publications, trade literature, advisory leaflets, press cuttings, standards, patents, etc.

Having sorted out those items which are going to be properly catalogued, the librarian has to decide which of the many details on the title page she will include on the catalogue cards. The details which must be included are the author, title, publisher, date of publication, class and accession number. Some librarians also like to include the number of pages and place of publication, and assigning a class number is done at the same time.

At this point the librarian should try to think carefully about the sort of headings which are needed and the kind of questions which might be asked in searching for the item in question. The two most common questions are:

(1) Which books do you have by a particular author? Or: do you have a certain title by such-and-such an author?
(2) Which books do you have on a certain subject (e.g. Irrigation in Agriculture, Transactional Analysis, Interviewing Skills, German Art, Southern History, etc.)?

The first question would be answered from the author and/or title catalogue, the second from the subject catalogue (these catalogues are generally interfiled into one dictionary catalogue in the United States, although in Europe they are often separated). Thus the details given on the card are important, though they do need to be kept simple. If in doubt, the librarian should refer to the Anglo-American Cataloguing rules.[1] For the most part, however, the librarian in the one-person library is obliged to rely on his or her common sense, and consistency in choosing headings is of primary importance.

All three catalogue entries (author, title and subject) need the following information included on the card or in the masterfile entry:

(1) Author(s).
(2) Title. The details for the title are taken from the main title page of the book and *not* the cover or the flyleaf. Details included after the colon (usually subtitles) are included, as they are often helpful.
(3) Place of publication. This information will either be found on the main title page or on the reverse of same together with date of publication, copyright

date, etc. It is included here because the reader may want to know if there is any foreign bias to the book.

(4) Publisher. This is included because certain publishers have certain strengths and may or may not be authoritative in a specific subject area.

(5) Date of publication. This is usually on the title page or reverse of same. Here the librarian must be careful to pull together the correct date and the correct edition. The reader may only want a book which is very up to date, or he may be happy to refer to a particular edition of a few years ago.

(6) Edition. If the book is not a first edition, the edition, if known, should be mentioned. Here the librarian must be wary of the difference between edition and impression. For the edition, the work may have been revised and updated, not necessarily by the author. The impression notation simply means that the book has been reprinted exactly as it was in the edition cited, with no changes. There is therefore no need to note impressions, but *editions are important.*

(7) Number of pages. This should be noted, as some readers want a short, concise text so as to be able to read up on a subject generally. Others may prefer a more lengthy text. It is also a help to the busy one-person librarian to know if he or she is searching for a fat text or a small pamphlet when searching the shelves. To make this task even easier, some librarians even describe the physical appearance of the book, but this step is not necessary in most small libraries.

(8) Number of volumes. If there is more than one volume, the number should be noted.

(9) Location. This can be done by noting the class number or mark on the *top left-hand* corner of the card, and the bottom right-hand line on the author and title cards. The reader is then guided to the appropriate place on the shelves.

Thus a *basic* description consisting of all these items is now on all three cards, but the *headings* are alternated.

When all this information has been entered in the accessions book or on accessions cards these can be photocopied and the photocopy given to the typist or input operator, if there is one, while the important accession document remains in the hands of the librarian. In the true one-person situation obviously the librarian is the typist or input operator, and such a photocopying step is unnecessary.

Thus we have a picture of the accession document (or 'access number' as we described it earlier for computerized catalogues) as the main masterfile from which the other files are read. For the form of author entries, title entries, subjects, etc., we refer the one-person librarian to the various standard library tools listed in the bibliography which have been created to guide the librarian in making whatever choices are necessary for compiling these entries. Again, we suggest that the librarian working alone strongly consider the use of CIP data which appears in the front of books. Using this information, even if it means an occasional variation from the specific way in which materials are arranged in the library in question, will provide a good short-cut in technical processing. One does not have to be locked into the format chosen for the CIP or the BNB data. The one-person librarian, looking for a way to get the material catalogued and to the users as quickly as possible, is free to use as much or as little of the available information as is necessary. It should exist as a guideline or model, not as an end in itself.

## Classification

Classification is a subject which is discussed more subjectively than cataloguing, which can be an advantage to a one-person librarian. When not kept under control, classification can be the most difficult and time-consuming part of running a one-person library. Early on in the operation someone has to decide (or perhaps has decided) whether the library is to be a browsing library or a closed-stack library. If the users are to have access to the shelves the materials must be sorted and stored in such a way that relatively similar materials (by subject) are kept together. If the users are not to obtain materials for themselves and the librarian is to do the fetching (which is not the usual situation in one-person libraries), the classification of materials does not necessarily have to follow any specific subject scheme. Thus, theoretically at least, the librarian in this latter situation can choose whatever scheme suits her. Practically speaking, of course, this cannot be allowed, for even the librarian searching for materials will want like subjects to be with like subjects, insofar as it can be arranged.

Assigning a class number to a book takes a fair amount of intellectual effort and it pays to classify only those items which cannot be drawn together by any other method previously shown. Classification is done so that items on a similar topic may be drawn together on the shelves, and it is often necessary to scan the item or even to read it fairly extensively before a class number can be assigned. The most important thing to remember when choosing a scheme is how it is going to operate for the librarian running the one-person library.

*Librarians are strongly recommended to use a recognized scheme of classification,* of which there are several excellent ones. The one-person librarian should beware of homemade schemes which are alleged to be easier to use and to understand. These are rarely satisfactory, and sooner or later they break down. The librarian must remember that the accepted classification schemes are the work of experts who have devoted many years of study to them and their development, and are designed to permit regular amendments to them. None of these schemes is perfect, but they have been thoroughly thought out, and are usually more useful for the small library. For the one-person librarian who is tempted to create his or her own scheme for the library, there are several warnings which should be heeded:

(1) It is not as easy as first imagined.
(2) It is very time-consuming.
(3) *Any* scheme constantly needs updating.

The librarian would be making trouble not only for herself but for her successor, who would unfortunately inherit a scheme that was probably no longer useful, and the entire library would have to be reclassified under an existing and accepted scheme. As anyone knows who has borne this task (and both authors have), this is a time-consuming, expensive and frustrating exercise. If materials are classified properly, order comes to the bookstock, books on the same subject are drawn together and books on related topics are nearby. More general works on a topic will precede more specific works. The most important point to remember about classification is so obvious that we are embarrassed to repeat it: *a good classification scheme will enable both the librarian and the users to find the materials easily on the shelves.*

As has already been mentioned, certain types of materials (e.g. annual reports, reviews, serials, trade literature, town guides, standards, etc.) only need to be arranged alphabetically A–Z, or, in the case of standards, in SI order. This procedure saves a lot of work, and provided shelves and drawers are labelled clearly and correctly, any reader would be able to find items easily. Other items which can be arranged thus are press cuttings, advisory leaflets, college prospectuses and catalogues, course brochures and any similar pamphlet material. Journals can be arranged in title and date order, as can newspapers. Remember one simple rule: *do not classify anything unnecessarily.*

A good classification will work only if there is a good alphabetical subject index relating to it, and while in most libraries in Europe the subject catalogues are separated from the author and title catalogues, in the United States the practice is to avoid separation whenever possible so that the user has to look in only one place. This combination of author, title and subject files into one large dictionary catalogue is discussed fully by Piercy.[2]

Finally, in discussing various schemes we should not forget the librarian herself. If the librarian actually *reads* some of the books that she has in the library, with the aid of good memory and some luck and the classification scheme chosen for the library, she will be able to go to the shelves and retrieve the item when required.

It is necessary that the librarian compare existing classification schemes and keep one important point in mind: *keep it simple.* Non-professional staff, to say nothing of users, find complicated schemes with difficult filing rules, cross-references, etc., difficult to use; even for the professional librarian, until the scheme is used often enough for him or her to have acquired a certain familiarity with it, a complicated scheme can use up valuable time and make the work more difficult. Sometimes, in a small library using a perfect version of a scheme – such as the Universal Decimal Classification – the many cross-references and extra cards in the catalogue will take up almost as much space as the bookstock. It is the librarian's job to simplify such a situation.

## References

1 *The Concise AACR2,* 2nd edn, Michael Gorman. ALA/CLA/LA, 1981.

2 Piercy, Esther, *Commonsense Cataloging* Wilson, New York, 1965, pp. 161–166.

# Chapter Eleven

# Personnel considerations

What kind of people work in one-person libraries? There are certain established ideal qualities: self-motivation, the ability to work – alone – under pressure, an interest in and an understanding of the goals of the parent institution of which the library is a part, high standards of excellence not only in one's professional and clerical tasks but in one's personal goals as well, and, of course, an ability to get along with everyone. Where do we find such paragons? Do they exist? In this chapter we shall attempt to discuss some of these professional characteristics, and we shall also explore some of the various employment situations which are available to the one-person librarian, and suggest how some of these may or may not be of use to the person running a one-person library.

The role of the library in the parent organization has already been discussed in a previous chapter, but we should yet give some consideration to the role of the librarian. Who is this person who has been hired to manage the organization's information unit? What role does he play in the administrative hierarchy of the organization? Indeed, what role does he play in productivity, in services, in operations? To find the answers to these questions we must look at what the parent organization expects of its one-person librarian.

Every organization needs to have information in order to survive – not for nothing do Japanese companies hire 'information-gathering' experts. It has to be the right information at the right time. In other words, the information must be good and opportune. Remember that information of one sort or another is needed every day, several times a day, by many different people for different reasons. The librarian/information officer in a one-person library acts as a kingpin between departments of an organization. If you look at the diagram you will see that all of the people in these boxes will know about their own responsibilities but they will not know so much about others. This limitation puts them at a disadvantage. Added to this, they will certainly know very little about the thousands of published and online sources from which information can be obtained. They are not trained in obtaining information – you are. By doing so you will have to liaise with all departments, and by helping each you will gain good insight into the workings of your library's parent organization.

Malcolm Tunley suggests that:

> the problem in special libraries is one of diversity. There is a tremendous range of types of special library and the size of operation may range from one-man library/information units to systems with several dozen staff of

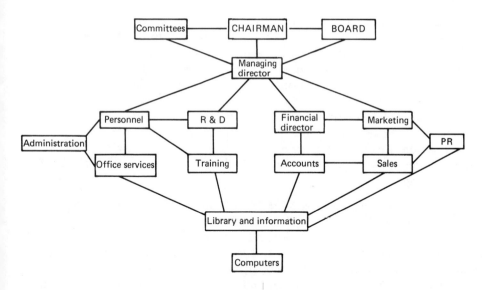

various kinds and possibly branch libraries. There are, however, some unifying factors which apply in most cases. Special libraries are concerned with *information*, regardless of the form in which it comes – even if it is word of mouth; the emphasis on education, recreational and preservatory functions is much less stressed (or is non-existent) than in other kinds of library. Special libraries are often relatively small in their resources, size of staff, stock, space, etc.; they are limited to the subject coverage of the parent body. The approach is often pragmatic and utilitarian: the motto of the American SLA is 'putting knowledge to work.' Supplying information may take a high degree of expertise and the suppliers are more likely to be held responsible for the competence of the service given than in other types of library.[1]

By pulling together the information needed by various departments you will enable them to work better with one another. Make sure that you get this point across to management, because it is often taken for granted. The thing to do is to make sure that the library is not simply in existence because 'it seemed like a good idea at the time' *There is room for a good librarian in any organization which wants to be efficient.* Make sure that you stress the idea that information is important, so that your library will be given sufficient funding and status within the organization. Having come to this point, Wilfred Ashworth suggests that

> ... the ideal situation is for the head of the library service to have managerial status through which he will derive the necessary knowledge (directly as part of the management team) of the the continually changing aims of the organization, of the potential for future growth and of the constraints under which the organization has to operate. This will enable him to assess which information can be used profitably, and also that which is unlikely, from lack

of proper resources, to be exploitable. The nature of his work subjects him to a constant flow of new information from outside, and this makes him one of the best-informed people on the staff about external developments in the organization's field of interest. As a manager, he would be able to use this information more directly in policy making, and not merely be a passer-on of information who might distort or fail to use it. The fewer steps there are in the transfer of information the better, as there is always the risk of distortion or inaction. The librarian's task is to use the knowledge that he acquires from his position to enable his unit to tap the most appropriate sources of information and select that part which has the highest potential for exploitation.[2]

In a one-person library this ideal is pretty hard to live up to. It seems to be uncommon, judging by the various surveys done, for a librarian who works alone to achieve this high status. However, one must work towards the ideal. It may take many months, even years, to enlighten your management about the importance of information to the organization and, what is more, about the necessity of having someone with the right qualifications doing this important job. In the process Alan Armstrong suggests that you should join the 'thrusters' in the organization.[3] Keep away from the 'sleepers', as they can do a lot of harm. In making information work for you and your users you may have to put together a package, or you may be asked to find out a straightforward fact. Accuracy is the aim here. You may make your company a million, or save it a few thousand, with a suggestion or some information which you provide. Package facts neatly, and always let your user know that the library has supplied it by attaching a compliments slip or other means of identification. In many ways you are in a privileged position because you are approached by all departments in various aspects of their work. You may provide company figures for the marketing department at one moment and a map for a messenger the next. Dr Johnson said: 'Knowledge is of two kinds. We know a subject ourselves, or we know where we can find information upon it.'[4] For your parent organization the latter place ought to be your library and information service.

For some reason there has been a perception that many one-person librarians see themselves as a much-maligned group, but this is not the case. In a survey conducted by the authors the responses were surprisingly positive. While some few respondents indicated that they felt that their roles were not completely understood or that they were subject to hostile or antagonistic users or management, the great majority (85.4 per cent) made extremely positive replies when asked how others in their libraries' parent institutions viewed their positions and rated their performance. A theme of appreciation for their professionalism ran through the responses, as did a sense of pride in what they are accomplishing. Because these insights are valuable, some representative replies follow:

'Am regarded well. Enjoy good rapport with students.'
'I believe my performance is highly rated after working hard for five years. It was only then that I was put on the same level as, say, the administrative director.'

'At first they were stunned at the president's decision to make an appointment, then I turned out to be energetic, well read, and effective in the library, and the faculty would brag to visitors about their "brilliant young" librarian. I was good, but maybe not as good as they thought I was. The last director had been a dour individual, and I looked good when compared with him.'

'I believe that I am perceived as bright, educated, helpful, witty, unpretentious, and management fodder.'

'Those who are observant and are aware are impressed that so much gets done; they recognize that there is too much for one professional.'

'Well received, and am surprised by the effectiveness I am beginning to project.'

'With respect and fairly high for bringing order to collections and for being someone who listens.'

'Professional colleague. Very high performance.'

'Position has respect. Staff thinks librarian knows *everything*. My performance seems to be approved by both clients and co-workers.'

'Highly. View me as a professional and closer to their ranks [scientific staff] than those of administrative assistants or secretaries.'

'I am appreciated and my services are noted frequently by faculty and students.'

'I feel that most people feel that I do an adequate job, an excellent job.'

'High. I try to be aware of the areas of interest in all departments so that I can give an intelligent response.'

'View position as valuable and rate my performance as good.'

There were, nevertheless, negative responses, but most of these seemed to convey either attitudinal problems or managerial or supervisory conflicts. The former might also be described as personality quirks on the part of the one-person librarians (e.g. 'Some think I'm doing a great job. Others, however, and correctly so, think I'm the pits'). Other negative responses clearly indicated a lack of managerial support or interest:

'Most are very unfamiliar with the library.'

'Never been evaluated. No communication. My professionalism is a thorn in their side.'

'With ambivalence. At first they perceive me as librarian and try to deal with me as such, then see that I don't have the prerogatives I should have and that creates confusion.'

'The internal users are the least appreciative of my services. They know little about the functions and services of a special library. External users [800] are far more appreciative and say so. I have been paid and treated as a clerk despite the fact that I have core curriculum in library science.'

'Those who frequently use the library respect the job and appreciate the services provided. Staff members who never use the library probably feel that the librarian and her job are of little importance.'

What conclusions can we draw from these responses? Primarily, it appears that the perception of one-person librarians of their status is considerably more positive than formerly thought. At the same time, these librarians seem to believe that if they do good work, are secure in their professional accomplishments and convey to their users and managements a certain level of enthusiasm and interest in their work their status in the institution will be high and they will be held in esteem by their colleagues and managements. Unfortunately, this belief is not always justified. The job description can be another good guide for determining one's role in the parent institution. When you were hired to be the one-person librarian for your company or institution how was the position described to you? Is there a written job description or were you invited to 'come aboard and we'll work out the description as we go along'? Such vague presentations are not uncommon, but it is to the librarian's advantage, and to the parent institution's, to have a written description of the duties and demands of the position. The job description should include . . .

> . . . job title, line responsibility, salary grade, a detailed description of the job itself (including performance standards and any special characteristics) and a note of qualities and qualifications desirable in the holder. However, in a special library, because it is usually small, it is particularly desirable to build in flexibility and scope for job development within the job description to reduce the need for debate if it becomes necessary to alter the task distribution or to meet changing circumstances.'[5]

As a minimum there should be a statement of the basic duties in the library ('the librarian is responsible for the orderly arrangement of the books on the shelves', 'the librarian is responsible for ordering, checking in and routing periodicals to the research staff', 'the librarian is responsible for providing bibliographies upon request', etc.). with some general statement alluding to the librarian's professional discretion for determining how these duties are to be performed.

## Work sharing

All one-person libraries are not run by a single individual, as contradictory as that statement may sound. For various administrative reasons a one-person library may, in fact, require more than one employee. Work sharing is one such situation. This has been practised only occasionally in the past, but now that so much of the workforce is made up of working mothers it is becoming more and more accepted by management as an alternative to not filling the position, or filling the position with inferior staff because the best people are not available full-time. In fact, while the practice may have been created to accommodate working mothers, Patricia Lee, in an article edited by Anna Marie McKee and Laura Scott, lists other equally good reasons for work sharing:

> Most people at some point in their careers would like to work less than full time: some because they are raising a family, others because they want to

further their education, some to pursue two careers, and some to postpone complete retirement. Job sharing enables employers to retain those valued employees who might otherwise leave to pursue other interests. With job sharing, employees can stay and still have time for other productive activities, or extra leisure ... as the eighties progress you are going to see more older workers sharing jobs ... we're going to lose the baby boom glut, and we're going to have a real gap in skilled workers ... And on a smaller level, you're going to find a lot more men who really care about spending time with small children and participating more fully in the development of their families. These are the men who are very broad-minded and liberated and they really want full participation at home. And these men are going to be utilizing job sharing, too.[7]

Simply defined, work sharing is one job shared by two people, or we could say it is an employment concept which helps two people reduce their hours in an interesting job according to their own needs. It is a voluntary agreement whereby two people share the responsibilities of one full-time job and share the pay and benefits between them according to the hours that each works. Lee defines it thus:

Job sharing is permanent part-time work with a full-time career-oriented structure. It's two people sharing the responsibilities of one job with a prorated salary, and the work is divided by hours, by experience, or by areas of expertise. It is a collaboration between two people to restructure a job that cannot be reduced in hours, and it provides the possibility for sharers to trade work time for time to respond to their personal needs.[6]

According to some, job sharing 'appears to be the answer to the questions: How can we meet the changing needs of today's workers in terms of the new lifestyles of the 1980s? How can the needs of the workplace and family be reconciled?'[7]

There are administrative advantages as well:

One of the advantages of job sharing is that it has resulted in a lower rate of absenteeism. Employees have more time for personal affairs and can trade off with partners in times of illness. It also provides continuity on the job during vacation periods or other times when someone may be absent. Job sharing is also an important tool to prevent burn-out ... Job sharing is also a means to strengthen affirmative action plans: to hold on to older employees, to bring women back into the workplace, and, in some cases during layoffs, it has been utilized to retain women and minorities.[8]

In one-person libraries work sharing can be found in small public libraries, in corporate libraries and in association or organizational libraries. Generally speaking, the two librarians work separate schedules, with minimal overlapping of time, perhaps only a few minutes each day as the 'changing of the guard' takes place. For administrative purposes the positions are sometimes considered as two part-time positions, although Lee makes a case for avoiding that characterization ('... one of the big things we promote in job sharing is that we don't call it part-time. It's less than full-time, but it's not part-time'[9]). There has been some movement on the part of personnel administrators to consider each position separately; Notowitz also make a persuasive case for employers to consider the two positions as separate administrative entities:

> The question of benefits is what separates job sharing from part-time work, which generally has no fringe benefits. Job sharing, when viewed as one job shared by two people with the existing benefits divided between them, often manages to satisfy the job sharers' needs, while not increasing the employer's cost for benefits. Employers receive the expertise of two professionals and the job sharers have control over arranging their lives, thus increasing job satisfaction ... Many employers are reluctant to pay any increased costs of full health coverage for two job sharers instead of for one full-time worker.
>
> ... these higher costs were offset by the slightly lower salaries (from the division of tasks) and greater productivity (from less absenteeism and fewer turnovers).[10]

McKee and Scott even cite an employer who accepts totally the concept of work sharing to the extent of prorating benefits ('Each member of the team gets complete health coverage and the rest of the benefits on a prorated basis'[11]).

Each of the two employees involved in a job-sharing situation will, of course, have certain strengths, and the workload is usually divided up according to who does each task best. Thus one of the two might be better at book keeping, ordering and processing, while the other might be better at book selection, public relations and reference. In all cases, however, both employees should be equally capable of performing all the tasks outlined in the job description. Also, we must recognize that job sharing is not for everyone. First of all, it is 'not necessarily a work arrrangement that one wants to stay with all one's working life. And, frankly, you cannot expect to advance in a job as quickly as if you were working full-time.'[12] Finally, the personalities of the two individuals must be considered as much as their separate strengths and weaknesses. The job sharing will not work 'if you had it between two individuals who both want to "run the show"'.[12] Lee goes even further in describing the best kind of employees for such a working relationship:

> You need someone with an ability to gear up quickly and learn fast, somebody who can work independently, who has good communication skills, scheduling flexibility, a willingness to consult, ability to set priorities, and ability to cooperate and collaborate. I would add – sometimes a sense of humour.[13]

There is no way to get around the idea that in a one-person library the efficient functioning of the library and the organizational success of the department are directly reflective of the librarian. If the two people sharing the single job are not compatible the job-sharing experience will not work and the mission of the library will not be accomplished. If they are compatible, the employing organization will find itself with the best of all worlds: a 'staff member' (i.e. two people) who complement one another for the benefit of the organization.

Before committing oneself to a job-sharing arrangement, it is wise to think about the pros and cons. There are advantages for management and for the job sharers, but there can be disadvantages which have to be weighed carefully. Advantages to the worker include the following:

- Hours can be worked to suit domestic arrangements,
- Income is better than for more mundane part-time work.
- More opportunities become available for better-paid professional jobs.
- There is more time for study and outside interests.
- There is more flexibility of hours worked, and arrangements can be altered to suit.
- Job sharers can pool their ideas, interests, contacts, skills, etc. (in other words, 'two heads are better than one').
- There is a division of labour, and skills can be divided accordingly.
- In the United Kingdom employment rights are unaffected as long as you work a total of sixteen hours per week or more.
- For women, job sharing makes it easier to return to work after maternity leave.

The disadvantages are:

- Job sharing only really makes sense in a professional position because of the resultant low salary – more mundane posts will scarcely provide a living wage.
- You could lose some of your benefits such as holidays, pensions, insurance schemes, etc., unless you are careful at the time of employment to have these included on a pro-rata basis.
- Other employment rights (contract, protection against unfair dismissal, etc.) could be affected, and these should be carefully checked before entering into any agreement to participate in a job-sharing plan.
- The job-sharing employee has to make sure that he or she is not working three-quarters of the job instead of half.
- You may find yourself spending a disproportionate amount of time travelling to and from work, and if management insists upon strict adherence to a particular schedule (as is often necessary in libraries) you will have less flexibility.
- You will have to make sure that there is overlap time in order to communicate with your fellow worker, or else things may start to go wrong.
- Job sharers, especially women, are often regarded by management and other employees as part-time workers.
- If one of the job sharers should leave, that half of the job could be lost through cuts, thus putting additional pressures and stress on the remaining employee.

It would seem that library jobs are ideal for job sharing. Libraries often have to be open for long hours and staffed at meal times. In fact, lunch hours can often be the librarian's busiest time. In a one-person library one job sharer can be left free to attend important meetings and conferences (or even visits to the dentist) while the other keeps things going at the library, and there is more time for part-time study in order to gain additional professional qualifications. There is also less sense of professional isolation, as there is a handover period when job sharers can exchange ideas. Working in a one-person library is often exhausting physically, and job sharers in such libraries remain fresher, especially in the latter part of the week. Tedious chores are not so mundane when someone else will also be doing them, and going on vacations does not mean that the librarian will return to a desk piled high with daily mail problems. Finally, when two librarians share a professional post there is no need to replace and train new staff as often as before, and the library benefits from their growing experience while the staff remains more stable.

The concept of work sharing, while unusual when compared with standard practices in the workplace, is becoming more and more accepted. In fact, a recent case proved that full-time work cannot be required. An English employment appeals tribunal ruled that an employer's refusal to allow an employee 'to work part-time for a corresponding cut in pay was indirect discrimination under the 1975 Sex Discrimination Act'.[14] The idea of work sharing may be an employment practice whose time has come.

## Contracts

The question of contracts often comes up when a librarian is being considered for a position, and while contracts are not included as part of the standard employment procedure in some institutions in the United States they are required in the United Kingdom. A librarian thinking about taking a job in a one-person library might give some thought to the idea of a job contract and consider whether or not one should be requested. A contract of employment is an agreement between the one-person librarian and the employer. In the United States a contract can be a signed document or it can be a simple verbal agreement; whether a contract is written or verbal will depend primarily on the type of institution, since a verbal agreement is just as binding and must be respected as seriously as a signed, written document as long as the specific details of the contract are agreed upon by both parties. Obviously, it is in the interpretation of these details that parties sometimes later disagree, and this is where a written contract is a protection for both parties. Most one-person librarians are employed in small institutions, so in the United States the agreement between the employer and the librarian is most often going to be a verbal one. Nevertheless, it is to the librarian's benefit as soon as possible to prepare a memorandum of record, just to keep on file, of the points agreed upon, with a copy of this memorandum given to the employer as well.

For the British librarian work contracts are important in your job. Make sure that as a one-person librarian you have a proper contract of employment drawn up before you accept a post. Read it carefully, and do not sign it until the implications are fully understood. Talk over with the personnel department anything you do not understand, and if you are still unhappy, take the contract to your solicitor. In the United Kingdom, the rights for individual workers are contained in the Employment Protection (Consolidation) Act 1978. These include the right to a written contract of employment, protection against unfair dismissal, entitlement to redundancy pay and maternity pay, and the right to reinstatement after maternity leave. Job sharers working over sixteen hours per week also have a right to all these benefits.

It is also interesting to note that under this Act a new employee must be provided with a written statement setting out certain details of his employment within thirteen weeks of joining the company or parent organization. This does not apply to part-timers working less than sixteen hours per week, but part-timers are entitled to a written statement once they have worked eight hours or more a week for five years.

The clauses that this statement or contract must contain are well set out in *Croner's Reference Book for Employers*[15] under the heading 'Employees' rights', and you should read this section for your own satisfaction before signing any contracts which have been drawn up. The British Institute of Management also provides a good *Guidance Note*[16] on the same subject, and this can be obtained from the information centre at Corby, Northants.

The Library Association publishes an excellent series of leaflets on recommended salaries in various categories of libraries, and its leaflet No. 7, *Recommended Salaries for Library Staff in Commercial, Industrial and Other Specialised Library and Information Services*, sets out guidelines and even states that:

> Some libraries and information units are operated by a single professional librarian, with or without clerical support. In these cases a whole range of professional skills and expertise is concentrated in one person and this should be recognized when arriving at a salary level.[17]

# References

1 Tunley, Malcolm, *Library Structures and Staffing Systems*, LA Management Pamphlet No. 2, 1979, p. 49.

2 Ashworth, Wilfred, *Special Librarianship*, Clive Bingley, London, 1979, p. 17.

3 Armstrong, Alan, *Introduction to Information Work*, Unpublished course papers.

4 *Oxford Dictionary of Quotations*, 3rd edn, OUP, 1979, p. 276.

5 Anthony L. J. (ed.) *Handbook of Special Librarianship and Information Work*, Aslib, 1982, p. 39.

6 McKee, Anna Maria and Scott, Laura, 'Job sharing: a speech by Patricia Lee and panel discussion', *Journal of Library Administration*, **3**, 2, 77 and 85-86, 1982

7 Notowitz, Carol, 'Job sharing for the 80s', *School Library Journal*, **28**, 6, 33, 1982.

8 McKee and Scott, op. cit., p. 78

9 Ibid, p. 85

10 Notowitz, op. cit., p. 33.

11 McKee and Scott, op. cit., p. 83.

12 Gardner, Frances, 'They try job sharing', *Syracuse Post Standard*, 31 March, D-5.9, 1981.

13 McKee and Scott, op. cit., p. 80.

14 'Women at work: a servant of two masters', *The Economist*, **291,** 7343, 23 June, 58, 1983.

15 *Croner's Reference Book for Employers*, Croner Publications, UK.

16 British Institute of Management, *Guidance Notes on Employees Rights*, available from BIM, Corby, Northants, UK.

17 The Library Association, *Recommended Salaries for Library Staff in Commercial, Industrial and Other Specialised Library and Information Services*, The Library Association, London, 1985-1986.

# Further personnel considerations

A continuing conflict in one-person libraries is the problem of non-related duties. This situation occurs when supervisory personnel ask the librarian to perform duties which are not part of one's professional work, and are often not related to library work at all. These tasks can range from the simply menial (being in charge of the staff coffee-pot for the floor where the library is located) to such professional (albeit non-library) activities as editing the organization's staff newsletter or, in a small museum, running the educational programme for members and their children. How do you cope with these demands on your 'library' time? The answer must come with an analysis of these 'extra' duties and a recognition of when they were assigned to the librarian. If duties were performed by the previous librarian they should have been included in the job description, in which case you would have been justified to request a discussion of the duties and perhaps, through negotiation, could have convinced management that such non-library-related activities should be done by another (non-professional) staff member. If, however, these duties were not discussed with you prior to your employment you must decide if they are objectionable to you, if they will interfere with the efficient performance of your library duties, and if they can be performed by some other person. If your answers to these questions are affirmative you must request a meeting to discuss them with your supervisor and you must make some attempt to renegotiate your position. Finally, if these non-library tasks are assigned to you as extra duties after you are already on the job, again you must decide how objectionable they are to you and whether you can include them in your regular work load. In any case, you should discuss these tasks with your supervisor to determine if they *must* be performed as part of the library's operations and, if so, how they can be worked into your previously assigned duties.

The very subject of one-person librarians performing non-library-related duties is one fraught with emotion, for the prevailing wisdom is that a one-person librarian, almost by definition, is overworked and does not *ever* have enough time to do all the tasks required in running the library alone. Such may not always be the case, however: increased efficiency may free some of the librarian's time for other duties. Certain small organizations (law firms, churches, small businesses, etc.) may need the services of a librarian only part-time, in which case non-library-related duties must be assigned to justify full-time employment. In such cases, however, it is management's obligation to explain clearly, from the beginning, that extra duties can be expected of the librarian.

What happens when the librarian refuses to accept extra duties? There is always the possibility, when a special situation comes up in a library, that the librarian might need to request extra help. But what if one has consistently refused to do extra work oneself? Obviously, the difference here has to do with frequency. An *occasional* request for help from the librarian is not out of line, and neither is the *occasional* cooperation of the librarian when asked. It is the regular request, or the addition of new, non-library-related duties on a permanent basis, which should be questioned and seriously negotiated with management.

Finally, it is important to remember that these tasks are not being requested, or done, as personal favours. One of the worst things a supervisor can say to an employee is 'I have a favour to ask you' or 'I have something I would like you to do for me', and then assign a task which has nothing to do with one's agreed duties. In such a case the employee is obliged to remind the supervisor that such a request is not acceptable and that the 'favour' cannot be performed without damaging the working relationship the two people have with one another. In the workplace one does not perform a task to ensure that another task will be performed in return. The work is there to do, and it is the librarian's obligation to educate management, if necessary, in what is and what is not acceptable in a professional situation.

In some institutions in which the library is run by one person the institution is small enough for the entire staff to work together, and such duties as collecting gift funds, planning staff get-togethers, etc., fall upon the librarian in his turn, because this is the way things are done in this particular organization. Here the librarian has no choice but to go along willingly, just hoping, like every other staff member in the organization who gets roped into such situations, that the work for which he is responsible will not suffer because of the demands of these 'extra' duties.

When asked how they feel about such extra duties many librarians respond that they do not especially like doing them but that sometimes it is politically expedient to accept them. Collating an annual report, for example, or planning an educational programme might be perceived by the librarian as demeaning and not especially 'professional', but by others in the organization such tasks would be seen as appropriate for a librarian, for they are, after all, 'intellectual' and the librarian is usually considered, especially in smaller organizations, the resident 'intellectual'. By agreeing to do them the librarian is recognized as a team player, an asset in the special library world, where the librarian does not often have an opportunity to show that he or she is a willing member of the 'team'.

## Additional help in the library

For most one-person librarians lack of time is perceived as their biggest problem. While some observers, especially, perhaps, management or supervisory personnel, contend that a properly structured library can be run by one person (depending, of course, on such factors as size of collection, requests for services, level of reference or research services, etc.), there are a number of situations in which the librarian simply cannot get all the work done and will require some form of additional support. Such tasks as an annual inventory, the disposal of non-current, unretained periodicals, preparations for the occasional book sale or the shifting of a sizeable collection all require more manpower than one person can supply. How does the one-person librarian deal with these special temporary needs?

There are various approaches. If the parent organization is large enough that there is a personnel 'pool' upon which various departments can draw for special projects and assignments, this is the obvious source of temporary help. If such employees are not available management must be approached for funding some kind of temporary employee, obtained either through the librarian's own contacts (friends, colleagues, a local agency which supplies library temporaries) or through a company or institutional personnel department. In either case, it is the one-person librarian who must determine when additional help is required and then make a case to management for temporary staff. The request itself should not be made in terms of a special favour. The need for staff must be explained in clear terms, demonstrating precisely that the work to be done is part of the ordinary work of the library and not a passing fad or fringe job, and that the completion of the tasks involved will result in better service in the library. The classic approach to getting an inexpensive extra hand in the library has been the use of student assistants. Long accepted in secondary-school libraries and in college and university libraries, student assistants have been utilized in almost every non-professional capacity. Even smaller departmental libraries in larger universities have no compunction about hiring student help, and the trend has now become so popular that we see student assistants (often euphemistically referred to as 'general assistants') being utilized in small corporate, museum, church and synagogue, health-care agency and law libraries. The reason is obvious: student help is cheap. Beatrice Sichel has considered student employees in a paper she wrote for the *Journal of Library Administration*, and while she lists several advantages for having students on the staff, the primary one is financial:

> There is substantial differential in the compensation offered a permanent staff member and a temporary student worker. In the typical library, the hourly wage rate for para-professionals ranges from $4.00 to $6.50 per hour. Fringe benefits, which include paid holidays, vacation time, sick leave, contributions to insurance and retirement plans, and logevity bonuses, increase the cost of compensation by another 22.6%. Student workers generally find the minimum wage (currently $3.35 per hour) acceptable.[1]

There are other advantages to having a student on the staff, however. Sichel points out that student staff are useful in keeping the library open more hours than would be possible with only one person on the staff.[1] For the one-person library, however, the prime advantage of having a student on the staff, even if only for ten hours a week, is having someone to help with the drudgery.

Students can do routine tasks, and if you are fortunate enough to have a good assistant you can teach her to shelve books, sort pamphlets, file reports and generally assist in all the myriad duties which pile up. A good student assistant can even be taught to perform quasi-professional tasks such as shelf-reading and inventory checking, if she is interested in library work and seems to take to it. The very fact that there are duties, even occasional ones, which the librarian does not have to perform and can count on having someone else do, can be a tremendous boost for morale for the librarian in charge of a one-person library.

In the United Kingdom there are a number of industry-based training schemes which may be of help to the single-handed librarian or information worker. The Manpower Services Commission oversees most of these, and details can be obtained from them.[2] The Commission's 'New Training Initiative' sets out various objectives, including the development of skills training for young people at different ages and moving towards the point where all young people at the age of 18 have the opportunity of either continuing in full-time education or entering a period of planned work experience combined with work-related training and education.

The best known of these training schemes is the Youth Training Scheme (YTS), which is open to all 16-year-old school leavers both employed and unemployed, to some 17-year-olds who are unemployed and to some disabled young people up to the age of 21. The scheme offers a different approach to vocational training in that it offers experience of different types of work and high-quality training on and off the job, a chance to learn new things which will help in work and everyday life, and a certificate regarded by employers as a valuable asset. There are periods of planned work experience and a minimum of thirteen weeks off-the-job training. (One-person librarians should take note of this last point; if you are very busy, having a worker disappear once a week to attend college can be inconvenient.) YTS trainees are also entitled to holidays (at least 18 days a year) and may want to go on vacation just when you need someone to cover for you. Bear in mind also that you are expected to train these employees, and this means giving them not just the tedious jobs which you have not the time for yourself but some of the more interesting tasks which are within their capabilities. Training takes much time to complete properly, and you have to weigh the pros and cons of these schemes. A bonus, however, is that if you find a young person who is capable and interested she may be taken on as a permanent employee at the end of the training year, and may go on to take qualifications such as the City and Guilds of London certificates of occupational education for library and information assistants.

Another way of getting someone in to help is by persuading your employer to let you take on someone under the Department of Employment's 'Young Workers Scheme'. This has been devised to encourage employers to take on more young people in full-time and permanent jobs at rates of pay which reflect their age and relative inexperience. There are certain conditions which your employer will have to honour and these are set out in leaflets describing the scheme. Provision of training is not a condition, and you will therefore be able to be more flexible in your approach to allocating tasks. It helps, of course, if you can provide some training so that the young person taken on has a better understanding of job which she is completing.

In the United Kingdom you may wish to supervise a candidate for admission to licentiateship of the Library Association. Anyone wishing to enter the list of Licentiates of the Library Association must fulfil certain conditions, one of which is to have undergone a period of supervised post-examination training under a Chartered Librarian who is on the Register of the Library Association. This training programme lasts for one year and enables the trainee to gain practical experience in professional work.

There are various objectives of this approved service:

(1) To introduce the graduate to the professional working environment.
(2) To enable the graduate to gain experience in professional practice in order to complement the theory already studied at library school.
(3) To give the graduate an opportunity to gain knowledge of the wide range of work available within the profession.
(4) To enable the graduate to gain new skills and knowledge.
(5) To provide the graduate with opportunities for professional and personal development.
(6) To develop in the graduate attitudes to professional work which reflect high professional standards.

Again, if you decide to use such staff you are going to have to train and supervise the person, but in this case you have the advantage of knowing at least that the employee is more interested in the job that she is performing, and that she will already have a level of professional expertise which will not be found in young people taken on by way of the various other schemes of training. If you yourself are not chartered, external supervision is acceptable and can be arranged with the Library Association.

Another source for temporary help in the not-for-profit sector is volunteers. Certainly those who volunteer their services in a one-person library cannot be asked to perform tasks for which the library should be hiring paid employees. Such tasks as those described above (inventory, shifting books, etc.) are not appropriate for people who are giving their time and energies simply because these tasks are part of the business of running a library. The library and its parent organization must be prepared to pay to get these tasks completed. However, tasks (usually those which might not be considered absolutely essential by management or supervisory personnel but which would enable the library to be of better service) can be assigned to volunteers who, when properly trained and supervised, can make a significant contribution to the library's work. Such tasks as sorting and arranging archival materials, preparing simple descriptive bibliographies for certain collections, sitting at reception desks, answering the telephone, etc., can be handled by trained volunteers. Guidelines for using volunteers in libraries are available from the American Library Association (ALA),[3] and Harold Jenkins has written a useful article which spells out many of the advantages and disadvantages of using volunteers.[4] The best guide to using volunteers, however, came out in 1983 in the form of a

'Library Journal Special Report (#24).' Prepared by Alice Sizer Warner, *Volunteers in Libraries II* is a basic text which dispels many of our preconceived ideas about volunteers and their use simply because Warner's guidance is based on information she received from some 700 respondents to questionnaires mailed to libraries of all types and sizes. She sees the growth of volunteerism as a natural phenomenon, something that was bound to happen in this decade:

> The 1980s decade brings with it as well a political atmosphere where macro economics is having visible and often drastic effect on mini (and not so mini) libraries. 'Volunteerism' is now not only the wonderful pioneer pitch-in spirit, it is the unwritten law of the land.[5]

She begins by asserting that there is agreement today that 'the single most important reason for a volunteer programme is public relations', and people come to the library to work as volunteers for a variety of reasons: civic responsibility, need for structure in their schedules, the desire to meet new people, to obtain hands-on job experience, especially to have references they can use when looking for jobs, to get out of the house and, frankly, because they are bored, to fill time in their lives, to do something active in retirement.[6]

Can a volunteer programme be of use to the one-person librarian? No single answer can work for all one-person libraries, but before plunging into such a programme to get people to help with some of the jobs that just do not seem to get done there are a few basic guidelines which Warner offers:

> The first step, for any library bent on careful exploration of whether and how to use volunteers, is carefully to define and review the goals of the library. Is the library accomplishing what it has set out to do? If not, what are alternate, feasible ways of reaching goals? Might a volunteer labour force be a workable solution?
>
> It is a good idea to gather as much information as possible about how other libraries, particularly libraries either nearby or approximately the same size, are using volunteers. Also, in early planning stages, a look should be taken to see if there already exists a community organization devoted to helping with volunteers and to finding and pre-screening volunteers.[7]

The one-person librarian should also ask herself if there is enough work, and whether the volunteers would help or hinder the efficient operation of the library. Will the public relations gains be worth the effort that goes into working with volunteers? If the answers are negative, the librarian will do better to look elsewhere for extra help.

## Sex discrimination in the one-person library

There is one insidious stereotype which will not go away, and it affects librarians, both male and female: 'Librarians are women, and as women they are weak, helpless and ineffectual.' This perception is, of course, another form of sex discrimination. Virginia E. Schein provides a definition of it in the opening sentence of her study of sex role stereotyping on ability and performance: 'Sex role stereotyping refers to the belief that a set of traits and abilities is more likely to be found among one sex than the other.'[8] It is a situation which plagues our profession more than most, because librarianship is a traditionally female profession.

There have been studies to attempt to determine the reasons why males proportionally outnumber females in leadership and managerial positions, but there are no significant conclusions yet. Kathryn M. Bartol has done some work on the subject, and she reports to the library profession:

> ... the research is quite consistent in indicating that sex is not a valid predictor of managerial effectiveness. Female and male leaders appear to engage in similar leadership styles, to be equally satisfied in managerial roles, to have subordinates who have equal job satisfaction levels, and to achieve equivalent job performance with their task groups. Furthermore, there is evidence that managerial talent is equally distributed among working males and females. This means that across a variety of work situations where there are more females than males in similar positions, we should expect to find, on the average, proportionately more females than males with managerial potential. In the case of libraries, this should translate into numbers of female and male directors of libraries in proportion to the number of females and males in the library profession. The numbers of female and male library directors are clearly not proportional to the numbers of female and male professional staff members in the library field.[9]

What does this mean for the one-person librarian? First of all, since most one-person librarians are women it means that they must learn to be aware of what it is that makes people treat them like 'the girl in the library'. While this is not the place to go into an analysis of sexism on the job there are certain characterizations which, when recognized, make it easier for the one-person librarian to deal with users, corporate executives and, especially, female secretarial and clerical staff. A light-hearted article directed at male executives offers some conclusions as to how men and women differ in the workplace. Although there is a risk of oversimplification, we repeat some of them here because recognizing them can be helpful to the librarian working alone. First of all,

> Men tend to be better at office politics than women, in the sense that they seem to understand they have to get themselves and their work noticed. Men are also better at working with people they dislike, if that's what it takes to get the job done. Women are inclined to believe that if you do your job well, the organization will treat you fairly.[10]

In reacting to criticism men immediately begin to explain why the circumstances of the situation made it impossible to do the job properly. Women take it personally. According to the author, Walter Kiechel III, the big difference is in decision-making, because it is this function that sums up or explains several other differences:

> Women are painstaking, seeking everyone's opinion and trying to build consensus; they want their own views listened to carefully in any deliberation. Because women dwell so on all the disastrous consequences that may ensue from a decision, they are less willing to take risks. Male behavior in making decisions can be summed up in a phrase: Go for it. In the parlance of behavioral science, men are interested in outcome, women in process.[10]

On the positive side, this may explain why women are so successful in running one-person libraries.

## Stereotyping of librarians

Most people who come into the library have a preconceived notion of what a librarian is like. For many reasons, all of them too complex to go into here, librarians are perceived as not quite like other people. They are thought of as shushing maiden ladies, as sad introverts who must escape into their books to get away from the rest of the world, or as pernickety types who are more interested in protecting the materials in their care than in letting anyone get to them. Of course, these are all ridiculous variations and intellectually the user knows this, but the generalized perception he brings into the library is not a positive one. This user expects, either subliminally or actively, to conduct his business in the library with a considerable amount of condescension, restraint, tolerance and, perhaps, awe, since the library is a place where one goes when one needs some information, but one does not take it 'seriously'. Or if one does, one certainly does not take seriously the person who has been employed to run it. There are reasons for the stereotypes of our profession, and the best analysis and discussion of the subject is to be found in Pauline Wilson's excellent study, *Stereotype and Status: Librarians in the United States*.[11] Wilson correctly contends that the stereotype comes about because, like all stereotypes, it is based upon a truth, the simple truth that 'librarians *are* charged with the responsibility of ensuring that the library is a functioning organization, that it works and works well for those who need it. And that perhaps is not without cost; part of the cost may be reflected in stereotyping.'[12] Wilson illustrates this idea with a long quotation from one of the respondents to the study on stereotyping in which she was involved:

> There is a limit to the concessions we should make to redeem our image. We can afford to let the noise level rise a bit more (if they can stand it, so can we); ... we can wear two strands of beads and let our hair down; we can ... be patient teachers to those who consider the catalog an enemy fortress; ... we can sit on the floor between the stacks with our researchers and pore over materials; we can confess to being no more than fellow students, on a slightly higher level, rather than acting as an authority. We can do all that.

What we *can't* do is to say: 'Come in you dear children and take all the current magazines, never mind who needs them after you', or 'Here are shears, clip all the reference books you want'. We can't overlook the rowdies who prevent others from serious study, or the spoilers who stick bubble gum in the earphones and exercise their pen knives on the stacks. We must watch our doors and check one hundred good readers to detect one bad one; we must insist on ID's to know who comes through our doors and to deter the thief. We are keepers of books and other media, not for our own satisfaction, but because we owe it to the reader of the future to preserve these things in order to serve him, too.

What we also cannot do is to say to our workers, 'Never mind the exact spelling or alphabetical order', or 'Relax when you shelve, a few digits off isn't the end of the world', as some of the new work ethics seem to go.[12]

What do we do about the stereotype of the librarian? Wilson provides the answer in a remarkable piece of perceptive advice: stop talking and writing about it:

Not only do librarians perpetuate the stereotype by keeping every librarian aware of it through journal articles, they indoctrinate new entrants into the profession early. Masters students are permitted to do theses on the stereotype as well as various classroom exercises probing the personality of the librarian. This practice not only disseminates the stereotype and gives it an unwarranted gloss of scholarship, it ensures that these new entrants into the profession begin their careers with the stereotype firmly implanted in their consciousness.[13]

Should we take Wilson's advice? Certainly in the one-person library there is no need to talk and write about stereotype, for the one-person librarian has a unique opportunity, through excellence of service and a positive attitude, to do more to dispel the stereotype than almost any other kind of librarian. It is an opportunity that should be grasped enthusiastically and when, in professional groups, the subject of the poor, downtrodden librarian comes up, the one-person librarian should take advantage of the situation and explain why the stereotype is not important. The one-person librarian, more than anyone else, is in a position to leave the problems of professional stereotyping for other librarians to grapple with. The energy and resources which the one-person librarian brings to the profession are needed elsewhere.

## References

1 Sichel, Beatrice, 'Utilizing student assistants in small libraries', *Journal of Library Administration*, **3**, 1, p. 36, 1982.
2 Manpower Services Commission, *The Youth Training Scheme* (Details from the Manpower Services Commission, Moorfoot, Sheffield, UK).
3 American Library Association, Library Administration Division, 'Guidelines for using volunteers in libraries', *American Libraries*, **2**, April, 407-408, 1971.

4  Jenkins, Harold, 'The library volunteer: volunteers in the future of libraries', *Library Journal*, **97**, 15 April, 1399-1403, 1972.

5  Warner, Alice Sizer, *Volunteers in Libraries II*, Library Journal Special Report #24, Bowker, New York, 1983, p. 4.

6  Ibid, pp. 10-11.

7  Ibid, p. 12.

8  Schein, Virginia E., 'Sex role stereotyping, ability and performance: prior research and new directions', *Personnel Psychology*, **31**, 259-268, 1978.

9  Bartol, Kathryn M., 'An addendum to the sex structuring of organizations: the special case of traditionally-female professions', *Journal of Library Administration*, **1**, 2, 90, 1980.

10  Kiechel, Walter, III, 'Beyond sexist management', *Fortune*, **110**, 8, p. 283, 1984.

11  Wilson, Pauline, *Stereotype and Status: Librarians in the United States*, Contributions in Librarianship and Information Science, Number 41, Greenwood Press, Westport, Connecticut, 1982.

12  Ibid, p. 29.

13  Ibid, p. 38.

# The business of librarianship

There is a philosophical approach to librarianship, most particularly to one-person librarianship, which must be considered by anyone going into a job in which he will be the only person on the staff with responsibility for the library or information service for a parent organization. This has to do with the concept of running the library as a business. We are often tempted, especially in a small library, to treat the 'behind-the-scenes' work of library administration as if it were someone's hobby or passing interest, but long experience has taught that in the library world, as in any other service profession, the acceptance and adherence to the same practices of management and fiscal responsibility as those of the business world are imperative to the efficient and orderly fulfilment of the library's purpose. There is no other way of saying it: a library must be run as a business, and succumbing to the temptation to treat library administration as anything less is not only a disservice to the library's users and the management of the library's parent organization or governing authority, it is a misuse of the funds and responsibility entrusted to the librarian.

An initial intellectual step which will pay positive rewards throughout one's career is recognizing that the library is a business even though the 'product' is the providing of information, a service which is difficult to quantify and often, especially in libraries which serve not-for-profit organizations (small public libraries, church and synagogue libraries, museum libraries, etc.), difficult to justify to the laymen who sit on committees and boards or who are in managerial or supervisory positions in the parent organizations of which the library is a part. Nevertheless, attempts must be made to impress upon these people the businesslike make-up of the library and to encourage them to accept the fact that the library is not a cosmetic department which is tolerated and condescended to.

How do these attitudes arise among management and supervisory personnel and even with users? How do they decide that the library is not as important as some of the other departments of the parent organization or, indeed, some of the other service departments? Part of the reason has to do with a managerial reluctance to deal with any department that does not produce a profit as a serious part of the organization. Libraries have traditionally taken in money, used it for 'running the library', a highly specialized and esoteric task (at least as far as the layman is concerned), and at the end of the fiscal year produced no discernible profit. In these very simplistic terms, management and supervisory personnel cannot help but wonder why it costs 'so much' (no matter how little the cost!) to run a library. Never mind that the parent organization probably includes other service departments that are just as costly and provide as little – or less – return. A library, simply because so many people have preconceived notions about what one is and so little understanding of what is required to run one, is not *supposed* to cost anything, and when it does turn out to be expensive much effort is required on the part of the librarian to justify the cost.

Fortunately, this attitude is changing and certainly, within a few years, will be considered dated and unproductive. It is now generally agreed that times have changed, and sociologically speaking we have left the age of industry and entered an age of service. The providing of information is a service which has come into its own, and for the last ten years or so management has begun to accept the fact that running an organization depends almost solely upon the quality of information it has to make decisions. Therefore information has become respectable, and we are finding more and more parent organizations willing to pay what it costs to have available the highest-quality information. When this involves the use of an organizational library the manager of the library is in a position to seek and often be given the requisite funding.

The other side of this happy picture, unfortunately, and more to the point for our discussion here, has to do with size. Most one-person librarians are employed in organizations which are small, and in the smaller companies, businesses, schools and organizations, especially those with a traditional library to provide traditional services, the impact of the information age has not yet been felt. It is a fact that smaller organizations tend to take longer than larger ones to acquire new managerial methods, operational techniques, organizational approaches and, particularly, the utilization of technological innovations. The reasons are obvious: new things cost money, and, especially in the small organization, if things are working all right now ('we have always done it this way') there is little or no motivation for change. This is not to suggest that change for its own sake is good. However, change and innovation, when applied in such a way that the work of the organization is done better and, more important, in such a way that the employees feel rewarded and compensated beyond their salaries, provide obvious benefits.

If we are entering an age which is accepting the cost of information as a part of doing business, how does the librarian in a one-person library put himself in a position to encourage management or supervisory personnel to accept the idea that running a library is a valid and reasonable place to invest funds? First of all, we literally treat the library as if it were a small business. We organize the library along what we have called businesslike lines, keeping appropriate records, setting up proper accounting procedures, making distinctions between tasks that are necessary and those that are not, using jobbers, outside agents and other such time-saving entities whenever possible and, generally, managing the library as if there were going to be a cash payment for the services rendered.

Before discussing these businesslike procedures in detail, however, we must analyse the attitude of the person who runs a library as a business. The one-person librarian already has certain skills (or, if management is generous, these may be learned on the job): basic accounting, record keeping, marketing or promotion, etc. In addition to these, however, there are certain personality traits which the librarian must have, and Shirley Echelman has listed them in her provocative essay on running a corporate library as a business. She regards six traits as necessary for the management of a corporate library, and it is our contention that these requirements also apply to a one-person librarian:

'First – an analytical intelligence ... the capacity for walking a problem through your mind, step by step, examining each step as it is made, and arriving at a conclusion based on careful examination of all available possibilities. This is a very different way of approaching a problem from that employed by a person with a creative intelligence. Creative intelligence, that ability to make leaps of imagination and understanding, often produces a fine reference librarian, more often a painter or a mathematician, but a strong dose of analytical intelligence is much more important for a library manager.

Second – self confidence ... considerably buoyed by a good grasp of management skills ...

Third – flexibility ... that quality which allows one to be persuaded by fact and reason, but not too easily ... The manager may enter a situation in which he thinks he has an absolutely clear view of what is going to occur. However, a rigid adherence to that vision often means that adequate solutions are bypassed if they do not quite fit the original view.

Fourth – a highly developed sense of humor. Not much elaboration is necessary on this point. After you encounter your fifth corporate executive in as many days who asks sweetly when the library is going to buy the latest porno classic, you will know exactly what I mean.

The fifth and sixth qualities are complementary, but not quite the same. They are patience and a high frustration threshold. Working through a problem, be it a year's budget or the floor plan of a new library, with colleagues whose interests may differ greatly from yours, whose job it may be to keep your budget down while you are convinced that it must rise, for example, can be an excruciating exercise in patience. And since the nature of the corporate experience is to balance departmental against overall goals, frustration is a frequent occurrence.[1]

If the library is not part of a corporation or business but part of a non-profit or not-for-profit enterprise (e.g. a church, historical society, club, professional association, etc.) it will present special problems, for the prevailing wisdom has not always been to treat such an institution – or its library – in a businesslike way. In 1978 William H. Newman and Harvey W. Wallender III recognized that not-for-profit enterprises were beginning to seek help from the business world in running their organizations, but they also recognized that these enterprises are different from commercial institutions. Newman and Wallender described several characteristics of not-for-profit organizations, among which are several especially applicable to libraries, especially small ones. For one thing, service is intangible and hard to measure in such an enterprise.[2] In the one-person library the service provided (e.g. research guidance, finding the right book for a user, quick-answer reference responses) is given on a one-to-one basis between the librarian and the user. Management is seldom involved in services provided by the library, and there is no tangible way to quantify the results that are achieved. There are no productivity standards, no counts (except for *numbers* of books borrowed, questions answered, etc., and these statistics are hardly representative of the bulk of work performed in a library, especially in a one-person library), and the measurement of performance is a subjective experience on the part of those who come into the library. Newman and Wallender also point out that not only is the measurement intuitive, but the people who are judging have varying expectations.[2]

At the same time, what Newman and Wallender call weak 'customer influence' comes into play, for the user leaves with his or her answer, or book, or report, or referral to another library. That user, no matter how grateful he or she might be to the librarian who helped, is highly unlikely to share that gratitude with anyone else, whether management, other users or the man in the street.

Third, Newman and Wallender refer to something they describe as the intrusion of 'resource contributors'. In the one-person library these are users who stand around, read a lot and, when they have time to kill, offer advice or suggestions on library policy and procedures. Even worse, they may be board or committee members or people who make heavy financial contributions, and even though they are not qualified to manage a library, they may think they are.

Finally, Newman and Wallender recognize charismatic leaders and/or the 'mystique' of the enterprise as constraining characteristics on managing. All of us have experienced, especially in smaller organizations, the 'dynamic and forceful individual' who seems to be in charge of the enterprise. The enthusiasm is needed, and can bring many other active and useful people into the organization, but from the professional library manager's point of view it must be weighed against the work that does not get done while dealing with all this enthusiasm.

The mystique Newman and Wallender refer to can be an additional burden in a library, though, conversely, it can be the reason the librarian was drawn to the organization in the first place. A librarian whose personal interest or hobby embraces the subject matter collected in the library can have a fine time at work, but the efficient management of the library is going to be left behind if the 'librarian' is there, as, for example, in a church library, to use the collection for writing inspirational novels and not to care for the collection. When this mystique is coupled with that aura that surrounds libraries in general, that 'good feeling' that many laymen have about libraries and books, the one-person librarian may very well find himself working in a situation akin to working in a sanctified place. The librarian must recognize that such a situation is not really part of the professional library world and should not be passed off as such. As Newman and Wallender state: 'Once established, the mystique defines a respected role in society. The mystique sets the character and values decision-makers are expected to follow.'[2] It is easy to get too wrapped up in the ambience of one's job and forget about efficient management. The solution to the problem is to be found in the person who has the job of running the library:

... the critical task is integration. The interests and values of contributors may differ sharply from those of scientists, prima donnas, and doctors who actually create the services of the enterprise ... A special need arises for people in buffer roles, who can relate to both inside and outside groups and can promote agreement on actions to be taken. This integrating task is especially difficult in enterprises where the service is intangible and the objectives are multiple and shifting.[2]

In the one-person library the librarian can be the integrator, if he is willing to take on such a challenge as part of the operation of the library.

## The budgeting process

Sylvia Webb poses a fundamental question that must be answered before we can begin to define budgets and describe the budgeting procedure: 'Was or is there a separate budget; who has overall responsibility for it?'[3] In the one-person library the librarian must determine who provides funding for the library and if the librarian is to have any input into the funding decisions. If the library is part of a corporate parent organization, funding decisions may very well not be made with the librarian's advice. On the other hand, in a small public library or historical society the librarian may be the only person who is in a position to know how much is to be spent in the library for its operations and services. In either case, it is important for the librarian to know how much influence he is to have in the budget procedure, and to plan how to use that influence to the best advantage.

Budgets are defined in different ways by different people, and many library management experts have tried to come up with a workable definition. Evans, in *Management Techniques for Librarians*, says that budgets are

... simply plans of action expressed in terms of cost. These costs may be dollars or man-hours, or machine-hours, or some combination of these factors. They do not have to be stated in dollars and cents. *Budgets are estimates of what management thinks it will cost to carry out a plan of operation for the organization during a specified period of time* [emphasis added].[4]

Sinclair, on the other hand, speaking of small public libraries, puts the emphasis not on the plan of operation but on the cooperation between the librarian and the board:

'The most important part of library business in which the librarian and board work together is the preparation of the budget. A budget, like much else in library management, is made easier by careful planning. The year's budget might be considered a programme for the coming year's activities with price tags attached to the various items. If librarian and trustees are agreed on objectives and have worked out together a long-range plan for library development, preparation of a budget becomes a matter of determining how much of the programme can be attempted in any particular year in light of current costs and local financial conditions. If the long-range plan has been approved in principle by the appropriating or taxing body or by planning officials, as well as by the library board, preparing the budget and securing approval become even simpler.[5]

Blagden, writing on financial management in Aslib's *Handbook of Special Librarianship and Information Work*, defines a budget as

... The mechanism by which funds are granted ... In putting forward proposals for funding it is, of course, important to spell out the overall role of the library and information service in supporting the goals of the host organization, and to specify in some detail exactly how this role will be translated into practice.[6]

When we turn from the strictly library considerations we find that the definitions and procedures are not much different. Gross and Warshauer, accountants writing for non-profit organizations, offer these basic steps:

1. A list of objectives or goals of the organization for the following year should be prepared. For many organizations this process will be essentially a re-evaluation of the relative priority of the existing programs. Care should be taken, however, to avoid concluding too hastily that an existing program should continue unchanged. Our society is not static and the organization that does not constantly re-evaluate and update its programs is in danger of being left behind.
2. The cost of each objective or goal listed above should be estimated. For continuing programs, last year's actual expense and last year's budget will be the starting point. For new programs or modifications of existing programs, a substantial amount of work may be necessary to accurately estimate the costs involved. This estimating process should be done in detail since elements of a particular goal or objective may involve many categories of expenses and salaries.
3. The expected income of an organization should be estimated ... Organizations are often overly optimistic in estimating income. This can prove to be the organization's downfall if there is no margin for error, and realism must be used or the budget will have little meaning.
4. The total expected income should be compared to the expense of achieving the objectives or goals.
5. The final proposed budget should be submitted to the appropriate body for ratification ... This should not be just a formality but should be carefully presented to the ratifying body so that, once ratified, all persons will be firmly committed to the resulting plan of action.[7]

As Gross and Warshauer emphasize, these steps may seem so elementary that to repeat them is unnecessary, but experience shows that many one-person librarians do not give the budget process the time and consideration it requires. It is not a matter of choice: either the steps are taken or the library budget is not properly prepared.

The obvious theme running through these definitions, regardless of emphasis, as well as in all other approaches to budgeting procedures, is the concept of planning. Yet planning is a time-consuming activity, and the one-person librarian is often constrained by lack of time, so the prospect of setting aside time to plan the library's activities and to include in this planning a study of costs and available funding is often daunting. Yet Evans offers good reasons why we must include time for planning in our work schedules:

1. Planning conserves time, a critical factor in any organization. Developing workable plans requires a great deal of time and effort. Carrying out activities also requires a great deal of time. Employees at all levels are confronted with a dilemma – how to find time to carry out the duties required and still have time to plan. Something always seems to be shortchanged in the pressure to do everything. Sometimes there are too many things to do and too few people. More often, however, it comes back to a problem of poor planning. If intelligent plans are drawn up at the outset, taking into account the resources available, there will be time to plan. Time for planning will have been included in the original plan because it is so critical for continued success.

2. Planning is the only way to combat uncertainty and accommodate environmental changes. Some managers, and many librarians, are willing to sit back and wait for lightning to strike before they make any move . . . When supervisors do not examine their operations, and do not plan for some of the more obvious adverse situations that could develop, they will spend too much time dealing with little problems. Work flow may be efficient as the time procedures are set up, but as time goes on the efficiency may fall off because of changing needs.

3. Planning focuses attention on organization objectives. Even when planning is poorly done, it cannot be carried out without some consideration of basic objectives . . . In many organizations the real objectives of the organization are lost in the haste to do 'the real work' – the day-to-day procedures that are easily understood and rather easily performed. Staff members may begin to resist the need to go back to and examine objectives, because they feel this interferes with the real purposes and function that they perform.

4. Planning is a critical element in gaining an economical, efficient operation. Planning as a procedure-formulation activity requires consideration of the efficiency and consistency with which work is being performed. It directs the efforts of the organization to achieve a coordinated work flow, and it helps to reduce the number of snap judgments that are made.

5. Planning is a major factor in the control of the organization. Plans provide the standards by which to measure performance, to ensure that the organization is going in the direction that it is supposed to be going.[8]

Thus we begin by going back to basics: what is my library supposed to be doing? According to Murray S. Martin, who edited *Financial Planning for*

*Libraries,* libraries must 'return to their basic role – the collection and organization of information'.[9] This requires that each one-person librarian plan his budget in terms of the library's role in the parent institution, how it is expected to perform that role and how much it costs to perform that role. If we are doing things in the library that are not part of that mission, perhaps we need to stop and question if they should be paid for from library funds. Martin then suggests that we reassess the role of libraries within the professional world, recognizing that the publishing world is changing (and with it the library world), so part of our request for materials must include funding for non-traditional expenditures such as increased interlibrary loans, online services, free or inexpensive copying facilities, contracted services, etc. Finally, as Martin says, we must place our money 'where it is most needed'.[10] This means that we must first fund the essential services and projects, and we must question, coldly and unemotionally, services and projects that are marginal (even if they are our favourites).

In Martin's book on the subject, Harold R. Jenkins has written a piece advocating an 'umbrella' concept for public libraries that can be applied to one-person library operations. Jenkins is an optimist, who takes a positive attitude to budgeting, and suggests an approach which 'covers planning, controlling, organizing and detailing each projected step of a contemplated action leading to a specific objective. Obviously budgeting should not be seen as an unwelcome constraint but rather as a welcomed opportunity to see one's way into the future.'[11] Can this optimistic approach work in the one-person library? Yes, if the one-person librarian is willing to take planning and budgeting work seriously. It is not easy, especially in organizations where the library is considered unimportant by management and supervisory personnel, but if the librarian is willing to take on the extra challenge of proving to management that the library is a serious part of the organization, educating and stimulating those people to see the library as the serious and responsible part of the organization that it is, the extra time and effort will not have been wasted. Various types of budgets are recognized for library work. The most commonly accepted is the line or formula budget, which, as Evans points out, usually means operating expenses,[12] although the line budget also includes another category – capital expense or capital outlay. The operating expense usually covers, according to Evans, the following items:

(1) Books and materials, 20-30 per cent.
(2) Salaries, 60-70 per cent.
(3) Utilities, 1-2 per cent (if included).
(4) Maintenance, 4-5 per cent (if included).
(5) Supplies, 4-5 per cent.
(6) Travel, 1-2 per cent.
(7) Insurance, 1-2 per cent (if included).

Other types of budgets include the performance budget, which Evans describes as 'based on functions, activities, and projects ... a financial plan prepared, analysed, and interpreted in terms of the services and activities themselves', and which he applies to library work by pointing out that the

> ... ultimate objective of a library is to provide service. The library's profit is thought of in terms of the degree to which its services are used and the satisfaction derived by the patron. Thus, the budget, which explains expenditures in terms of accomplishments and results rather than strictly in terms of objects, can be very useful because it is oriented toward the real goals of the library.[13]

Performance budgeting, while beneficial in many respects, does present some problems. According to Blagden in the Aslib *Handbook*, there are two: the performance budget 'can be a very time-consuming exercise and some of the decisions regarding the allocation of costs to different services will be done on a somewhat arbitrary basis'.[14] Thus we have a classic conflict for the one-person librarian, who would like to use the budgeting procedure which would most accurately reflect the work done in the library but, unfortunately, is limited by the very same restrictions which Blagden describes.

There have been attempts to determine just how much it should cost an organization to support a library. Ashworth suggests the following formula:

> The cost of running a special library is a matter of extreme variability in practice. Managements should not think of allocating less than one fiftieth of their total research budget to the library; and for the fullest service, covering every type of information dissemination, at least one thirtieth to one twentieth should be the aim. The latter figure would be for smaller organizations, as there is a minimum size of library which would be viable to support an innovative team. For this a moderate collection of textbooks (say 5000 volumes), a small intensively selected reference stock (200 volumes), and at least 200 current periodicals, amongst which would be sets of relevant abstract journals, would be essential stock. This would be supported by pamphlets, patents, reports, standard specifications, etc., as appropriate. Such a library could be maintained by one person, though the addition of more staff would be highly desirable – and essential as soon as the library increased appreciably beyond the minimum size.[15]

It was Gordon E. Randall who put into perspective the various components of the budget for the special library. Budget construction, for Randall, consists of three major parts: salaries, book costs and subscription costs, and the minor budget items of binding, supplies and travel.[16] Randall quotes Ruth Leonard in suggesting that salaries should range between 50 per cent and 70 per cent of the total budget, a range that Randall suggests is justified because 'the demands placed on the library staff vary depending on the disciplines to which the library users belong, the nature of the information requirements of the users, their geographic dispersion in relation to the library, and the service traditions of the installation'.[16] Randall's two guidelines for determining book costs can be quoted directly:

> For each library borrower, the library should plan on having to acquire two to three books per year. A more logically derived number can be obtained by determining the number required to keep the book collection on the current side of obsolescence . . . In an established collection it is necessary to replace 10% of the book collection each year if the average age of the titles is to be less than ten years old.'[16]

Obviously, the type of collection and the use to which the materials are put will seriously affect the formulae; a library in a historical society is not necessarily going to replace books at such a high rate, and a library in a technological organization is going to replace books more quickly, in addition to reports, journals, etc., which will probably take up more of the collection. Certainly each one-person librarian is going to have to study the situation in his particular library and make budget decisions accordingly.

The costs for periodicals, as Randall points out, are difficult to predict, although there are some guidelines (he suggests 1.5 to 2 subscriptions per borrower[16]). These figures are complicated today by the availability of much periodical and report material on-line, so that while budgets must include the costs of subscribing to the particular utility or utilities needed in the library, the number of journal subscriptions will vary with the kind of institution served by the library.

Randall reports that binding should be equivalent to '80–150% of the titles on the subscription list'.[16] Supplies are purchased based on what understanding is operative with the corporate or institutional supply department and how much material specifically needed for the library will be purchased from other sources. Travel expenses cannot be generalized, but the practising professional librarian who keeps up with the literature and makes a point of participating in his professional organizations will know in advance approximately how much should be requested for profesional travel, particularly since nowadays most professional organizations schedule their meetings and conferences far in advance.

Finally, there are a few basic tips which should be remembered by the one-person librarian who is contemplating an annual budget proposal. After we have read all the appropriate literature on the subject, after we have had conversations with our users and our supervisors, we might give some thought to the following:

(1) Question *everything*. Before your supervisor or manager asks why something is in the budget, be sure you can justify it yourself (and if you think it can be deleted from the budget, suggest deleting it – do not include it just because 'it has always been there'). Be ruthless.
(2) Be realistic, and be attuned to what is going on in the parent institution. If this is the year that profits or income are down, do not ask for funding for a marginal item.

(3) On the other hand, do not restrict your planning to available income. If the item is important enough – and if you do a proper job of recognizing and reporting its need – management just might find the money for it.

(4) The library is a business. We must employ the same procedures regarding hours of service, staff involvement, purchasing, user relations and cost effectiveness that we would employ if our users were purchasing – for an established price – the services we give them for free (after all, *somebody* - - town citizens, corporate headquarters, university administration – is paying for these services; the difference is that we do not see the money directly).

(5) Keep it simple. As we have said before, try to eliminate the layers. If we simply think of budgeting as using our available funds to best advantage we can cut through a lot of the rhetoric.

(6) Look for substitutes. If there is a cheaper way of doing something, try it. Leasing equipment, for example, can be cheaper in the long run because you are not trying to get service or parts for obsolete machinery. Similarly, using a periodicals agency, even for a small list, saves time. Look for short cuts.

(7) Proselytize. Be political. There is nothing secret about the budget (or there should not be), so if you need to speak with someone about it, go ahead. If there is a user who can be helpful, seek his help. Management might well approve a microfilm reader-printer if the users have made it known that they need one. Have some of them write letters. Your library can use its supporters. If people write fan letters to you, write back and ask them if they would be willing to help you seek additional funding for the library.

(8) Finally: Read. Listen. Learn. If you know a manager (or another librarian) who is especially skilled in budget work, get to know him or her better to learn what contributes to that department's success. Look for budget articles in the professional media. If you don't have extensive accounting background, seek out books like G. Stevenson Smith's *Accounting for Librarians and Other Not-for-Profit Managers*.[17] Another useful title is the previously cited *Financial and Accounting Guide for Nonprofit Organizations*, by Malvern J. Gross, Jr., and William Warshauer, Jr.[7]

The budgeting procedure does not have to be the negative practice it is for some librarians. For the one-person librarian, it can be an opportunity to plan for the year ahead as well as opportunity to promote a positive relationship with management and supervisory personnel, who can be educated to see the library as the serious and responsible part of the parent organization that it is. At the same time, perhaps in connection with the preparation of the library annual report, the preparation of the library budget documentation can be an excellent opportunity for the librarian to review his work of the past year and to anticipate what is to be achieved in the next.

# References

1   Echelman, Shirley, 'Libraries are businesses, too', *Special Libraries*, **65**, October/November, 411, 1974.

2   Newman, William H. and Wallender, Harvey W., 'Managing not-for-profit enterprises', *Academy of Management Review*, **3**, 1, 24-31, 1978.

3   Webb, Sylvia P., *Creating an Information Service*, Aslib, London, 1983, p. 10.

4   Evans, G. Edward, *Management Techniques for Librarians*, Academic Press, New York, 1976, p. 100.

5   Sinclair, Dorothy, *The Administration of the Small Public Library*, American Library Association, Chicago, 1979, p. 60.

6   Blagden, J., 'Financial management', in Anthony, L. J. (ed.), *Handbook of Special Librarianship and Information Work*, Aslib, 1982, p. 55.

7   Gross, Malvern J. and Warshauer, William, Jr, *Financial and Accounting Guide for Nonprofit Organizations*, John Wiley and Sons, New York, 1979, pp. 316-317.

8   Evans, op. cit., pp. 101-103.

9   Martin, Murray S. (ed.), *Financial Planning for Libraries*, The Haworth Press, New York, 1983, p. 4.

10   Ibid., p. 5.

11   Jenkins, Harold S., 'Returning to the unified theory of budgeting: an umbrella concept for public libraries', in Martin, op. cit., p. 75.

12   Evans, op. cit, p. 226.

13   Ibid., p. 227.

14   Blagden, op. cit, p. 63.

15   Ashworth, Wilfred, *Special Librarianship*, Outlines of Modern Librarianship, Clive Bingley, London, 1979.

16   Randall, Gordon E., 'Budgeting for libraries', *Special Libraries*, **67**, January, 8-12, 1976.

17   Smith, Stevenson G. *Accounting for Librarians and Other Not-for-Profit Managers*, American Library Association, Chicago, 1983.

# The library office

In this chapter we will discuss two related subjects: office tasks and procedures, and planning the library layout to facilitate those routines.

## Procedures

The secret of success in any office is the establishment of procedures. Most librarians with graduate training are not experienced in or taught office procedures, and many come to the one-person library situation lacking what in many offices would be considered basic training. Obviously, many procedures which necessitate specific forms and files will be dictated to the librarian because of the requirements of the governing or legal authority which has responsibility for the administration of the library. Many others, however, will be created by the librarian. This is especially true for the one-person librarian, who often does not have a procedures manual simply because no-one has ever put one together. Whether we write them down or not, though, we are following procedures all the time, and it is wise to create a manual or at least the beginnings of one. There are various reasons for this, the primary one being that the same librarian is not always the person running the library. Also, once a decision has been made to do a task in a particular way, it is not always easy to recall the procedure, or the reasons for the decision, if the task does not come up again for a while.

Though she was writing specifically for the librarian or information officer engaged in setting up a new facility, what Sylvia Webb has to say can be of benefit, especially to librarians working in one-person situations, who have some difficulty with the requirements of paperwork and administrative record keeping:

Administrative procedures and records are viewed by some as necessary evils to be put to one side for as long as possible. Why not reverse that and set them up so that they work for you? They can be seen as positive assets and provide ways of finding required information in the shortest possible time. They are your means of cutting through the necessary and ongoing administration which accompanies the setting up and running of an information service.

There are two basic rules to be observed when setting up procedures. The first is to keep a written note of each procedure for future reference; and the second is to keep all procedures simple. Simplicity is most important from the point of view of the initial time and effort involved in setting up the procedure, and that involved in its ongoing use. It will also enable future modifications to take place easily as the service develops and changes are required.[1]

Accounting procedures for the one-person librarian are fairly basic and will be determined, in large part, by the accounting requirements of the parent organization. Some organizations will give the librarian almost absolute power over the expenditure of library funds, with an annual audit, while other firms and institutions will require that each purchase order be approved by a supervisor or someone on the management staff. In all cases, good record-keeping is essential. The two basic texts which the librarian in a one-person operation can benefit from using are Gross and Warshauer,[2] for non-profit organizations, and Murray on general financial planning for libraries.

Bookkeeping in the one-person library does not require accounting expertise, but simply calls for knowing what the current status of the library account is. For Gross and Warshauer:

> Bookkeeping is the process of recording in a systematic manner transactions that have taken place. It is that simple. There is nothing mysterious or complicated about bookkeeping. It is simply maintaining records in a manner that will facilitate summarizing them at the end of a period in the form of financial statements. For small cash basis organizations there is little need to know a great deal about accounting theory. Common sense will dictate the records that must be kept.

In the one-person library, even simple bookkeeping is one of those tasks which usually fall into the category of 'when I get round to it'. The successful one-person librarian will set aside a particular time near the end of each reporting period to gather together the invoices (which have been filed in one particular place as they come in), payment vouchers (or the cheque book, if he or she pays the bills directly instead of sending them to an accounting office for payment), cash receipts and any other documentation. Being systematic is vital, for the task cannot be undertaken in a haphazard manner, and the materials must be easily accessible. Gross and Warshauer contend, correctly, that book-keeping is simply common sense, and that 'anyone can devise a simple book-keeping system that will meet the needs of a small, cash-basis organization'.[2] We do this with our personal finances and most of us are not even aware that we have set up a 'bookkeeping' system. Certainly the one-person library employee can do the same at the office; it is simply a question of taking the task seriously, setting aside a particular time for it and, often enough, overcoming a negative attitude toward it. Many people, especially those who work alone, tend to dismiss accounting with remarks such as 'I never was able to handle money', which is really an excuse for avoiding a task that is perceived to be difficult and time-consuming. In the one-person library, handling the daily finances is simple as long as it is done in a systematic manner. The rewards of doing it on regular basis are two-fold: the librarian who keeps the books has a better grasp of the library's finances and, more important, has control of how and when the money is spent. Control, according to Diane Cole Eckels in her essay on the special librarian as manager, is

> ... the primary concern in the execution of the budget ... Accountability in managing the fiscal resources allocated to the library is the focus of this part of the budgeting cycle. Periodic financial reports should indicate where to cut back spending if necessary. The flexibility allowed in spending depends upon the authority granted the librarian,[4]

It must be noted that while many one-person librarians do not have the authority to make major spending decisions, periodic financial statements give the librarian control over what can and cannot be recommended to the management personnel with the authority for spending. Financial statements reflect trends, both short-term and long-term, and the librarian who knows how to read statements – who, in fact, contributes the information that is included in them and who does it in a systematic manner – is the librarian who is in control of planning for his library.

Gross and Warshauer record only three steps involved in bookkeeping for a small cash-basis organization, and they are worthy of inclusion here:

> 1. Recording each transaction in a systematic manner when it occurs. In a simple cash basis system only cash transactions are recorded. This recording could be on the checkbook stub or, for organizations with many transactions, it might be an entry in either the 'cash disbursement record' or the 'cash receipts record' ...
> 2. Summarizing transactions so that all 'like' transactions are grouped together. This summarizing can be informally done on a simple columnar worksheet, or it can be more formally handled in a system in which transactions are posted to a formal book called the 'general ledger.' In either case, the objective is to bring 'like' transactions together.
> 3. Preparing financial statements from the 'summary' prepared in step 2. These financial statements can be a simple listing of all the major categories in the summary or they can involve some re-arrangement of the figures into a more meaningful presentation. In either case, the financial statements are the end product of the financial system.[2]

The librarian who works alone will find that following these simple steps will put him in the position of knowing what is going on with the library's funds at just about any given time, and will, in the long run, make the management of the library easier. We have already mentioned that a distinction between clerical and professional tasks in a one-person library is not possible, and the daily routines must be handled on a daily basis. One of the great temptations of working alone is to put off for a day or so those routine or administrative tasks which should be done every day, but in most cases these are exactly the kinds of tasks which pile up and which, before too much time goes by, require a major effort to complete. One of the essentials of good time-management is the early and quick completion of routine 'housekeeping' duties each day. Good time-management also means making sure that the proper tools and equipment are available; the loss of time in searching out needed forms or tools make a routine job much more expensive than it need be. Keep a checklist or inventory of necessary equipment and supplies and set aside a certain amount of time each week to see that all is in order.

Creating a good public image is also part of the librarian's job. Although formal stationery and notepaper will probably be provided by the parent organization, the library should have its own stationery as well, or at least an adaptation of the organization's stationery, with reference to the library and the proper telephone number. It need not be expensive to create good-looking notepaper and other library forms in-house. To send out messages written on scrappy pieces of paper creates an image of equally scrappy service. Handwritten formal correspondence gives the same amateurish impression. After all, the managing director or the general manager do not do it, so why should the librarian? If you have a printing or audio-visual department within the organization it can produce such items as compliments slips, reminder letters and similar informal forms on the standard stationery used by the parent organization. Special library forms can be ordered from various library supply houses, and all supply houses offer materials which can be customized with the library's name and other pertinent information.

As we have said before, outside jobbers and agencies expedite some of the more time-consuming library activities. The two most popular examples are jobbers for providing books and agents for providing magazines. There are two major factors to be considered when dealing with book jobbers, and both have to do with their efficiency. First, they provide fast delivery. In a larger bureaucratic library, users will grudgingly accept the excuse that 'the book has not come yet', but in the one-person library the success of the operation is based as much on the perception of the service as on the service itself, and the first place a library is judged is in its responsiveness to the needs of its users. There may be cases where the librarian who works alone will pay a little more than the price offered by one of the major book jobbers simply to get the materials faster. In the long run it is worth it. Second, will they accept telephone orders? Many requests for new materials can be better filled if they can be ordered when needed rather than waiting until the standard time for sending in an order.

Using an agency for obtaining magazines and other periodicals is slightly different, for in this case the library will probably not obtain a discount but will pay a little more for the service than the actual price of the subscriptions. The service is well worth the cost, however, especially for one-person libraries, since this allows the librarian to make out an annual list and submit one invoice for payment instead of handling a separate file for each individual title. While this seems obvious, there are managements which discourage using periodicals agencies because of reported problems in subscription fulfilment, missing issues, etc., but the conscientious librarian can set up a procedure, as part of the regular check-in routine, which enables him or her to know when a title is missing or not received, and the agency can be notified. In the long run, using the periodical agency is well worth the extra cost.

The repair and care of books and other library materials is best left to someone other than the librarian, but in a one-person situation the librarian is going to be expected to know how to handle minor tears, loose or broken spines and similar minor problems. Of course, any serious repairs and binding will be done outside, probably through the use of a commercial binder for such things as the repair of current books and the binding of periodicals, and through the use of a local conservator-bookbinder for valuable items. For routine repairs, however, the librarian would do well to spend a few hours in one of the basic conservation and repair programmes offered from time to time through library schools and museums.

## Layout

Space planning is not always the librarian's privilege but each of us, at some point in our careers, has the chance to renovate or redesign a facility, or install new and different equipment requiring a change in the physical arrangement of the library. Occasionally, the librarian is moved by the parent organization into a new space. When these opportunities come along there are certain choices which must be made.

Aaron Cohen and Elaine Cohen, recognized as authorities in space planning for libraries, suggest that three elements are needed for the successful planning of a library space: the aesthetic, the functional and the behavioural: 'To separate any one of these elements from the others in the various stages can cause a breakdown in usability'.[5] It will be necessary for the librarian to exercise a certain amount of assertiveness here, for as the plans for the project are drawn up, management and designers will tend to 'forget' to seek the opinions of the librarian, and the criteria for decision-making are in danger of being removed from the functional and behavioural. When there is to be a new library facility the librarian should do all he can to be part of the design team, at least as an advisor to that group, so that the functional and behavioural needs of the library and its users will not be lost among the aesthetics. To this end, Cohen and Cohen suggest that the planners, 'beginning with the program stage', consider the following:

1. The program should be followed; the place should ultimately function as expected – within reason. This may sound logical, but it often is not the case in real life . . .
2. The facility should be comfortable – or behaviorally usable – for both users and staff. The users should find the library inviting, of course, but it is not mandatory that the staff be relegated to subterranean spaces and treated as second-class citizens.
3. The facility should be attractive. Although we have complained mightily about aesthetics running rampant, on the other hand, beauty plays a

significant rule in the functioning of a library. A library housed in a structure that is ugly and ill-kept says something about the management and staff, such as disorganization and poor morale.[6]

Setting up a library or information service, hiring a person to manage the service and buying equipment are expensive processes, made even more so by lack of careful planning. Books, journals, furniture, equipment and computers are not cheap, and too many libraries have been set up in the past by managements who have had little idea of what is really involved, leaving the librarian to struggle in an inappropriate environment or without proper managerial support. Working conditions must be pleasant and reasonably comfortable if the output of the staff and the users is to be good. There is nothing worse for efficiency and motivation than cold, draughty, dingy surroundings.

Having said this, and assuming that management has realized the present and future value of the new facility, the first step is to choose a setting for the library. There is, of course, a discrepancy between the ideal and the non-ideal situation, but the one-person librarian will want to try to influence management's decision on the location of the new service. A fairly spacious area is needed, and *not* at the end of a long corridor (forcing staff to walk considerable distances). See that the area is well lit, airy and comfortable. The atmosphere should be neither too hot and dry (sleep-inducing for the staff!) nor cold and damp (bad for the books and the health of the staff!). Temperatures around 20°C (68°F) are about right. If old, valuable books are to be stored these must, of course, be kept in a proper atmospherically controlled space, with a cooler temperature and the correct humidity.

Heating ideally should be the warm-air circulating kind, preferably electric, as gas causes condensation problems. Radiators are a nuisance, as they take up valuable wall space where bookshelves or filing cabinets could be placed. Air conditioning is obviously very desirable not only for comfort for users and staff but also because it reduces dirt and condensation, but many older buildings and office blocks do not have this luxury, especially in the United Kingdom, where the temperate climate makes air conditioning somewhat extraneous. Without air conditioning, cross-ventilation is a necessity.

Lighting is also most important. Daylight, coming over the shoulder for staff sitting at reading tables, is best, but obviously there must be some form of artificial lighting for winter and evenings. Fluorescent lighting is the best as it casts no shadows, but it is tiring for the eyes. Large windows help in this regard, but can cause a greenhouse effect in the summer. Therefore Venetian or vertical linen-strip blinds should be fitted to keep out strong direct sunlight.

Before any shelving and furniture is put in place, consider the flooring. An important point (often taken for granted) is the strength of the floor. Can it support the weight of a large number of shelving units and filing cabinets? Books and journals are very heavy, as every one-person librarian knows who has staggered about under large piles of them. The floor must also be covered with tough carpeting to absorb noise. The carpeting should be strong enough to resist marks from heavy shelving and equipment, and it should also withstand fairly heavy traffic from users and staff. Synthetic carpets can build up static, however, which must be considered if audio-visual and electronic data-processing equipment is to be situated in the area.

There are various types of shelving available for the one-person library. Metal stack shelving, though not as smart looking as wooden shelving, comes cheaper and is easy to install. It comes in standard grey, 36 inches wide and in two heights, 6 feet 3 inches, 7 feet 3 inches (approximately). Two units can be placed back to back where necessary. Shelves are usually a standard 10 inches deep and there are six to a standard unit, and shelving should be adjustable for variations in book size. The advantage of wooden shelving, aside from its aesthetic value, is that it absorbs noise better when shelving books. However, it is considerably more expensive than metal, although the option of acquiring second-hand wooden shelving might be explored.

Get hold of various library suppliers' catalogues and compare what they have to offer in the way of equipment, furniture and shelving. Ask other people in similar libraries, and do not be rushed into hasty buying. The cheapest is not necessarily the best. Remember that the library will be there long after you may be, and though bookstock will be updated regularly, furniture and equipment may not. Shelving should be placed around the walls in well-lit situations with island units – on casters if possible – in central locations. If there are separate windows, shelving can be placed end-on to make the best use of light available. Do not place shelving against the light if at all possible; dingy, badly-lit bookstacks and filing systems are not conducive to browsing. A minimum of 4 feet should be left between bays of shelving to allow two people to browse in comfort. If, for reading purposes, a chair and table are placed between the shelving, the space should be approximately 5 feet 6 inches. This may seem a little generous to some, but cramped, overcrowded conditions are not very comfortable, and it is annoying to users working in the library for others to be continually squeezing past them.

It should be remembered that each shelf should be no more than about two-thirds full, not only to allow for growth of stock but for the books to be easily put away. Bookstock and files should not be squeezed in so tightly that spines are broken and corners become dog-eared. Use a book-end per shelf for support (left to themselves, books tilt and fall over, thus damaging the spines). A standard six-shelf 36-inch-wide unit will therefore take approximately 200 average-size books.

The library should have enough shelf guides to give a reasonable idea of what is where – the sliding metal ones with card inserts on which one may write or type are cheap and cheerful. Some book-ends – usually plastic or metal – have slots for card guides to be slid into place.

Journals should be housed either on a display rack or in boxes on standard shelving, preferably a mixture of both. The more popular journals may be displayed on sloping racks – the current issues on display, with back numbers stored away underneath, available when the shelves are raised and pushed in. If back numbers are to be stored on standard open shelving the library should invest in journal boxes. The folded flat cardboard boxes are cheapest, come in various sizes and can be labelled quite easily. They are also useful for storing items such as government papers in filing cabinet drawers. Plastic journal boxes are better looking and come in a variety of sizes and colours, but are more expensive. They can be colour coded, which is quite useful for stocking back runs of magazines. Journals can, of course, just be stored in piles, but piles of journals inevitably take more room, because they are often in disarray and are not protected from dust and dirt.

Unless the library or information unit is to have very little in the way of conventional bookstock and is to rely on a computer terminal, a library counter is still probably a good investment. It forms a focal point for the room, as well as acting as a useful work surface. The desk of the average one-person librarian is usually far too cluttered to double as a counter, which should be the place where items can be laid out and details taken of books, journals, files, etc., that are to be borrowed. The counter will also have useful shelving space underneath, ideal for timetables, maps and all the other reference materials which often do not come in the form of a book and which need to be referred to quickly. These, like reference books, are kept separate from the bookstock so that some enthusiastic soul does not remove an item just when it may be needed most. Try to put the counter near the door so that clients may walk in and know immediately where to come for help. It will thus act as a useful depository for items returned when the librarian is not around. On the top will go the necessary items of what goes in and out of the area, journal and book cards and call slips housed in trays or desk card boxes, and the date stamp or light pen, or whatever equipment is needed for the circulation of materials. Wooden trays with sprung wooden blocks can be used for filing book cards, and 5×3 inch desk card boxes if one uses the call-slip method.

Another important item is the card catalogue, if one is used. Which type is chosen will depend on the space available, for it can stand on a desk or table top or it can be free-standing. Like shelving, card catalogues are available in wood, and most traditional libraries have them. Metal catalogues are cheaper, but they are not as easy to use and one must beware of sharp corners when filing cards. A card catalogue is still the quickest and easiest method of tracing an item, although microcomputer technology does allow even the one-person librarian to print out a book catalogue with some frequency. Nevertheless, though you may eventually get the data on the cards transferred onto floppy or hard disk, it is still quicker to check in a card catalogue to see if you have a book by a certain author. Thus, when purchasing this important item, allow for expansion and have plenty of spare drawer space for housing such things as the subject index, if a dictionary catalogue is not incorporated into the library's procedures.

The person in charge must have somewhere to sit and work. Purchase as large a desk as you can afford. A one-person librarian needs space for reference books, diary, telephone, typewriter and all the other working paraphernalia. Some one-person library employees hide the telephone, but it is much more convenient on the desk or counter. Fit the desk into an easily seen corner and make sure that your chair is adjustable and ergonomically comfortable – a one-person librarian with backache is not very useful. A swivel chair with an adjustable back is good for typing. Finally, a small filing cabinet should be next to the librarian's desk, if the desk does not have a file-size drawer or two, so the librarian can have at hand materials for continuing projects. Keep the desk top relatively free. A good rule of thumb to *attempt* (but not likely to be consistently realized) is to have on the desk only the materials for one task at a time. Obviously, few one-person librarians are every going to be working on only one task at a time, but the very idea of trying to keep an orderly desk projects a sense of organization and control, not only for the librarian but for users who come in to visit the library.

A few easy chairs should be provided for readers browsing amongst the journals or studying timetables. If they are encouraged to feel comfortable and at home when they visit the library they will make better use of the library and its services. Also, depending on the types of services offered by the library and the number of users, there should be at least one table and chair, with a reading lamp, so that serious readers can come in and work without necessarily taking materials to another office or building. Some seating should also be provided for visitors.

Space must be allotted for special equipment, audio-visual materials and electronic data-processing equipment, and supplies must be provided for. Generally standard library or office-supply vendors have furniture and cabinets for these items. Just be sure, when you are considering adding new equipment, that the library office is properly situated for the additional power supply and other site considerations.

Finally, every library, regardless of the type of service offered, needs a notice board or bulletin board, ideally situated near the entrance, where reminders can be posted for visitors and users alike. This can be one of the library's most successful public relations tools, and should be chosen and kept up with care.

Space planning is not easy for libraries, yet while the librarian may not have design or engineering skills he will know what is needed in the library. Cohen and Cohen explain it clearly:

> Libraries are furniture- and equipment-intensive facilities. The interior design aspects – furniture and equipment layouts, people and material traffic patterns, work flow, lighting, acoustics, and even color – affect how users and staff work in the library. Obviously it is easier to find something in a well organized facility than in a poorly organized one. It is easier to concentrate in a quiet space where the lighting is adequate than in one that is perpetually noisy and dimly lit.[5]

# References

1 Webb, Sylvia P, *Creating an Information Service*, Aslib, London, 1983, p. 24
2 Gross, Malvern J. and Warshauer, William, Jr, *Financial and Accounting Guide for Nonprofit Organizations*, John Wiley and Sons, New York, 1979, p. 469.

3 Ibid.
4 Eckels, Diane Cole, 'The special librarian as manager', in Jackson, E. (ed.), *Special Librarianship: A New Reader*, 1980, p. 168.

5 Cohen, Aaron and Cohen, Elaine, *Designing and Space Planning for Libraries: A Behavioral Guide*, Bowker, New York, 1979, p. 3.
6 Ibid., p. 6.

# Library services

Librarianship is a service profession. As we have said over and over again, the role of the library is to get the information to the user, and whether it comes from a collection managed by a one-person librarian or from another collection or source to which the user is referred, the goal is to provide the services which our users need to meet *their* goals.

What are those services? Actually, the list is not so long, although the specific duties involved in creating and providing those services are numerous, and in the one-person library the numbers seem even greater than they are, simply because all the services are provided by the one employee.

Library services include reference and enquiry work, the lending (and borrowing) of materials and the selective dissemination of information (SDI). SDI entails scanning journals, current awareness, compiling bibliographies and reading lists, abstracting and indexing and, of course, photocopying. Some of these duties have been mentioned briefly in previous chapters, but here we will give a more detailed picture of the skills needed in reference and enquiry work.

## Reference and enquiry work

In his paper on reference and information work Kenneth Whittaker says that the purpose of this work 'is to allow information to flow freely from information sources to those who need information. Without the librarian bringing source and seeker together, the flow would never take place at all, or only take place inefficiently.'[1]

Of all the duties that a librarian or information worker performs, direct personal assistance and help with reference queries are probably the most visible and the most consciously appreciated by a library user. The user may not care about the classification system by which you arrange your books and journals or the system you use for ordering new materials, but he or she does appreciate being helped with a problem or a project. The user appreciates what the library provides, even if that appreciation is not always expressed to you. All librarians should therefore try to guarantee willing and efficient service in this area. If you do, your users will return to make use of the service, and they will also cease to regard the librarian by the unhelpful stereotype of a person too busy and too preoccupied to help.

According to our survey of one-person librarians it does seem that helping readers with their enquiries is one of the librarian's favourite activities. Indeed, Ruth Finer, in her paper on reference and enquiry work, says that this kind of work

> . . . is often considered the jam on the bread and butter of library routines. It is in searching for, identifying and providing the information required by a user that many people who work in special libraries and information units get real job satisfaction. There is something particularly pleasing about using one's skills and experience to supply information that otherwise might not have been traced.'[2]

Obviously, when working in a one-person situation a large proportion of time is spent on this work. Sometimes it seems that there are not enough hours in the day to complete all reference enquiries properly, and it is the constant complaint of one-person librarians that they have to spend perhaps ten minutes on a query when they feel that it actually deserves a much fuller exploration. Frustration results all around. So somehow you must organize your day so that the right amount of time is spent completing each reference query as it comes along. The key to this is, once more, to establish priorities, thus tackling an enquiry step by step so that no valuable clues are missed.

It is a well-known fact that some people are very nervous about approaching a library for information, and that some are equally arrogant and think there is nothing new that a library can tell them. Coupled with that is the attitude of some highly qualified users, especially staff in a corporate or research organization, who think that librarians do not have the technical competence to answer their questions. One-person librarians must overcome these obstacles and impress their personalities on the library service. They learn to be calm, unflappable, firm and pleasant in dealing with their assorted users who seem to range from the barely literate to the know-it-alls. Above all, a good reference and information worker needs informed common sense.

As your user starts to describe the problem, do not assume that what he or she appears to be asking for is what is actually required! If you do, you will have committed a cardinal sin in information work: taking a question at face value. A good reference and information worker will follow with these steps.

First, ascertain who your user is, his or her department or job title and telephone number. You may, of course, be well aware of these facts already, but nevertheless jot them down. If you get many queries in a day you may not be able to remember who asked what. At this point it is probably a good idea to have a printed supply of enquiry cards on hand, stamped with running numbers. If the question sounds as if it is going to turn into a long and complicated enquiry you may prefer to jot all the points down on paper first, and later note the details onto the card to serve as an *aide-mémoire*.

The next thing to do is to listen to what your client has just said and how he or she has framed the enquiry. Occasionally the user is articulate and able to convey exactly what is required, but it is much more likely that the person has had difficulty in framing the question or even coming to the point and being specific enough. Why does this happen? Gerald Jahoda[3] suggests that when an individual recognizes that he or she has an information need, something like four steps – which are all to a certain extent unconscious – go through his or her mind: the information need is present but has not been consciously expressed; there is a vague feeling that he or she should know something; this uneasiness causes a conscious recognition of an information need; and the user will then translate this need into a formal statement. Only then will this be expressed as a query to the librarian or information worker

Sometimes the question is posed at the second stage, before it becomes clear in the user's mind what he or she really wants to ask. This is why so many questions are vague and ill-defined. It is difficult to ask about what you do not know.

There are yet other reasons why a user does not frame his or her questions as well as he or she might:

(1) He does not realize the depth and extent of the literature coverage in the library.
(2) She does not want to be too technical because of a fear that you might not understand.
(3) He feels that the question might be too elementary to bother you with, or if the user is a senior member of the staff, there might be a feeling that it is beneath him to ask what is perceived of as a favour from someone who is not graded as highly as he is.
(4) The matter is highly confidential, and the user is worried about how much information should be disclosed to the librarian.

At this point, the librarian's skill as a communicator should take over. Jahoda suggests that each time a query is received it should be broken down into the 'wanted' descriptor and the 'given' descriptor.[3] For instance, when a user comes in and says 'I'd like some information about pigs' the wanted descriptor is 'information' and the 'given' descriptor is 'pigs'. The question is very broad, so you must narrow it down through further discussion, asking questions to clarify the nature and purpose of your user's query, and at the same time encourage the user to be more forthcoming and express his question in more exact terms. By careful questioning you can begin to get to the specifics. 'I'd like some information about pigs' is delightfully vague. On closer examination, what the user really wants may turn out to be information on pig health, or even a specific disease of pigs. This stage of the reference interview is very important, because if you have a misunderstanding about what is required things can get pretty embarrassing, or at least frustrating.

As you talk, note the points down on your reference enquiry card. At this stage, do not feel foolish about asking the user to spell out any difficult technical words or jargon which he may be using, or to repeat facts, especially if you are on the telephone. Do not make assumptions – an enquiry about 'china' could be about the country or a request for details on pottery. Also, ask the reader to explain any technical points which you do not understand. We cannot be experts in all things, and no user minds enlarging a little on his subject. If your user really is in too much of a hurry to elucidate, then look up the details in an encyclopedia afterwards and proceed from there, referring back to the user to make sure that you are on the right track.

The next step is to decide what category of enquiry the question falls into. In the reference and information world, queries usually fall into four types:

(1) *Administrative directive enquiries.* 'Can I borrow a pencil?' 'What time is it?' 'Do you have a train timetable?' 'Where is the bathroom?' This type of query scarcely needs to be answered by a qualified librarian, but all librarians are frequently asked these things and one must deal with them politely and patiently.

(2) *Author and title enquiries.* Here, the user is seeking a particular work, which is why proper title and author entries are so important in the catalogue. With good guidance the user should be able to find what is wanted by herself. However, when she cannot be specific enough, or when the author or title is not known, she may come to you and ask for 'a French-English dictionary' or 'a map of Paris' or 'the article in the *Financial Times* last week about the merger of company X with company Y'. Here is where a detailed knowledge of the holdings of the library joins with specific bibliographic training to help the librarian, especially when you get an enquiry about the 'government report on non-departmental government bodies'.

(3) *Fact-finding enquiries.* Sometimes known as quick-reference or ready-reference queries, these require a limited amount of help in that once the answer is found the user does not require anything more. Nevertheless, the librarian should be no less sympathetic to questions of this sort, as statistically they form the bulk of questions received in libraries of all kinds. All that the user wants is an unambiguous factual answer, but he will be delighted if you can give it quickly and efficiently. However, remember one golden rule here: do not attempt to answer such questions off the top of your head. The temptation is great, if you know the answer, to impress the user, and it is easier and faster. But if you should blurt out a quick answer and it turns out that you were wrong, even with the best intentions in the world, you will find yourself in a highly embarrassing position. Always check the facts in an appropriate reference book. Memories can be hazy, and if you send someone away with the wrong information you will lose not one but several users. The grapevine is notoriously effective in spreading the word about 'the mistake in the library'.

(4) *Material-finding enquiries.* Often known as 'subject' queries, these are much more open-ended in nature. Examples could be 'What is the difference between management and administration?' or 'What do you have on growth deformities in cattle?' or 'What has been written on artificial insemination in sheep?' Thus what the library users require here is a range of information on the topic they have chosen. Small technical and business libraries run by one person get many queries of this type, and there is a lot of work that goes into answering them. In such cases different users may require different answers to the same questions. For instance, one member

of the staff, new to the subject, may only require one or two well-written but fairly elementary articles on a topic to start him off, whereas another may want a detailed search, sometimes online, in order to determine exactly what has been written on a topic before he begins further research on it.

You, as the librarian, can ascertain how far your reader wishes to investigate her topic only by careful questioning, and by observing her reactions. Here, careful judgement is necessary, and this comes with experience. You soon learn when not to inundate users with information and when to instigate a very detailed search. Tact and sensitivity are the watchwords here, and you will learn from experience when to bring a search to a conclusion. The user may have to accept an answer which is not quite in the form that she expected. This is often the case with statistical questions when the answer will not be quite as exact or up-to-date as expected. However, the response, in all cases, must be the best that can be provided by your particular library.

Denis Grogan suggests that there is a fifth category, what he calls a *mutable enquiry*.[4] This type of query suddenly changes its nature during the course of its investigation. So an apparently simple query such as 'Can you get hold of a copy of *Dairyman's Monthly*? may cause problems when it is discovered that there is no such title in existence. You will therefore have to refer back to the user with a complete list of titles of journals on dairy farming, from *Ulrich's*, say, and let him decide, perhaps with a little prodding, what it is that he really wants to see. Users are frequently vague about these things, often listening to radio programmes with half an ear, or hastily scanning journals, all the while thinking that they have a clear picture of what they have taken in. Things can be even more vague if a colleague has passed on the information over lunch. Again, tact and patience are the key.

Unless it is part of the job description the one-person librarian draws the line at original research and investigation. This is the job of the research worker, whom the librarian more often serves, and as much as it would present a great challenge to work on this type of project, you would find yourself doing what someone else in the organization is paid to do. It is the librarian's job to make their work easier by carrying out searches, etc., but coming up with actual ideas and projects is for other staff.

Then there are the unanswerable questions, such as 'Does God exist?' or 'What will happen if I fall into a black hole?' These cannot be answered from the existing literature. It is surprising to find, too, that dates of birth for many famous people are uncertain, and that facts on certain topics have just never been gathered together. So what at first may seem like a simple question may be unanswerable. Further searching will prove fruitless, and the user must be told as tactfully as possible.

Having sorted out what type of question we think the reader is asking we now have to ask ourselves the following:

(1) Is this a real question?
(2) Is the subject recognized?
(3) Is the query unambiguous and complete?

(4) Is the amount of information wanted specified?
(5) Is the level of answer specified?
(6) Are there potential constraints of language, time period, place or type of publication?
(7) Is the question answerable in the time available?
(8) Does the query contain inaccuracies?
(9) Is there an acceptable answer in the literature?

Once you have sorted out all this, and have asked your user to clarify any points which you are not sure of, you are ready to start the investigation proper. One very important point to remember at this stage is to ask the user if he has already consulted any sources before coming to you. This will save time and trouble. At this point, certain skills come into play: the ability to know where to start looking for information, based on knowledge of reference books, bibliographies, etc., and personal attributes such as tact, sympathy, intuition, resourcefulness and confidence in your ability to handle the query. These cannot be stressed too much when undertaking reference work. The good reference and information worker has put himself in the shoes of the person whom he is trying to help, and often almost has to do the thinking for the user. It is even more important to conduct this reference enquiry in full if the question posed needs to be answered by an online research. These searches are expensive to conduct, and you therefore need to use your connect time effectively. If logic is not applied to your search technique there will be many 'false drops' and references thrown up which are useless to the question being asked. Proceed from the general to the specific and from the most recent literature backwards.

The second and third types of enquiry can usually be answered from a core collection of reference works such as dictionaries, yearbooks, directories of associations, bibliographies, such standard reference books as the *World Almanac, Whitaker's Almanac* and *Statesman's Yearbook*, and, of course, from your own catalogue. You will also have other specialist works according to the subject coverage of your particular library. If you need to know more about the workings of Parliament and government information in the United Kingdom then *Parliament and Information* by Dermot Englefield[5] should be in your collection, as this gives an excellent overall picture of what goes on in the various libraries sited in the Houses of Parliament, how the various standing committees work, and the information needs of Members of Parliament as well as those of all the many bodies and businesses outside Parliament which report information. It also gives an excellent description of the workings of the House of Commons and the House of Lords, and a list of books and journals about Parliament and parliamentary publications. Because the workings of the British government are a mystery to the average member of the public (and to the average librarian!), this book goes a long way towards dispelling some of the mystique. More information can be found in the quarterly publication by Vachers and in the annual *Civil Service List*. We mention these publications because questions about government procedure and publications are often difficult to answer and can cause more problems than any other type of reference question.

As we have suggested, the fourth type of reference enquiry, the subject enquiry, needs more effort. Supposing, therefore, that your enquirer wants some information on a specific disease of pigs. You learn that he has not tried any previous sources and so you will commence from 'square one'. It is worthwhile at this point to check in any good, standard, up-to-date work on pig husbandry as a starting point. This may be all the user wants. However, in the case of a technical expert this is unlikely – she probably already knows the symptoms of the disease and actually wants to find out what, if anything, has been written on its diagnosis and cure. Again, you can only discover by careful questioning whether she wants to be more specific. Having done this, you will need to start searching journal indexes and abstracts either manually or online. Here again, the method depends on the types of journals taken in your library, and whether the articles contained in these are sufficiently in-depth for her needs.

If you have good indexes to your journals, and are aware of some likely sources, an online search may need to be constructed, and will certainly be more cost-effective than a protracted manual search. In an online search you can work faster by combining the various key-words exactly in the way needed by the searcher. Only experience will tell which method is best. If you are not online but suspect that this type of search would be useful, there are various bodies which will do a quick, reasonably priced search for you. Some of these are the Online Information Centre at ASLIB, the Science Reference Library in Holborn (London), the Commonwealth Agricultural Bureau at Farnham, Surrey, and, as discussed later, international commercial search firms such as Information on Demand and FIND/SVP.

Another point to remember is to ask your reader 'How urgent is URGENT?' or, in the United States, 'Do you really mean RUSH?' Different people have different ideas of what the terms mean. You may have to stop everything to do this search, or you may have a day or so. If, however, he says, 'Oh, there's no hurry,' still make an attempt to get the information as quickly as possible. Not only does it get the job out of the way, a fast response demonstrates that you are efficient. Users are impressed by this, even if they do not need the information immediately. Grading enquiries helps you get the 'urgent' requests out of the way first.

Having ascertained that your reader may need his information fairly promptly – if not yesterday! – you can complete the search by whatever method is the most cost-effective. If the question is of the 'quick reference' type you will likely have done it on the spot. If it is a subject request he will have left the matter with you to deal with, and only expect you to refer back if the search throws up something which you are uncertain about. This can happen when a query becomes 'mutable'. Keep in mind also that you need to know if the user is going to be satisfied with a stack of photocopied articles thrown up by the search or if a state-of-the-art report is expected. Would the user be satisfied with an up-to-date technical book on the subject or does she want you to search conference proceedings, theses, 'grey literature', etc.? Remember, if your search comes through online you will have to consult it to attempt to sort out the likely articles and reviews, especially if they are not contained in your own library's holdings. Sometimes titles of articles can be very deceptive, and it is here that you need to develop good search techniques. Other indexes may need to be searched on microfiche and the original articles obtained 'blind', which can pose the same problems.

At this stage you must approach your user for some feedback. Gather the results of your labours, be they a simple address or telephone number, a section from a book, a print-off from an online search, a collection of photocopied journal articles, a patent search or a complete compilation consisting of several sources from abstracts, grey literature or whatever, and discuss your findings with your user. You may have given her exactly the results she requires, you may need to search further, or you might, by producing an item of which she was not aware, start off another chain of thought. Serendipity plays no small part, especially in the work of a researcher. Remember that information often has to be re-packaged in a form which can be quickly digested by a busy user. In nearly every case, information found by the librarian has to be manipulated into the form required by the user, and some findings have to be discarded as irrelevant.

When the enquiry has been completed you can finish writing it up on your query card, with details of the steps necessary, the results and the time it took to complete the work. The card can then be filed in running number order, and will not only provide you with useful statistics for your annual report but will serve as a record should you receive a similar query again. In fact, a box of these cards is a useful weapon in proving to management that your time is well spent. Any query can be noted on the cards, from a simple 'author and title' to 'Impossible!' Use them also for interlibrary loans and requests for items from your monthly bulletins and accessions lists. The cards can also be used to record hard-to-find addresses until you find time to transfer them to your address files, and also form a record for the number of online searches which you may perform, or give details of how often you use online services to answer a query. The card file is also useful for sorting out the number of 'quick-answer' reference queries, which shows you how much time is spent on more in-depth enquiries. If you need to do much photocopying you can make a note on the cards. In other words, if you make the cards work for you, you will give yourself the statistical information you require to evaluate how your library is being used.

In discussing reference work we must not lose sight of the 'referral' aspect of library work. The librarian in a one-person library may know of a library or other outside source which might be able to provide the information on a topic which is not covered in his or her library. In fact, it has been said that an information service could be run with just a telephone and the local telephone directories. Naturally, they are more useful in the hands of a skilled librarian. However, when your own sources do not cover a particular topic it is the moment to refer your user to another source, or to contact that source personally if you are not too pressed for time.

# Lending materials

Another service provided in practically all one-person libraries is the circulation of materials for use away from the library. It is a good idea when working in a one-person library to keep the charging methods simple, and to allow readers a reasonable reading time so that you do not constantly have to be sending overdue notices. About one month seems reasonable but each library's clientele is different, and for some one month may be too long for a book or other material to be kept from other users. If a user is working on a special project the loaned material could be put on long loan (say, six months), with the proviso that if anyone requests any of the material it must be returned to the library when the borrower is notified. If accurate circulation records are kept, this situation should create no special problems.

Journals present slightly more of a problem. Some libraries do not circulate journals but merely display latest editions of journals on racks, and notify interested persons when they have arrived at the library. This has the advantage of bringing people into the library on a regular basis and works well if everyone is on the same site. However, if users are frequently busy away from their base of operation, or scattered around the country, difficulties may arise. In this case it may be easier to circulate journals with lists of interested users clipped to the front, or extract items which are of use to various members of staff. Another approach might be to write a weekly current-awareness bulletin with short abstracts of relevant recent articles and circulate these. If journals are circulated, users must have the importance of timeliness pressed upon them. It is no use receiving a weekly journal two weeks after publication because another user was away on holiday or forgot to read it. The librarian must make sure that either users or their secretaries pass on journals promptly. Only then will the system work well for everyone.

A useful tip for one-person libraries has to do with returned materials which have been checked back into the collection but have not yet been shelved. Most one-person library employees save the shelving for a scheduled time, usually when the office is quiet and, depending upon the amount of material circulated, on some sort of rotating schedule, usually once a week or so. If instead you store returned materials in a busy and heavily used area of the library you will find that browsers will look these over and some will be re-borrowed before they must go back to the shelves. It may seem like a silly and rather unprofessional idea, but if browsing is part of your users' activities in the library, you will find that they enjoy looking over these materials. Why do they do this? No-one knows, but it probably has something to do with human nature, the pleasure of reading something one knows someone else has used recently. Obviously, such a scheme will be wasted on highly technical materials called for only for specific projects, but the bulk of returned material is perfectly suitable.

An important consideration in reviewing circulation services performed in the one-person library is interlending and interlibrary loan, two terms which mean the same thing in the United Kingdom and the United States, respectively. This is an important part of the library's services, and in the one-person library the interlending work is especially valuable in acquiring resources that are not available in the library itself.

Ferguson and Mobley tell us that interlibrary loan 'occurs everywhere in the library world because there is no such thing as an all-inclusive library'.[6] They go on to tell us why interlibrary loan has become a standard practice:

> 'To a special library the borrowing privilege has always been vitally important. That library characteristically has a small collection in a limited subject area and is bound to need other materials from time to time: (1) materials outside its subject field, (2) materials needed only occasionally, and (3) materials which cannot be purchased or (4) materials which are not practical to purchase.'[6]

There are a few points which should be kept in mind when a one-person library employee is using interlending to augment the collections. The primary consideration, of course, is a recognition of the fact that interlibrary loans are a privilege, and no one library is obliged to lend to a borrowing library. While professional courtesy requires that most of us try to aid other librarians whenever possible, it is an accepted fact that, especially with regard to special libraries, the lending is done by the larger libraries and the borrowing is done by the small ones. While those who work in small libraries, including one-person librarians, would be more than happy to participate in lending materials from their collections, because of the limited collecting activities of these libraries they do not have what the larger libraries need. So the one-person librarian is usually the borrower, and is thus placed in the position of wanting to reciprocate but being unable to.

Another point to remember about interlibrary loans is that there exists a formal procedure for borrowing, namely the Interlibrary Loan Code developed by the American Library Association and, in the United Kingdom, the policies organized by the British Library Lending Division. Produced as the result of many years of varying kinds of experiences by all kinds of librarians, these procedures provide direction and guidance to libraries who wish to avail themselves of the collections of other libraries. In fairness to all lenders and borrowers, these procedures must be adhered to.

Unfortunately, many one-person libraries are too small to benefit from some of the local schemes, so for their librarians it is best to rely on the informal borrowing and lending of materials or, when necessary, formal interlending. On an informal basis you can ring up a library or colleague whose collection is likely to contain the item which your user requires and simply ask to borrow it, offering to send the appropriate form, postage, etc. If you cannot locate the item after a few telephone calls you should resort to whatever union catalogue arrangement is available in your area. If you are lucky enough to be serving a library which participates in one of the local consortia or networking arrangements (e.g. METRO in the New York metropolitan area), familiarize yourself with the procedures and try to use them often enough to justify your membership of the organization. There are a couple of ground rules to keep in mind. First, if the purchase price of the book is under a certain amount (usually agreed upon by practising librarians in the area), you should not try to borrow the book if it is in print. Also, keep in mind that the costs of the loan, considering the paperwork and staff time spent on checking details, typing the form and envelope etc., can be a deterrent. If the book is not too expensive and is in print, it might be better to purchase it for the collection. Obviously, more expensive materials, such as textbooks, should be borrowed whenever possible, particularly if they are going to be used for only one specific project.

This last caveat does not apply, however, for photocopies of cited journal articles. Since these constitute the bulk of interlibrary loan requests it has become common practice to provide a photocopy instead of lending a volume.[7] Also, the speed of obtaining these is often more important than the cost. However, it should be remembered that in the United States the CONTU guidelines (provided by the National Commission on New Technological Uses, created by Congress in 1974) limit photocopied loans in one year to five copies of one periodical title not more than five years old.[8]

So remember, try your local sources first when needing to borrow, but do not spend hours ringing round in order to save the cost of the BLLD form or the interlibrary loan effort. This is false economy. Also, as a courtesy to lending libraries, if you borrow a book two or three times, it should be considered for purchase.

It is a good idea to borrow expensive items to assess them before actually going ahead and ordering them for stock, as you could show them to relevant users and seek an opinion. Most people are very positive and like to give help if approached in the right way, but this requires a good instinct.

In order to keep a record of the various items which are borrowed, and the various sources from which these items come, a loose-leaf file can be split up into sections for the various libraries used. On each page, the following records are included:

Date that an item is requested.
Title of the item requested.
Name of the user requesting the item.
Date that the item arrives.
Date that the item is due back.
Date on which the item is returned.

It is useful to note that readers can be asked to return the item borrowed for them a little before the due date, so that the borrowing library can have time to return it by the date of return given by the lending library. This seems only courteous when the other library has gone to the trouble of helping out the borrowing library.

It should be unnecessary to mention that you should stress to users that they take good care of books which are borrowed for them through interlibrary loans. It might be worth putting a note on the book stating that it has been borrowed from an outside source and that you would appreciate their taking good care of it. Some tact is called for here; presumably your people know how to handle books and other library materials. The point is to get this across without seeming to make too many rules and regulations.

Before sending out requests to other libraries in written form make sure that as many of the bibliographical details are as correct as possible. This helps the lending library to trace the item quickly, and means that you get more efficient service. If your library does not subscribe to *Books in Print* or to the *British National Bibliography*, or if you are not online with BLAISE or BIP, try calling a local public reference library to ask if someone there will check the bibliographical details for you. If you have correct bibliographical information you should get a much quicker response to your requests.

If a library is unable to supply the requested item immediately your request will probably be put on a waiting list and your user can be notified that the book will not be quickly forthcoming. If the book is needed urgently, purchase should be considered. This is one of the many things to be weighed when using an interloans service – cost saved against the speed of service.

In the last few years commercial document delivery has become a viable alternative to interlending, especially for special libraries. Commercial document delivery, as provided by such firms as Information on Demand, FIND/SVP and others, can seem expensive to the one-person librarian accustomed to doing all the telephoning around and filling out of interlibrary loan forms, but when the success rate of commercial delivery firms is compared with the staff time spent in locating and obtaining the material, this method can more than pay for itself, especially as it frees the one-person librarian for less routine tasks. There are various ways to incorporate commercial document delivery services into the library's operations, primarily by having management consider that the costs of such services can be handled the same way as those of using other jobbers and agencies are handled, i.e. in lieu of hiring staff to provide better service for users. Additionally, if the one-person library charges off services to the different departments of the parent organization, the actual costs of the delivery can be charged and the expenditure does not have to be part of the library budget.

Photocopying is a most useful service but it is very time-consuming in the one-person library. Certain decisions have to be made: do you locate the photocopier in the library, where everyone can walk in to make copies, or does having the machine safely down the corridor mean that you have to track up and down constantly? However, management is probably going to have as much to say about the location of the photocopier that serves the library as the librarian is, especially if that machine is used by other departments for non-library copying, so this is one area where the one-person librarian is going to have to weigh the benefits of one solution against the liabilities of another. No matter where the machine is located, one thing is certain: photocopying is not going to go away, and you, as the one-person librarian, are almost bound to have a large amount of this work to do. It is part of the job, and while you should do what you can to encourage users to do their own copying, there will be times when seemingly more important things will have to wait while you stand at the copier churning out documents for a user.

There are some basic guidelines for photocopying which should be observed, and one of the best quick guides is in the article 'Photocopying without (much) damage' by Anthony J. Amodeo.[9] It is especially necessary in the one-person library for the staff member to set a good example for users by showing them how to copy properly (particularly in a corporate or commercial library, where there may be a pretty high level of disdain on the part of the users about the care of materials they want copied). Amodeo gives eight rules each librarian should memorize:

- Select copying machines carefully.
- Always fully support the materials being copied.
- Never allow a book to be flexed over 180 degrees.
- Use two people (including a staff member, i.e. yourself) for copying oversized materials, atlases, etc.
- Watch out for undue pressure exerted on materials to 'get a good copy'.
- Limit the number of pages which can be copied from any one volume of irreplaceable material.
- Reference books should be copied by the staff, not by the user.
- Have space nearby for holding materials which have been copied.

Finally, the one-person library employee should keep in mind a quote from Amodeo, worth repeating here:

> '... it has been shown time and time again that, once convinced of the importance of conservation, patrons do become conscientious about photocopying, shelving, and general handling of library materials – provided, of course, that the librarians and staff set a good and conscientious example.'[9]

## Selective dissemination of information

The selective dissemination of information (SDI) has been described by Grieg Aspnes as a sophisticated service in which 'the special library reviews the current literature, filters from it items of significance and sends these directly to various individuals according to their personal interests.'[10] Aspnes characterizes SDI as a valuable service, but the special librarian is also warned against its dangers: it can be haphazard and inconsistent, and whoever 'does the scanning and selecting must keep up with the ever-changing interests of many individuals; inevitably some will be forgotten or neglected, and significant items may be missed or their value to certain persons may be overlooked'.[10]

The whole point of SDI is current awareness, and such a service can be useful to professionals in any business or field of work if it keeps them informed of what others in the field are doing, of meetings, conferences, special programmes, etc. However, such service is only valid if the professional who received the material wants it and uses it. Aspnes warns, by quoting Henry Mintzberg who had written about managers in the *Harvard Business Review*, that managers strongly favour the verbal media for their information, they skim their periodicals in seconds, they want to have their information in 'soft' form, not hard copy, and they piece their information together, from 'odds and ends'.[11] Having said that, however, we must recognize that many other managers and professionals still want to participate in a current-awareness programme for their information. For them, the whole purpose of current awareness is to save time, as it supplements the supposedly haphazard reading which professionals, for lack of time, tend to do. A good current-awareness service increases a user's habitual use of information in his work. By providing the current-awareness service, the library in turn gets feedback about the needs of its users and can better plan and organize its services.

For a one-person library which includes SDI as part of its services to users, items to scan include journals, reports, conference papers, newspapers, standards and patent specifications, and, as secondary sources, abstracts, indexes and critical reviews. Professional, academic, trade and society journals provide literature that is not so timely, but they can be useful to the one-person librarian for retrospective searching. The main thing for the librarian to remember is that he must keep in touch with the users to determine, on a continuous basis, if an SDI service is relevant. A questionnaire can be helpful, but a simple tear-off slip or an interview can be just as useful. In other words, as far as the SDI service is concerned there is no substitute for feedback.

Scanning journals is an extremely useful and time-saving service which your users will appreciate. This also requires a little practice, but with practice comes ease. You will soon learn to acquire a 'feel' for items which may be useful to your users, and then you can mark these up. As already mentioned, marked-up journals can be passed to staff with circulation lists clipped to them, or can be tagged, displayed in the library and staff notified of useful articles either by reminder slips or by a short current-awareness bulletin. Users can then come into the library to read the articles if they wish.

A current-awareness bulletin keeps users informed of all the latest news and articles on a topic on which they may be working or have an interest. Try to write a bulletin on a weekly basis, keeping it to one or, at the very most, two sides of a sheet of paper. Give short abstracts – just a couple of lines will do – on items which may be of interest to your users. Make sure that the journals and newspapers containing the articles are readily available and then send the bulletins out on a regular basis – Friday would probably be best.

This service really does fill a large gap, saves users valuable time and can be used to demonstrate to management how worthwhile your services are. If you are really short of time, you could copy journal content pages, but as titles of articles often can be somewhat misleading, it really is worth considering the extra effort to compile a much more effective current-awareness list.

When sending out lists of additions to the library – probably on a monthly basis – it is also worth considering writing two or three lines about a book, journal or pamphlet, so that your users can see what it is really about and whether it will help them in their work. Keep your writing short and pithy. No-one thanks you for wordy and lengthy lists.

Remember that abstracting in full is best left to the experts. It is very time-consuming to do properly, and it is much more sensible to use one or more of the specialized services which can be purchased commercially, either in hard copy or online. These abstracting journals are very valuable to staff, and to yourself, for keeping in touch in their fields, and should be scanned regularly. Bought-in services such as these, although expensive, are valuable for busy one-person librarians and their users, and the costs are quickly recovered in the time that they save and the number of items brought to light which might not otherwise have been discovered. Their only snag is that they are often out of date by the time they are published, and this is where your own current-awareness system takes over to keep users really up to date. Commercial abstracts are easy to scan, and it is relatively easy then to obtain copies of the articles requested by users, as most provide a back-up service.

Indexing journal articles is a very time-consuming job. Not only do all the journals taken have to be scanned on a regular basis and the worthwhile items extracted but these then have to be sorted and key worded. You will often find that another larger library in the same field may be doing this work because they have the necessary staff, and you may be able to use (for a fee) their indexing expertise. You may also find that other libraries, even if they do not provide printed indexes to journals scanned by them, will provide indexing systems for use by their own staff and will be pleased to answer your queries. For instance, in the United Kingdom the British Institute of Management Library at Corby, Northamptonshire, indexes many journals on management and related topics, and the staff is pleased to answer a query either by post or telephone. Similarly, the Institute of Personnel Management provides a service to libraries and members, and the list could go on. Find out about other services in your field and make use of them to supplement your own resources.

Reading lists are often requested in the one-person library. These can be compiled from the stock in your own library, either as a computer print-out if you have the facilities or, failing that, as a list typed from the relevant catalogue cards. Do not forget to include your non-book items which may or may not be catalogued, as well as any really relevant journal articles. Complete bibliographies take much longer to compile, and in a one-person library situation these are best purchased or borrowed from larger libraries with similar subject interests. They are very interesting to compile, of course, but you have to remember that time is money in a small set-up and it is more cost-effective to make use of the work already done by the staff of a larger library. Also, you have to determine whether your user wants to pore over a lengthy list of items or whether a short list compiled by yourself would be satisfactory.

Finally, in considering services to users some attention should be given to the subject of library access, especially when the librarian is not on duty. In the one-person library the hours of service are usually determined by management, and the librarian is hired to be there to assist users during those hours. Arrangements are made for the librarian's absence due to illness, holidays, attendance at professional meetings, etc., but what about when the librarian is not on duty, in the evening or at weekends? Is the library open to users at those times, with no staff member available? The answers to these questions, like most in the special libraries world, will depend on the patterns established in the parent organization. If the library is part of an organization in which research and information are part of the job for many of the employees, and evening and weekend research is also part of the operation of the business, library staff will probably be expected to be available for assistance or the materials in the library will be accessible, without professional help, and users will be expected to use materials carefully and to leave word, using an 'honour system', when materials have to be removed from the library. Obviously some materials will be locked up when the librarian is not on duty, to be used only during her hours of service. For those situations in which materials 'disappear' from the library only to turn up in the offices of thoughtless users some time later, the librarian is obliged to approach management about the security of these types of materials and to seek some appropriate solution to the problem. Basically, the solution will be arrived at by determining the role of the library in the parent organization. If the material is so valuable that all staff need to use it, management will probably agree to some special security arrangements or limited hours of service (or additional part-time staff to service the library at odd times). If the material in the library is not considered essential, there is little the librarian will be able to do to change things, except to get to know the users, know who is likely to have certain materials when they are not to be found in their proper places in the library, and approach them and ask for the materials to be returned. It is a question of clear communication between the librarian and the users, and of respect and concern for the materials which all users need. Frank discussions will usually determine what role these materials play in the work of the parent institution.

## References

1 Whittaker, Kenneth, 'Towards a theory for reference and information service', *Journal of Librarianship*, 9, 49-63, 1977.
2 Finer, Ruth, 'Reference and enquiry work', in Anthony, L. J. (ed.), *Handbook of Special Librarianship and Information Work*, Aslib, London, 1982.
3 Jahoda, Gerald, *The Librarian and Reference Queries*, Academic Press, New York, 1980, Chapter II.
4 Grogan, Denis, *Practical Reference Work*, Clive Bingley, London, 1979, Chapter II.
5 Englefield, Dermot, *Parliament and Information*, The Library Association, London, 1981.
6 Ferguson, Elizabeth and Mobley, Emily R., *Special Libraries at Work*, Library Professional Publications, an imprint of The Shoe String Press, Inc., Hamden, Connecticut, 1984, p. 52.
7 Ibid., p. 54.
8 Ibid., p. 56.
9 Amodeo, Anthony J., 'Photocopying without (much) damage', *College and Research Libraries News*, 44, November, 365-370, 1983.
10 Aspnes, Grieg, 'A philosophy of special librarianship', in Jackson, E. (ed.), *Special Librarianship: A New Reader*, 1980, p. 10.
11 Mintzberg, Henry, 'The manager's job: folklore and fact', *Harvard Business Review*, 53, July/August, 49-61, 1975, in Aspnes, op. cit.

# Automation: feasible or not?

For the one-person librarian the provocative title of this chapter introduces one of the most important considerations of our professional lives. In the mid-1980s there is no librarian who can avoid the subject of library automation. Despite protestations to the contrary, especially from those who oversee the financially strapped small libraries run by one person, one-person librarians will, in the next decade or so, be required to come to grips with the reality of library automation. The next few years will see the availability and adoption of electronic data processing as the standard for library record-keeping. Many one-person librarians, however, do not like the idea. Therefore before we describe in general terms what automation and information technology can do for the library and, most particularly, for the librarian, we should give some attention to the pattern of resistance that seems to have grown up, in both the United Kingdom and the United States, to the idea of electronic data processing.

Perhaps we should start with a definition of automation (or information technology, as it is also called), since the term is bandied about so much in the library and information science profession. 'Automation' and 'information technology' are terms used to describe the acquisition, production, transformation, storage and transmission of data by electronic means in forms such as vocal, pictorial, textual or numeric, so as to facilitate the interaction between people and between people and machines. The terms also refer to the applications and implications of these processes.

The reader will observe that nowhere in that description is reference made to replacing the librarian with a machine. Nor is there any reference to removing the books and other library materials from the shelves and storing their contents in a machine, or using the machine to ingest, absorb and analyse intellectually the information that is contained in the library collections. Artificial intelligence is a concept, yes, but for the one-person librarian and the users with whom she interacts and the materials which she manages in the library, the paperless, bookless and staffless library is so unlikely that it should not cause even the slightest concern.

Why, then, do so many one-person librarians resist? Some do not, of course. For those employed in libraries which support scientific and technical institutions, government agencies, academic departments, research and development organizations and business and corporate staffs, resistance has worn down. Acceptance has come primarily because, initially, leadership into electronic data processing was developed by management for other purposes and recognized to be of value in the work of the libraries attached to those institutions. Those who did resist, and who continue to resist, seem to do so for several very understandable reasons. First, it is human nature to resist something new: 'I have been running my library with a telephone and a typewriter and a card catalogue for all these years. It works fine.' Second, the cost of electronic data processing has been prohibitive, and many librarians in smaller units simply did not expect to see these costs come down appreciably during their careers. Third, the automation industry exploded on the scene. Companies came and went with amazing swiftness, and the confusion of choices in hardware, software, peripherals, supplies and, most important, of tangible results for the libraries was more than most one-person librarians were able to handle. Even if they were interested, they did not have the time to learn everything there was to know. Finally, we all tend to wait and see: with library automation, even if the supervising financial authorities were willing to expend the funds, the small libraries simply could not afford the luxury of trying new techniques and new systems without some idea of what the tangible results would be for the library. Caution was the watchword, for there was not enough confidence that the service would be improved to such an extent that it would be worth the extra time, trouble and expense involved in making such a drastic change. Most one-person librarians want to provide better and more efficient services for their users and, all other things being equal, they, too, would have joined the electronic revolution. However, things were not equal, and for the OMB/one-person library it was prudent to wait until the industry had sorted itself out.

That time has now come, and the resistance is weakening. The cost of simple automation equipment has come down to the level of other high-quality office equipment, and for the truly financially strapped library the hardware can be leased. Library software development continues, and by the end of the decade probably no library smaller than 50 000 volumes will have to create its own databases and have customized software written for it (as was the case earlier, since library software was developed primarily for large collections). The results are beginning to show: every issue of *Library Journal* has a column devoted to automation in libraries, and a second column about online databases, to say nothing of the many columns and articles written in the nearly two hundred other journals and publications devoted to libraries and library administration. Books proliferate faster than any librarian, especially the one-person librarian, can acquire them, much less read them. Information is certainly there for the librarian who wants it. No, it is not perfect, and yes, it is weighted with personal opinion and experiences, and, no, it is not presented in an easy checklist format for each individual one-person library, but these are small drawbacks. Librarians are, first of all, organizers, professionally trained to categorize and organize information and then, if called upon to do so, to analyse its content. They can surely do this for themselves on the subject of library automation.

Thus, new technology in many forms can be of great use to the one-person librarian. Not only will information technology (or IT) help you with many tedious clerical tasks, it can also make you more efficient at such tasks as literature searching and answering reference queries. No longer can the one-person librarian plead convenient ignorance of the technology, or state that management will not accept the need for the financial support for such equipment as microcomputers and the like. The one-person librarian of the future will have to know enough about the technology to be able at least to build up a good working relationship with an appropriate expert. It is even better if you can choose your own hardware and software, and be aware of the capabilities of each item and piece of equipment.

It is also possible that the organization for which you work may already have some equipment such as a mini- or microcomputer or a word processor which can be put to good use for the library, even if only on a time-sharing basis. All these machines have library applications, so it comes down to making a good case to management and proving that any task which you may wish to perform on the machine can be done more cost-effectively than if it were done manually.

Remember, too, that the new technology will supplement the old but not displace it for a very long time yet. This is simply because the average person – and that includes management and users – does not yet want the paperless office. IT in the library is going to replace only those tasks where the ability to 'plod' is needed. In other words, IT will expedite the more mundane tasks such as logging in journals and book order/accessioning, etc. For instance, even when you may have a large number of very relevant citations thrown up by an online search, most users will still want to see these in hard copy in order to read further than the abstract. We are not trying to be 'Luddites', but it is necessary to balance enthusiasm for new technology against the older, well-tried methods and take each case on its merits. What will suit one set-up will be wrong for another. Remember, too, that there is nothing like hard copy for reading on trains and planes. People seem to want paper, if only to be able to make notes in the margins! So despite proclamations from some members of the information world about the obsolescence of paper, libraries and books will be with us for a long time yet simply because there is nothing else which is so convenient.

Another factor mitigating the onslaught of technology is that the average library user does not want enormous quantities of data spewed at him out of the computer. He wants an answer to his query in digestible form and in the right quantity and format. This means that the librarian is needed to get the information into a usable form. If you can harness automation to help you do this, all the better.

Technology is simply a means to an end. It will certainly help everyone in the small set-up. For instance, using the example of online databases we can see that . information available does not stop at international boundaries but is worldwide. So technology which enables us to search easily information from, say, the United States or the EEC on a screen in our libraries is more than welcome.

# Information storage

Technology, of course, does not only mean computers. How can we use technology in a small library, and in what forms? Perhaps we ought to start with simple forms of information storage. Suppose, for instance, that you are very busy, are in a one-person situation, with no clerical help, and find it difficult to get out of the office for meetings or even lunch breaks. Have you thought of installing a telephone-answering machine? These are not unreasonably expensive, but will give you peace of mind when out of the office, and ultimately will ensure a more efficient service. Being able to leave a message means one less frustrated user, and you can ring back as soon as you are in the library again.

In the same situation, if you have no clerical help and are asked to give presentations to staff of your library's parent organization who might be scattered about the country, or at least not on the same site, think about having a tape, slide or video-cassette made about the work of the library and how the library serves the organization. This can be shown at meetings which you may not be able to attend because of pressures of work. Obviously, it is much better if you can get up and give the presentation, but having an electronic stand-in, if it is properly done, is better than not giving the presentation at all.

Possibly the next item which you may find yourself needing is a microform reader. These provide the all-important link betwen the user and the information that has been committed to one of the various microforms. It is the only form of equipment that the microform user will need, although for a library in which there are many periodical and newspaper files on microform, a reader–printer is appreciated by the users because, even if coin-operated, it reduces the amount of time needed for taking notes. Microfiche is probably the more common form of this medium. Microfiches are flexible sheets of film which contain a series of micro-images laid out in accordance with a standardized grid pattern. Some material comes in the form of roll film. The British Library still has many theses in this form. It is simply film in 100- or sometimes 200-foot lengths wound onto open reel, usually 16 mm size. Sometimes the film is on cassettes rather than open reel and this makes for easier access. Cartridges are even more common.

In the United Kingdom the best way to choose a microform reader is to read *What to Buy for Business*[1] or to consult the National Reprographic Centre for Documentation. This organization gives impartial advice about such items as microform readers, word processors, videotext, etc.[2]

There is also no harm in consulting a colleague who has purchased such an item, for he will give advice to help you avoid some of the more obvious pitfalls. For instance, some microform readers are designed to take both film and fiche, but are not so effective as a machine designed to take only one type of microform or the other. Whatever you decide to buy, see it demonstrated first, and go for the best that you can afford, e.g. a dual-lens, dual-carrier fiche reader which can search indexes and documents at the same time.

One last point: remember that the plus points of storing items in fiche are space saving and convenience of storage (less bulky than original documents) and ease of scanning for short items such as EEC documents, all types of indexes, course materials, etc. An excellent example in the United Kingdom of a document which appears in both hard copy and fiche is *British Reports, Translations and Theses*, which is received and scanned in print form but is discarded when the fiche form is received. Minus points to think about are that searching this medium becomes very tiring for the eyes and it is more cumbersome to refer back to previous pages, and therefore more difficult to take notes. This is especially the case when reading a thesis which is often transferred to film and has to be wound backward and forward to refer to points made. Nevertheless, microform is becoming more common because of shortage of storage space in libraries. The British Library no longer stores theses in hard copy for this very reason, and newspapers are being regularly transferred to this medium.

As we discussed earlier, photocopying is now a way of life in the library office. Although the earlier discussion centred around photocopying as a service for users, the one-person librarian will obviously choose and have available for office use the same-quality machine. The uses to which the copier is put in the office vary only with the imagination, time and talent of the librarian: certainly copies of documents, reports, correspondence for files, etc., as well as booklists, guides for users and, in fact, all materials which are distributed from the library office and which, without a copier, would entail printing costs using vendors outside the organization.

The utilization of the microcomputer for library 'housekeeping' routines seems to be an idea whose time has come. Some of the routine tasks in the library which can be performed much more expeditiously with the aid of a microcomputer include acquisitions, serials control and periodical check-in, circulation record-keeping, cataloguing (including online catalogues, catalogue card production, book catalogue production), accession lists, reading lists and bibliographies, indexing and keywording, in-house SDI, spreadsheets for budgeting, planning, access to online databases and, of course, word processing.

At present, not all small libraries will benefit from the use of a computer, but because hardware and software are becoming increasingly cheaper to buy or lease and install, the cost benefits to small libraries are becoming very attractive. Primary among the hidden cost benefits is the fact that computerized record-keeping makes it 'much easier to concentrate on the content of the collection, due to time savings and control of information'.[3] However, if you do wish to automate, you have to establish certain objectives, and to do so, you must ask the following questions:

- Can money be saved by improved efficiency? Will the exercise be cost effective?
- Will you be able to maintain the service by higher productivity?
- Can you extend the service as a result of automation?

● Will better controls result, e.g. more standardized calaloguing, better
  overdue records, etc.?

One strong point in favour of automation for the one-person librarian is that
using a microcomputer for some housekeeping duties will reduce the amount
of clerical work which must be done on a regular basis. Once the system has
been installed and is up and running it becomes less labour intensive, enabling
the one librarian to cope with an increased workload or, better yet, with more
professional bibliographic endeavours. Sometimes extra help is needed with
setting up the system, but this should only be temporary.

Frequently, small libraries tend to organize their own systems of housekeeping which can be tailored exactly to their own needs. This is because so
often when using large networks, for, say, cooperative cataloguing, small
libraries would not really benefit from joining in a cooperative effort because
their intake is too specialized to match the general coverage of a cooperative
system. Again, at this stage, when the one-person librarian is organizing in-
house systems, it is essential to have a working knowledge of computer
technology. It is necessary to understand how the computer can be applied to
the library environment, especially if you have to liaise with your own computer
department in order to describe your needs in the library. You may be able to
buy the software package you need off the shelf, but it is likely that you may
wish to adapt an existing system, so you will have to be able to tell the staff in
the computer department of your requirements and have an appreciation of the
problems involved in creating a suitable program for you. In a larger library a
member of staff might be appointed to liaise with the computer department,
but a one-person librarian has to become conversant with computer jargon. Go
on a course, learn the basics and then you should be able to ask the right
questions and make sure the original design of your program will allow you to
incorporate changes and extras.

One word of warning here: if you have decided to install a microcomputer for
your library you will be faced with a confusing array of choices. However, the
best thing is to investigate all avenues and choose the software first. If you
cannot get a program that fits, then have your computer experts write one for
you, because this comes cheaper than other custom-made software. Once you
have chosen the software, you can then eliminate certain types of hardware as
incompatible.

Before going any further here, read the British Library report by Trevelyan
and Rowat[4] on investigation of the use of systems programs in library
application of microcomputers. This gives various specifications and systems
flow-charts for such housekeeping routines as cataloguing and current
awareness in the library. Studying a document like this will help you to avoid
some silly mistakes.

Probably the best book written on the subject so far is *Introducing
Microcomputers: A Guide for Librarians*, by P. F. Burton and J. Howard Petrie.[5]
This is the first single source for information on micros in British libraries. It
covers the basics of computer technology, the importance of software,

hardware and software selection, and, most important, specification of microcomputers in libraries, which is very useful for beginners. Most helpful, perhaps, are the actual examples of how the applications are put into practice in various libraries. Another important and useful guide is *A Micro Handbook for Small Libraries and Media Centers*, by Betty Costa and Marie Costa,[3] which, as the title indicates, is especially aimed at librarians who work alone. Also of value are the previously mentioned columns on microcomputer technology in *Library Journal* each month,[6] regular articles which are short and to the point and which provide a wealth of information to the librarian familiarizing himself with the so-called mysteries of microcomputer utilization. There is also 'Computerized housekeeping systems', by Jane Eyre,[7] a good chapter in the Aslib *Handbook of Special Librarianship and Information Work*, which details the ways in which microcomputers can be used for these routine tasks in the library. Some of these applications are perhaps a little advanced for a small library, but there is much of relevance.

In addition to the monthly columns in *Library Journal*, a regular journal which is now produced for users of microcomputers in libraries is *Library Micromation News*,[8] produced by the Library Technology Centre, Polytechnic of Central London. This contains first-class examples of the use of microcomputers, actual case studies from various users who also tell of the snags involved and how problems were sorted out. You can write to the magazine if you have a problem and find another user who will put you right. The journal also covers online searching as well. The monthly newsletter *Library and Information News*,[9] published by Alan Armstrong Associates, contains many useful snippets of information in this field, as does Aslib's *Current Awareness Bulletin*.[10] Although the American newsletter *The One-Person Library*[11] purports to avoid featuring high technology as a regular subject, the use of automation in small libraries is often referred to.

## Information sources

When the one-person librarian is ready to start his examination of how these jobs can be performed more efficiently and cost-effectively with the use of electronic equipment, there are any number of sources of information which can be sought out. We have already referred to the variety of literature available about library automation, and the conscientious librarian will want to spend a considerable amount of time investigating what has been written on the subject. Also, one should form a habit of perusing the many articles and notes about automation in the professional press, even if one has no intention of getting into automation any time soon. Such reading keeps the one-person library employee up to date about what is going on, and it allows him to gain some familiarity and knowledge of the jargon of automation, which is a language in itself.

Another source for one-person librarians seeking information about library automation is the industry itself. Vendors have a wealth of knowledge to impart to librarians who are looking into automation, and there are ways to take advantage of their expertise. Such a list appeared in an early issue of *The One-Person Library*,[12] and although the subject of the article was the purchase of any sort of major equipment or appliance for the library, the advice is especially appropriate for one-person librarians considering an investment in library automation:

- Use salesmen as a resource. There is only so much that you can learn from brochures and catalogues. You are going to want specific answers to specific questions, and only a salesman can provide you with that information.
- Do not create an adversary relationship. Of course the salesman wants to make a sale, but he also wants to be helpful, so allow him to be.
- Make an appointment. If a salesman just drops in or if you receive a telephone solicitation (and it is a product you are interested in) tell him that you are too busy to talk, but you will be glad to make an appointment for some future time. This will give you a chance to collect your thoughts.
- See salesmen at the library. If the meeting takes place on your 'turf' you will be more comfortable. If the product requires a demonstration, see if it can be done at the library. If not, you should still have your initial meeting at the library and arrange for a later demonstration at the showroom.
- Be prepared. Before the sales call you should know something about the product. Have a list of specific questions written down and leave space between them to jot down the salesman's responses.
- Do not be afraid of appearing foolish. If you have a question, ask it. If you do not understand the response, say so. You are not expected to know everything about the product in advance.
- Do not worry about wasting the salesman's time. He gets paid for it. Take as long as you feel you need. If the salesman seems to be rushing you it is a clear sign that you should look elsewhere. On the other hand, do not feel that you have to buy something because the salesman has been pleasant and has spent a lot of time with you. If he does not make a sale, he loses a commission, but if you buy something you do not really want or need, you are stuck with it.
- Ask for names and phone numbers of other people in the area (particularly libraries) who have purchased the product. Contact them and find out if they are satisfied. Also find out if they have had any problems getting service for the product.
- Do not be afraid to talk about money. It is, after all, a major factor in your decision.
- If you are considering a large purchase, look into financing. You will pay more in the long run but you will not be putting a great strain on your budget at any one time. Be sure to check interest rates. Some financing is offered at rates as high as 20-25 per cent, which is unreasonable.
- If the salesman tells you that his product does not currently meet all of your requirements but his company is working on 'add-ons' that will be ready in a few months, politely (or not so politely) show him the door.
- If you are really interested in a product, ask the salesman to prepare a formal

proposal tailored to your specific needs. If you feel more comfortable, tell him that you need it for your committee or board. Salesmen are always anxious to impress committees.

- If you mean 'no' say 'no'. This is one of the hardest things to do since it means 'insulting' the salesman, but it is better to do this than to waste his time making additional sales calls or preparing proposals if you have already made up your mind that you are not interested.
- If you feel that the salesman is not being honest, or if you feel that he is trying to pressure you, find another product. The product should sell itself. You should have a feeling of confidence that it meets your needs. The salesman should spend more time answering your questions than 'selling'.
- You may not have to buy the product at all. Ask the salesman about leasing. With many products the state of the art changes so rapidly that a product may be obsolete within a few years. Leasing allows you to keep up with changes in technology and without having to unload obsolete equipment.

Even with all this in mind, it is not likely that you will ever really enjoy sales calls. There is pressure on you to make the right decision and select the correct product. If you do not, it will be you, and not the salesman, who will be held accountable. Nonetheless, if you follow these steps you may find that the process is not as painful as you expected, and you certainly will be in a better position to make the proper purchase.

# Online searching

It would be impossible to examine in detail every way in which the library can take full advantage of automation technology, but one application should be discussed simply because its manual application is such an important part of library work. We are speaking of online searching, the technique of searching for information that is held on a database in a computer. Vast amounts of information can be retained in databases and the information retrieved almost instantly by entering search terms which will have been extracted from the records or from a thesaurus. As a result of this progress, information can be retrieved online much more quickly and efficiently than by using traditional methods.

Some systems are available through a direct telephone link, e.g. Datastream, or via a host computer with systems such as Dialog in the United States. There are directories of these databases which can be consulted. Some of the databases are bibliographic utilities set up expressly for libraries (e.g. OCLC and RLIN), although they are expensive, and smaller library units usually enter into a cooperative regional arrangement to take advantage of these types of databases.

Other databases, however, are primarily providers of information, and can be searched through the use of modems and dial-up utilities. Some of these are designed for home use, and the information will be of limited value to library patrons, but others can provide almost unlimited bibliographic and statistical data.

In studying the advantages and disadvantages of online searching, some of the questions to ask could be:

- What relevance does online searching have in my particular subject field?
- What does online searching offer me and my library that is not available elsewhere?
- Does online searching replace the traditional source of information or is it complementary?

There are several advantages over traditional search methods, and the Costas' book[13] lists these:

(1) The resulting information is more comprehensive.
(2) The information is current.
(3) Access to information is very fast and not as expensive as it seems. The hourly rate may seem high but few searches require that much time.
(4) Information may be multilingual and international.
(5) The information will be as specific as you want it to be.

Lucy Tedd[14] also made a list of the advantages of using online search services, and her findings are similar:

(1) Immediate access to a wide coverage of over 40 million records in 1980.
(2) Ability to access information not immediately available in printed publications.
(3) Online databases tend to be updated more quickly and more frequently than their hard-copy counterparts. Abstracting journals are often a year behind.
(4) Less clerical work involved, because the references are printed out.
(5) More effective searching because there are a greater number of access points in the record.
(6) Much faster searching – it is estimated that an online search takes on 5-10 per cent of the time taken to search a printed index.

These points are very much in favour of going into online searching, but there are some drawbacks:

(1) Lack of coverage in older material.
(2) Need for special equipment to access the services.
(3) Cost of online searching is not cheap and, unlike manual searching, is not hidden – the bills tend to arrive every month!

Will the addition of online searching as a service in the library be cost-effective? Are you going to be able to do enough searches to justify the equipment purchased or leased? Probably the best thing to do at this stage is to have some searches done by outside organizations such as Aslib, The Science Reference Library, BLAISE, The Commonwealth Agricultural Bureau,

Information on Demand or FIND/SVP. There is a list of organizations which will perform searches for you in *UK Online Search Services*, by J. Denuette,[15] and the monthly online column in *Library Journal* also frequently lists services available. Some databases will also provide free trials and demonstrations, and these all help you to evaluate whether online searching will be feasible or not. The thing to remember is that as long as you do not do it, there may be no perceived need for the service by your parent organization. However, when you do start providing the service you will find that there are many takers and more work is generated because you can solve more detailed problems. You could carry the idea of trying out various databases even further and undertake a limited-budget, short-term project whereby a number of services could be tested and evaluated in-house in response to genuine information needs.

Having come this far and discovered that perhaps you should take the plunge, what equipment are you going to need to access an online service? You will need a keyboard, so that instructions can be typed in, a visual display unit (VDU, or CRT, for cathode-ray tube) necessary to display the information received and a printer, so that information displayed on the VDU can be printed if desired. A microcomputer purchased for the library office will also have online search capabilities, with the addition of a modem to utilize the telephone lines.

Searching can sometimes be done 'offline', i.e. out of peak telephone hours, in order to save costs, but this can only be done if information is not urgently required. Most information will be needed fairly quickly and within office hours, and is therefore done online.

Finding out about databases in your subject area is not such a difficult proposition if you follow a few guidelines. First, in the professional literature of you library's subject area you have already probably been reading about some databases available, or at least about some of the information that is provided by the appropriate databases. You should then consult a colleague who deals with the same or similar subject areas to see for yourself. She will already have come across some snags and will be able to obtain a demonstration or two from colleagues who are utilizing databases for online searching.

A second line of approach is to read up on the subject as much as possible. Aslib has produced a publication called *Online Bibliographic Databases*[16] which is very useful and discusses all the better-known systems and subject coverage of each database. The Aslib Online Centre also produces a very useful booklet called *Going Online 1985*[17] which every potential searcher should read, as it covers just about every aspect and answers every question that a beginner would ask about getting into online searching.

In addition, previously mentioned publications such as *Aslib Information, Online Review, Chronolog* and *Library and Information News* will all keep you up to date in the field of online searching, as will the publications from Headland Press entitled *Which Database?*[18] and *Which Databank?*[19] In the United States there are directories of databases which list more than 2500 databases available. These are too expensive for the one-person librarian to acquire, but they can be consulted at major research libraries in most areas. Not only do these directories give coverage of the various databases, they also evaluate them. This is most important if you are to get value for money on a search, as often several different databases will give coverage of the same topic but the results and the coverage will vary.

Finally, of course, attendance at conferences and meetings where exhibitors are showing their wares is one of the best ways to see online searching in action and to acquire all the literature you need in the form of pamphlets, brochures, advertising broadsides, etc. Any meeting of the American Library Association, the Special Libraries Association, Aslib, the Library Association and numerous other professional groups will have vendors exhibiting, and meetings with these exhibitors alone make the trip worthwhile.

When you have evaluated your databases and decided which ones to use you will then require training. Several organizations in the United Kingdom do this, including Aslib at its Online Information Centre, the UK Online Users Group, the Central Information Services at London University, and the various databases themselves, such as BIOSIS and CAB. You can get half-day and full-day training at most of these centres.

Remember it is very important to obtain this initial training so that you can develop suitable search strategies for the various databases which you may be calling up. This does not just mean that you become familiar with the physical layout of the keyboard, passwords, etc., but rather the ability to understand what your user requires and structure the search accordingly. This is why we mentioned in our chapter on reference work that much importance should be attached to the reference interview, especially in preparation for conducting an online search. Then you can ascertain the specific terms and keywords in order to structure the search and make sure that the end results match your user's needs. You will also have to become familiar with the contents of the databases so that you can search the most appropriate one, and this comes with training and experience. Training will also teach you how to use the command languages, which may be in natural language terms or in codes and mnemonics. So when trying to convince your management of the advantages of online searching, make sure that you impress upon them that proper training in the use of databases will ensure more cost-effective searching.

It is not our purpose to describe in detail each of the online databases available to the one-person librarian, but looking at one in depth might give an idea of what can be done with online searching. In the United Kingdom much online searching is done through Viewdata, the best-known system being Prestel, which can be accessed through a television monitor. Note that the term Viewdata should not be confused with Teletext. The British Broadcasting Corporation (BBC) has many pages of Teletext available on a suitably adapted television set. This system is known as 'Ceefax'. Independent Television (ITV) has a similar set-up known as 'Oracle'. Teletext systems do not need a telephone line to access them, and contain pages of information on the weather, news, sports, etc.

Prestel is different, in that although the information can be obtained on a specially adapted television set it comes from several central computers via a telephone link with the user. So the cost of using Prestel includes the purchase or rental of a specially adapted television set, or an ordinary colour television (UHF) with adaptor and keyboard or alphanumeric keyboard, a telephone jack for which a small rental fee is charged, a standing charge for the Prestel line, time online, the varying costs of each page of information (many pages are free) and, lastly, the normal telephone charges. Prestel can also be accessed through a microcomputer via a service known as Micronet.

Once you have the system set up and have obtained your identification number and password from Prestel you are ready to start using the system, which is very simple. To call up an item from the thousands of pages available you put in the page number on your keypad. The computer then sends it down the telephone line and it appears instantly on your screen. Prestel puts out an excellent directory which is updated quarterly. This lists all the information providers together with their page numbers, and also has a subject index so that you can search for information on a particular topic. There are hundreds of independent organizations which are information providers, and some choose to put in their information under 'umbrella schemes' run by such organizations as the Council for Educational Technology and the National Farmers Union. In this way, charges to organizations for putting in pages of information are not so high. Many organizations also have response pages so that other Prestel users can make enquiries about services and publications or simply leave messages. There is also a system called Mailbox whereby Prestel customers can send messages to each other (for this you will need an alphanumeric keyboard).

In 1982 another step taken in the further development of Prestel was the introduction of Gateway. This new application opened the way to other computer systems. For instance, customers having accounts at certain banks can check the balance of their accounts through the bank's own computer with a minimum of fuss. It may be possible to link up with the Viewdata systems of other countries in the not-too-distant future. Some businesses keep their Prestel pages confidential by placing them in Private Prestel. This means that only users nominated by the owner of the page, i.e. the Information Providers (IP), can look at these pages. This effectively gives them their own private information system but without all the problems and costs of running it themselves. These private stystems are known as Closed User Groups (CUGs).

What sort of information is available on Prestel? The list seems to be endless. The first organizations which took to Prestel in a big way were travel agents, but now the system is used by hundreds of Information Providers in every walk of life. A glance down the indexes of the Directory shows that you can obtain financial, economic, statistical, travel, and agricultural information just by keying in a page number. There is information by country, advice for consumers, exporters, stockbrokers and even librarians! You can search the Daily List of Government Publications and order the items you need. You can also shop by Prestel (including buying books on business and computers), book a hotel, find out the exchange rate, the retail price index or buy a theatre ticket using your credit card. You can also print out pages of information for users and store information in the memory. After a very slow start the whole system now seems to be taking off.

There is one further factor of library automation that is worth considering and it concerns what can be accomplished in a library which is well managed, in which the librarian is enthusiastic, takes pleasure in helping the users and has the confidence to know that she is doing a good job. If this is the case before automation, the simple act of studying, evaluating, acquiring and implementing electronic data-processing equipment and services in the library will not alter it, except for the better. It even becomes fun. If we see the new technology as a challenge for the OMB/one-person librarian, if we take it on as we would any other exciting new venture in our professional lives, we will enjoy it and, better yet, we will have made a serious and lasting contribution to the better management of the library.

# References

1  *What to Buy for Business*, 11 King's Rd, London SW3.
2  National Reprographic Centre for Documentation, The Hatfield Polytechnic, Hertford, Herts SG13 8LD.
3  Costa, Betty and Costa, Marie, *A Micro Handbook for Small Libraries and Media Centers*, Libraries Unlimited, Littleton, Colorado, 1983.
4  Trevelyan, A. and Rowat, M., 'An investigation of the use of systems programs in library applications of microcomputers', *Library and Information Report*, 12, British Library, London, n.d.
5  Burton, Paul F. and Petrie, Howard, J., *Introducing Microcomputers: A Guide for Librarians*, Van Nostrand-Reinhold, London, 1984.
6  *Library Journal*, Bowker, New York.
7  Eyre, J. 'Computerized house-keeping systems', in Anthony, L. J. (ed.), *Handbook of Special Librarianship and Information Work*, Aslib, London, 1982.
8  *Library Micromation News*, The Editor, Library Technology Centre, Polytechnic of Central London.
9  *Library and Information News*, Alan Armstrong and Associates, Reading.
10  *Current Awareness Bulletin*, Aslib, London.
11  *The One-Person Library: A Newsletter for Librarians and Management*, OPL Resources, Ltd, New York.
12  Ibid., **1,** 8, December, 1984.
13  Costa and Costa, op. cit., pp. 101–102.
14  Tedd, Lucy, in Anthony, L. J. (ed.), op. cit., pp. 326–327.
15  Denuette, J., *UK Online Search Services*, Aslib, London, 1982.
16  *Online Bibliographic Databases*, Aslib, London.
17  *Going Online 1985*, Aslib, London.
18  *Which Database?* Headland Press, Hartlepool, 1982/1983.
19  *Which Databank?* Headland Press, Hartlepool, 1984.

# Promotion and public relations

All libraries employ some form of promotion or public relations, either overtly or not, but for the one-person librarian this is also a highly effective way of affirming the importance of the library to the parent organization. It is at the same time a good means of evaluating the librarian's professional worth. Just as people are not going to use a library they never hear about, so they will not value the librarian if they do not know what goes on in the library. In this chapter we will discuss ways in which to promote the library. The discussion of the reference interview in Chapter 15 describes direct communication between librarian and user, but there are other targets for productive communication as well.

To reach management, one universally utilized form is the *annual report*. Whether it be a ten-page printed and bound booklet or a one-paragraph heading over some statistics, the annual report is probably the single most important document the one-person librarian will give to management during the year. It is the statement which reflects the policies of the library, the accomplishments of the year and, significantly, goals for the future. It tells management what the librarian sees as problems and where the strengths of the library, as reflected by use, are to be found. Finally, it gives the librarian a tool to use in lobbying for changes, to build strengths and to eliminate weaknesses in the library operation. It is easy to underestimate the value of the annual report, to dismiss it as a bothersome chore, but management prefers to see the facts about your service in black and white. For the alert and dynamic librarian who runs a library without help it can be the most important task of the year.

It could be argued that items such as circulation figures are not necessarily an accurate record of what a small specialized library does, as you may help many users by compiling lists of references, giving them verbal help, photocopies, etc. The time taken to complete an enquiry is not reflected in the simple loan of a couple of books, for much searching in journal indexes and elsewhere may also have taken place. Therefore, for public relations purposes, and for reporting to management, you should keep a record of all work that can be quantitatively recorded. Not all enquiries received need be recorded, unless it is the policy of the parent organization to require such statistics, but you should be in a position to take spot surveys a couple of times a year and extrapolate the figures for the annual report.

It is important to prove to management that a good library or information service saves the valuable time of technical, professional and managerial staff. If you receive inadequate funding your annual report may go some way toward proving that more could be done if more money were allocated. Use the annual report to put forward a positive case for the library, as well as discussing what has already been accomplished. Use it to break down your budget and to show how it has been spent over the year. Management is always impressed by accurate costings and flow charts. Information is not cheap, and it might be a good idea to cost out the average query, or how much an interlibrary loan really costs, to set against the cost of purchasing an item for stock. Your management should be made aware of the fact that you are providing a cost-effective service and spending money wisely.

*Management briefings* by the librarian are also important methods of communication. Management is concerned with all operations of the organization, and while the library admittedly may not be high on the mangerial list of necessary departments, in an one-person library it is up to the librarian to sell the library, and he does this by first convincing management that the library's services are needed and appreciated. A good manager does not want to get involved in library operations – indeed, that is why he has hired a professional librarian to run the library – but he does want to know what is going on. Periodic briefings are invaluable to the manager, as they give a general picture of what the librarian is doing. The briefing does not have to be formal, but it is valuable for the librarian to let the manager know who uses the library, what interesting or useful questions are asked, etc. By discussing problems, special circumstances, policy and other issues, the librarian gives management input about his value to the organization, which is certainly advantageous to the librarian.

Another valuable communication format is the *written memorandum*. In most organizations the manager keeps a file of current activities in the library, and as long as the librarian does not flood management with trivia, memos about certain projects, programmes, etc., will be appreciated. The memo also serves the purpose of keeping management informed when a personal briefing is not possible. Because of heavy demands on her time a manager might not be able to meet with the librarian as often as she would like, and a memo ensures that the information is conveyed. Similarly, in a difficult situation when the librarian and the manager are not getting along, the memo 'gets it down in writing', a less emotional communication technique that has been standard operating procedure in such situations in the business world for many years. The librarian should also share with management some of the complimentary letters he receives from satisfied users. Of course, the best public relations for management and users is in the attitude of the librarian. In a one-person library a pleasant attitude is essential, because the librarian is the only one who is dealing with the user or the manager, and it is the librarian who will effect a pleasant or unpleasant reaction.

For the library's users there are several communications tools which are effective in bringing them into the library, and we shall discuss these with promotional materials, for they are, in essence, materials that promote the use of the library. Here again, the annual report can be the most useful of all, if it is well constructed and attractively presented. The users of the library are as entitled as management to know what the policies, services and goals of the library are. The report to users could have a different emphasis, but many one-person librarians find that one annual report can serve both needs, with perhaps some special annotations for the version given to users.

In dealing with users, as with management, attitude means much. The librarian who makes a user feel that his enquiry is welcome will find people attracted to the library. Good service is the best form of communication and promotion. In no place is it easier to grow stale, to become complacent, than in a one-person library, and it happens all the time. Without stimulation from the work, the users, colleagues outside the parent organization and management, the one-person librarian runs the risk of becoming so introverted and so limited that the work of the library will suffer.

Thus the one-person librarian faces special attitudinal challenges. Librarians working with other librarians have external stimulation, but for librarians working alone it is easy to let professional service slide, to get bogged down in day-to-day routine tasks. If the demands lessen, it is up to the librarian to create his own challenges. Index the organization's archives, if that needs to be done, or spend some time weeding a section that has been neglected for years. The librarian can create his own professional stimulation, and the library and its services will be better for it.

The terms 'library marketing', 'public relations' and 'promotion' are often interchangeable. Just what is the difference between them, and what does the library get when it engages in a public relations, marketing or promotional programme.

Public relations is not advertising. It is, according to a popular handbook for public relations for libraries used in the United States, an attempt 'to influence public opinion by conveying information that benefits the client through a variety of techniques that will result in favourable publicity . . . The benefits of public relations can be enjoyed only if the public relations are good and when the benefits are deserved. No public relations practitioner worth his or her salt can put one over for long on the general public or the media. Your honesty with the media is a powerful asset.'[1]

Marketing is something different, and can be, for the one-person librarian, one of the most important tasks that she can perform. We can define marketing as 'the process of identifying your customers' needs and then developing your business so that you can meet these needs profitably'.[2] Another definition, from the literature, is 'the performance. . . activities that direct the flow of goods and services from producer to consumer or user'.[3] Marketing is therefore seen as the most basic and indeed one of the most important skills the librarian needs. However, in a busy small library where the librarian may be occupied with tasks such as opening the mail, answering the telephone and processing the books it is too easy to assume that there is not time to promote the library, added to the fear of being inundated by requests for help. Keep in mind, however, that answering readers' queries and getting the right information to the right people with as little delay as possible is the primary aim of an information service. Since we are dealing with information anyway, and since the users are there, why not concentrate some of the effort on conveying information *about* the library to users and potential users? That is marketing, as defined above. Keeping a low profile will not do it.

Promotion combines marketing and public relations, for the dictionary definition calls it the 'active furtherance of sale of merchandise through advertising or other publicity', and offers 'publicity' as a synonym. If we agree that the purpose of the library is to get the information to the user, and if we agree that our goal is to provide information to as many users as can benefit from the information contained in the library, we may go further and think of the information as the 'merchandise' and its conveyance to the user as the 'sale'. Are we not, once again, advocating the techniques of the business world, where they apply, to the management of the library? Of course we are, and the library can only benefit from such an application. The 'community' which the one-person library serves, whether it be a town or neighbourhood, students and faculty of a department in a university, a research and development team in a firm, or a corporate headquarters, needs to be told frequently that the library is there for its use:

> Your library is one of the most treasured assets of your community. If, by using public relations techniques, you can strengthen that perception where it exists, and plant the seeds of that idea where it does not now exist, your library will reap the benefits.[1]

What are the benefits? Usage. There is no other word to describe what we are seeking here. Librarians and their managers want their libraries to be used, and the only way to get people to use them is to let them know what they can find at the library. People do not, generally, think about the library. By and large, there are so many other attractions for most people's attention that they do not automatically think of libraries when they are looking for some way to spend some time, or a place to go to entertain or divert themselves, or even, indeed, if they are seeking information. If they are reminded of the library they will respond, but they must be reminded, and frequently.

A caveat about promotion. There are some concerned with library work, both librarians and management, who contend that libraries attract those who need them or want them, and that any efforts to draw others to the library is not only disruptive to the library but can put such a burden on the staff, especially the staff of a one-person library, that the librarian cannot get her work done. Not so. The role of the library is to provide information, not to be a warehouse for books, and the more people use the library, the better the library is fulfilling its purpose. Yes, full usage might put strains and demands on the staff, on the bookstock, indeed, on the facility itself, but such usage is seldom realized, even when a full-scale promotional campaign is successful. If it were, then the librarian and management would find themselves in the enviable position of having to deal with success, at which point the librarian and management can decide how the library could be used less. Until then, most librarians, even one-person librarians, should concentrate their efforts on the other side of promotion: how to get *more* people to use the library.

As librarian, you may lack clerical support, perhaps because management does not perceive that it is needed. Meet this negative attitude on management's part with a positive response from yourself: a marketing plan. You must somehow convey to management that the library is a valuable asset which can save the valuable time of the professional and technical staff – as well as the management – of the parent organization, and should therefore be adequately funded and exploited to the full. This in turn means giving the librarian the necessary tools to enable her to do the job properly. All sections of management today are after funds, which are in short supply, and also extra staff, and the toughest emerge at the top of the pile. It is your job to be pleasant, well-informed and businesslike, but you must also be fairly ruthless in order to get what you want. Develop a thick skin and do not take 'no' for an answer. However, the thickest skin in the world will not help unless you obey certain basic rules.

In the first place, know your organization. The importance of this has already been discussed in previous chapters but it is repeated here simply because it is the *most* important factor to take into account when promoting the library. If you do not know the set-up of your organization, the company policy (if you are part of the corporate world) and the requirements of the users, your efforts will go for naught.

Consider the place of the library within the organization, and identify the goals of the company. If possible, try to become a member of the management team, director of library affairs or information services or some such role, or at least attend relevant meetings from time to time to make sure that policy statements, when published, are sent to you promptly.

Strategic planning is next: 'Strategic planning is a process. The process begins with the setting of organizational aims, defines strategies and policies to achieve them, and develops detailed plans to make sure that the strategies are implemented.'[4] Why do we plan? For many of the same reasons that we used planning in considering the library's budget: planning helps 'in determining the mission and goals of the library', identifying 'potential problems and opportunities', enabling the librarian to 'set the tasks for other boundaries of management, organization, implementation, and control', and, most important, it 'communicates, to those inside and outside, what the organization hopes to be'.[4] In this case the organization is the library, and the one-person librarian can, by planning, know where and how far she wants to take that library in its service to its users.

Librarians usually find themselves in one of three situations: starting up a new service, inheriting a run-down or under-utilized service or taking over a well-run and well-used service and keeping up the flow of good library services. There is a range of ideas for good publicity and marketing which can be applied to each of these situations. First, make a list of objectives and stick to them. The library should be able to (1) assist in providing information for company projects and reduce operating costs, and provide information to enable the company to make a profit (if that is the objective), and (2) be able to exploit literature fully, thus keeping technical and managerial staff well aware of what is happening in their fields. Here the idea of interviewing potential users, put forward by Sylvia Webb,[5] is a good one. Not only can you make yourself known to all members of the staff or community who may be or already are users, but you can also take the opportunity to explain what the service can do at the same time. Even in this enlightened age, many people, even professional staff in the corporate environment, do not know the extent to which a library or information service can help them. Interviews with individual staff do not take up much time and yet are a means of fostering good public relations. Another method is to get a group of staff together (new employees are a good opportunity for this) and give them a short talk, possibly illustrated with slides. In this way, the service, even if it is new, can start from day one. The library may not even exist physically yet you have stamped your impression on staff and given them the idea that you are willing to help. While waiting for the library to take shape, if it is a new service, you should be able to refer to files of information which you may have drawn from various offices into a central place. Until the service is physically set up, consider calling on other libraries in a sphere similar to your own, and using the facilities of any public reference libraries nearby. Make sure that the service supplied is tailored to the organization concerned. Remember: always start as you mean to go on.

From this you will begin to act as a central information point where all company information is stored. Thus you will be able to make available documents which might not otherwise be fully utilized. The main thing is to provide a quick and efficient enquiry point as well as an information-retrieval and dissemination system. Exploit every source that you have available – quick-reference works, books, patents, journals, online services – that are relevant to organizational needs and build up a good core collection of these.

We have said frequently that good performance is effective public relations, and while performance is undoubtedly the *best* form of public relations we acknowledge, at the same time, that performance cannot be the *only* form of public relations. You will need constantly to remind your users of the availability of the services in the library, and you must consider using promotional materials. The printed material coming from the library might be taken from a selection of the following: the annual report, a library guide, a weekly current-awareness bulletin, monthly accession lists, journal contents pages, abstracts from journals, bibliographies and reading lists, bulletin boards and articles for the organization's house journal or training newspaper. For a small public libary other promotional materials might be used, such as gift items with a library message, local newspaper and magazine publicity, or local television and radio advertising. The library guide might be entitled 'How to Use and Get the Best from Your Library'. You may think of a better title, but make it snappy and informative. The ideal guide comes in the form of a glossary, so busy users can scan it quickly to find areas of interest. If you do decide to compile the guide in this form there will need to be a short introduction giving a brief history of the library, its aims, hours of service and perhaps a short introduction to the staff. This should then be followed by the guide to the sources and how to use them, in alphabetical order. A short paragraph can be written about each topic.

You might also like to try compiling a weekly current-awareness bulletin. You may consider this time-consuming, but it really only needs to be one side of a sheet giving short abstracts (a couple of lines will do) of items which may be of interest. Send out the sheet giving these brief entries on a regular basis, and then photocopy the items at your leisure, so that staff can come into the library to refer to them. Booklists and monthly accession lists are also invaluable, for these can be compiled without much effort even if you are desperately short of time. However, you must aim at providing them regularly, even if your funding is minimal, as they are a valuable guide to what is new in the library. They can be annotated if you have time, and are best done in classified form. Add a colourful cover and a short introduction. If you have access to a word processor, use it for working up this accessions list. Using a microcomputer you can obtain an accessions list, monthly acquisitions bulletin, and catalogue cards (or catalogue data, if you do not use cards), all from one input. You will also be able to provide booklists on any given topic, which will be most useful for staff with special subject interests. Do not forget to include non-book material such as government papers, advisory leaflets, journals, etc.

Whether they are annotated or not, booklists or monthly acquisitions lists are valuable because they keep the image of the library before the clients and give them a feeling of knowing what is offered in the library, even if they are not immediately going to avail themselves of it. The booklist can also serve as an important statistical tool, a point well made at one of the annual Elizabeth Ferguson Seminars sponsored by the New York YWCA and the New York Chapter of SLA. Alice Norton, speaking on how to get people to use the library, remarked that the booklist can be a simple way of quantitatively evaluating how the library is used: we simply keep a record of the number of reservations that are made, and successfully filled, through the use of a regularly scheduled booklist.[6]

Other communications tools are received by users with varying degrees of success. Newsletters, with information about as the library and its history and some of the special collections, are always popular, especially printed descriptions of work by users based on research undertaken in the library (provided, of course, that the presentation of such a description does not conflict with any particular regulations or rules about confidentiality, a consideration in a library which is part of the for-profit sector).

Journal contents pages are a quick way of alerting users to items of interest. The only disadvantage is that the actual titles of articles are not usually annotated and can be misleading. However, if you are busy they are an excellent way of getting information out quickly. Provide a simple tear-off form at the back of the list. This will enable users to indicate their requirements and the relevant articles can then be photocopied.

Use a bulletin board, either free-standing or on a spare bit of wall space if that is the only space available. You can display posters, notices of meetings, information about other libraries, photographs of visiting guests, and more. It is also useful to display information about your organization such as social meetings, clubs or outings. This makes the library a welcoming place that says you are aware of what is going on in the organization. Try to keep the notices looking reasonably tidy, and change them regularly so that the users and other staff of the parent organization do not lose interest.

If the library is part of a larger organization, corporation or academic setting, make a point of contributing to your house magazine on a regular basis. If you can write something interesting about the library once a month or once a quarter, then do so. Suitable subjects are staff accomplishments, visitors to the library, projects completed, meetings attended, and any work which will benefit users. You could attach a short monthly report to the monthly accessions list, or send a short report to your line manager or more senior management on a regular basis. Finally, never forget to make sure that if your parent organization has an internal telephone directory the number of the library or information service is readily accessible where it can be seen by all staff. Post the numbered on the staff general notice board to remind everyone that you are there.

Promotion includes more than the printed word. Never underestimate the importance of your appearance and how you present yourself to the users. A pleasant, positive helpful attitude works wonders (do not forget to smile). It is unforgiveable to create the impression that everything is a lot of trouble – that is the best way to end up with an empty library. Do not occupy the users' time chatting for hours about purely social matters. They will be irritated because you waste their time, and wonder what you do with yours. As we have said before, mind your telephone manner and how the library and its services are presented when you speak on the telephone. Finally, try to dress neatly. This may sound elementary, but many unfortunate assumptions can be drawn by older management from weird hairdos and clothes to match. Keep these for outside the workplace, however much you may wish to express your individuality. Put your creativity into running the library instead. If your manner is brisk and businesslike, your dress should be the same, and your personality should be positive. Keep a sense of humour. Endeavour to make all who come to the library rethink their misconceptions that anyone who works with books is dull and boring. Instead, try to stamp your personality on everything you do. If you are successful, there will be people who dislike you, but the main thing will be to have the library busy and well used.

Nevertheless, it does pay to remember that however well you do your job, you will rarely succeed in getting 100 per cent of your potential users to take advantage of library services on a regular basis. Do not think that you have failed because one or two members of staff, despite your campaigns, never appear. There exists a hard core of chronic 'know-nothings' who cannot be reached by information campaigns. In fact, there is something about the uninformed that makes them harder to reach. All you can do when you meet these people is to keep working with them with charm and patience. If they are older, it is likely that they will be set in their ways and you will be unable to do very much. Instead, concentrate on those who want to be informed and make sure that they are encouraged to use the library.

# References

1  *A Guide to Public Relations for Your Library*, Data Phase, Shawnee Mission, Kansas, n.d.
2  Kofler, P., *Marketing our Non-profit Making Organizations*, 2nd edn, Prentice-Hall, Englewood Cliffs, NJ, 1981.
3  Alexander, Ralph S., 'Report of the decisions committee', *Journal of Marketing*, October, 202-217, 1948, cited in Eisner, Joseph, 'Beyond PR: marketing for libraries', *LJ Special Report 18*, Bowker, New York, 1981.
4  Sannwald, William W., 'A strategic marketing plan for public libraries', in Eisner, op. cit., p. 6.
5  Webb, Sylvia P., *Creating an Information Service*, Aslib, London, 1983.
6  Norton, Alice, Untitled remarks. A presentation delivered to the Elizabeth Ferguson Seminar, New York City Chapter, YWCA, and the New York Chapter, SLA, May 1984.

# Chapter Eighteen

# Afterword: why work in a one-person library?

If there are so many people working in one-person libraries why do we hear so little about them? Some have suggested – with tongue not so firmly in cheek – that one-person libraries are so busy they do not have time to write or even talk about their work. At one time this might not have been such a far-fetched idea, but nowadays we are not prepared to accept it wholeheartedly. For one thing, one of the purposes of this book has been to demonstrate that the one-person librarian can work alone and get the work done if she follows certain rules about time management, communication with management, business practices and productive interactions with the library's users.

Perhaps one reason we do not hear so much about one-person librarianship is that for many the job is an entry-level position, and those employees often move on to a multi-staff library before they have begun to deal seriously with or have been able to resolve the problems associated with their kind of work. Another reason might be that, in the past, the type of individual drawn to the one-person library was not assertive enough to get what she needed for the library. Certainly that has changed. A third reason probably has to do with the perception that non-librarians had of the profession. Prior to about 1965 or so, most managers and, indeed, many users had no concept of the professional skills needed to run a library, even a library which employed only one person. That perception, too, has changed.

If there are so many problems in working in a one-person library, if there are so many professional and, possibly, personal inconsistencies, why would anyone do it? Why would anyone, trained for a service profession, want to work alone, where the opportunities for professional service are obviously limited, where there is absolutely no possibility of professional advancement within the organization and where, quite frankly, if he is not actively fighting against it constantly, he can get lost in a morass of clerical and other non-professional detail? There are two reasons, both of them having more to do with the personality of the librarian than with the theoretical service orientation received in graduate school. First, there is definitely a lack of external pressure. For the librarian in a one-person library who does a good job, there is little of the harassing and political manoeuvring that characterizes many library positions. There is pressure, of course, but it is internal, based on a desire to do a good job and to keep up the good work. If the librarian wants to do so, he can make library his own little world, and as long as he does a good job, is competent and keeps the users satisfied, he can be professionally happy without added pressure. Sometimes we describe this lack of pressure with another term. We call it 'independence', and, as we saw in the chapter on professional isolation, independence is what attracts many people to their jobs in one-person libraries. So we can definitely include independence as a reason for working alone.

Another reason, of course, is appreciation. In the one-person library there is an immediate interaction between the user and the librarian, and even if the librarian is unable to finish the project and has to refer the user elsewhere, the user is appreciative and will usually say so, either to the librarian or, better yet, to his or her manager (and frequently to both). The one-person library is a good place to work if the librarian wants to be appreciated and to see the results of his work.

Certainly not everyone would enjoy working in a one-person library. It is a special world, one that might be alien to an academic intellectual, to a skilled administrator or even to a librarian who wants to make a significant societal contribution. Yet for those who choose it, the tight-knit and pleasantly rewarding world of the one-person library has its advantages that far outweigh the problems.

What of the future? We can safely assume that one-person libraries are going to be with us for a long time to come. There have always been small libraries, of course, and many small libraries have grown up in the last decade or so to meet the information needs of various concerns and organizations. Are things getting better for the one-person librarian? Probably. We sense a camaraderie among one-person librarians that did not exist before, or if it existed no-one talked about it. People are talking about what it is like to work alone, and they are starting up workshops and seminars and continuing education courses on the subject. They are reading and writing articles about their experiences, and learning about how to share resources and connect with one another so that they can make their libraries, small and limited as they are, available to as many users as they can find. So they are interested, and with that interest they are bringing a commitment to a higher level of work for their employers, a higher sense of responsibility and a sense of professionalism about their work, even among the many one-person librarians who do not have professional degrees.

Considering the advances in modern technology and the reluctance of contemporary management personnel to add staff to library and information units in an organization, it is unlikely that the proportion of one-person librarians in the profession will fall to less than the current one-third to one-half. In fact, it is probably safe to assume that the number of one-person library operations will grow, as management comes to realize that one excellent, efficient and enthusiastic librarian or information specialist is preferable to two or more who do not provide the same level of service for users. It is these committed, enthusiastic librarians who will bring to the profession a level of service that their employers cannot help but appreciate, because they will bring to the parent organization, the employing corporation, hospital, society or teaching facility, good library service, which is all they wanted in the first place.

# Index

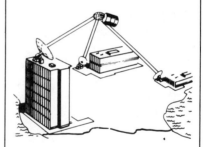